Oh, Our Fair Ones

A Memoir of the Life of LaVelle Holmes

LaVelle Holmes

LifeRich
PUBLISHING®

LifeRich Publishing is a registered trademark of The Reader's Digest Association, Inc.

Scripture quotations marked KJV are from the Holy Bible, King James Version (Authorized Version). First published in 1611. Quoted from the KJV Classic Reference Bible, Copyright © 1983 by The Zondervan Corporation.

This book is a work of non-fiction. Unless otherwise noted, the author and the publisher make no explicit guarantees as to the accuracy of the information contained in this book and in some cases, names of people and places have been altered to protect their privacy.

LifeRich Publishing books may be ordered through booksellers or by contacting:

LifeRich Publishing
1663 Liberty Drive
Bloomington, IN 47403
www.liferichpublishing.com
1 (888) 238-8637

ISBN: 978-1-4897-2829-6 (sc)
ISBN: 978-1-4897-2828-9 (hc)
ISBN: 978-1-4897-2830-2 (e)

Library of Congress Control Number: 2020911766

Print information available on the last page.

LifeRich Publishing rev. date: 07/02/2020

Contents

Acknowledgments...ix
Introduction...xi
Foreword.. xiii

Chapter 1   Early Beginnings 1
Chapter 2   Experiencing Pure Joy.....................................11
Chapter 3   Feeling the Arms of His Love 24
Chapter 4   I Loved You Before I Knew You 34
Chapter 5   Marriage 101...47
Chapter 6   Moving to Utah 56
Chapter 7   Knowing His Tender Mercies...........................67
Chapter 8   Taylorsville Years..74
Chapter 9   From Darkness into Light-Our Errand for
             the Lord 83
Chapter 10   First Call to Relief Society President 92
Chapter 11   Winter Quarters 111
Chapter 12   Woods Cross to Bountiful............................. 120
Chapter 13   The Fire 127
Chapter 14   Family Affairs 144
Chapter 15   Floods in the Eighties 152
Chapter 16   Troubles Times Turning into Blessings............ 158
Chapter 17   Hidden Wedges 167
Chapter 18   Our Very Own Rising Generation.................... 172
Chapter 19   A Season for All Things 179

Chapter 20 Second Birth 187
Chapter 21 Finding What They Did in Gunnison 196
Chapter 22 New Decade, New Century, New Life Changes... 202
Chapter 23 John says "Bingo" 209
Chapter 24 I Will Wait Upon the Lord 219
Chapter 25 Golden Keys to His Kingdom........................ 224
Chapter 26 I Can See Clearly Now.............................. 232
Chapter 27 His Spirit soared Like a Lion 236
Chapter 28 Love is a Many Splendored Thing 243
Chapter 29 Receiving My Gift of Charity and Love................. 249
Chapter 30 The Lord's Work Hastens; Miracles Still Happen ... 255
Chapter 31 No Bologna in Heaven 261
Chapter 32 Oh Our Fair Ones 267

Epilogue 275
Glossary 281

Dedication

I dedicate this book to the loving memory of my wonderful husband John. He taught me so much and in turn let me teach him as our love for each other, Jesus Christ, our Savior and loving Heavenly Father grew.

Acknowledgments

I acknowledge our nine children, their spouses and our grandchildren. Without them, I would not have the many experiences of my life that has brought me to where I am in this part of my journey through eternity.

I wish to thank my granddaughter Emilie Holmes Wheeler for being my first editor and a dear friend, Nicki Pugmire, for being my final editor.

Introduction

As far back as I can remember, I had a curiosity about God. About who He was, or what He was. I wanted to know where I came from and why I was here. These questions concerned me, and I wanted to find out as much as I could.

I was a shy young girl and often felt inferior to others. As I listened to people talk about the subject of religion, their answers were never satisfactory. It seemed they did not really care that much about learning about God. I said my prayers to an unknown being, believing they were being heard.

As I grew, I attended a nearby church. While I did not feel satisfied, at least it was something. However, when I was thirteen, I attended the Church of Jesus Christ of Latter-day Saints for the first time. It felt like I had come home. This feeling has never left me. I planted my feet firmly in this wonderful and ever-lasting gospel of Jesus Christ that I had been so blessed to find. I knew then as I do now that it is the gospel of our Savior, Jesus Christ, restored for our Heavenly Father's children so we can be blessed throughout the eternities.

Many things came into my life to discourage me, but a loving Heavenly Father taught me to use them to my advantage so that I could grow and realize my potential as one of His daughters. I knew that I could use them to become bitter or better. I chose the latter.

Several years ago, the thought came to me that I should share my story in hopes that if it helps even one of my posterity, friends, or associates to realize the love our Heavenly Father has for them, I would be pleased. I knew too that I was to title it: "Oh, Our Fair Ones."

All of us has a story; this is mine, and I share it with you. Yours may be more adventurous, exciting, and full of glamour and drama. Some of you may have shared these experiences with me and you may tell the same story your way and what you got out of it.

Some have asked, how can you remember these things? The answer is simple: I kept journals, notes, notebooks, and just things that I wrote down when a feeling came over me. How grateful I am that I did this, not knowing that someday I would put it all together.

The things that I want to share most with "Our Fair Ones" are my love of the gospel of Jesus Christ, my love of people, and the knowledge that there is a place where we came from, a reason why we are here, and blessings that await us if we choose to keep the commandments that we are taught.

LaVelle Parratt Holmes
2018

Foreword

Oh, Our Fair Ones is a story of faith, strength, and love. The passion that LaVelle Holmes has for both her religion and her family is evident as she shares her life story.

In this lovingly crafted memoir, we follow a young girl who desires to know who she is and what comes after death. She finds fulfillment as she is baptized into the Church of Jesus Christ of Latter-Day Saints, and continues to learn and love the gospel throughout her life.

This story is a woman's testament to the strength that can be gained through faith, service, and love. Through her experiences learning and living gospel truths with her sweetheart and nine children, LaVelle overcomes many challenges. Whether these come in the form of unexpected death, a fire that destroy her home, or kidney failure paired with multiple battles with cancer, LaVelle's sweet testimony shines through the despair as she shares how her faith and reliance on Christ led her and her family through even the darkest of times.

Readers learn of her diligence in serving and caring for family members, both living relatives and deceased ancestors, for whom she spent countless hours researching genealogy. She shares many personal instances where her connection to the spirit of God and her commitment to follow its promptings led her to have sacred experiences to further guide her on her mortal journey.

LaVelle's genuine voice will have readers laughing at her wit and mourning with her through the hardships faced by her and those she loves. Most importantly, readers will learn from a life lived in faith and commitment to the belief that no matter what circumstances people find themselves in, they can always control how they will react. The meaningful stories she shares testify that with faith and the right attitude, the burdens of life can be lifted.

Given LaVelle's commitment to her religion, many terms are used that may be unfamiliar to those not of her faith. In an effort to help readers better understand the terminology woven throughout her life's narrative, a glossary is provided in the back of this book. These descriptions are meant to provide context and clarity to the terminology found in this memoir, but more information about the Church of Jesus Christ of Latter-Day Saints can be found at www.churchofjesuschrist.org.

Those who have the opportunity to read this uplifting memoir will feel privileged for the glimpse into the life of LaVelle Holmes. The stories of romantic courtship, family adventures, tragedies, perseverance, and faith will leave readers feeling like they have met each member of the Holmes family. It is easy to get swept up in the magic of a life well lived full of love well earned, and I cherish the opportunity I had to enjoy and learn from her.

Nicholle Pugmire
2020

Chapter 1

Early Beginnings

"How many days until we leave, Mama?" my sister and I inquired as we watched our mother carefully wrap newspaper around her glass dishes.

Ruth was seven and I was five, and we were preparing to move to Richland, Washington from our home in Antioch, California. My father's family had recently moved there to start a new life. We kept up our questioning: How long would it take to get there? What were Grandma and Grandpa Parratt like? Could we take our dog Prince?

"Yes, we could take Prince," she answered. But she didn't have the answer to everything, such as whether we would see Brian again since we were moving a long way away. Brian was our next-door neighbor, and his mother and our mother were best friends. Both women stood on the porch and were sad together when Mother shared the news that we were leaving.

Ruth and I played a lot with Brian, but I mostly just tagged along because they were more similar in age. One of our favorite things to do was to go around to all the hedges in the neighborhood with jars in our hands and collect caterpillars. We fed them grass once we caught them and hoped they would turn into beautiful butterflies. To our dismay, they usually died.

My grandparents Francis Edger and Dolly Abagail Parratt had lived in Salt Lake City, Utah, most of their lives, where my grandfather worked as a paint contractor and a farmer. Their seven children were born and raised in their home in Salt Lake City near 400 South and 700 West. Each time a new baby was born, grandfather added a new room to the house and bought another cow. Grandmother told me she was not a good nursing mother, and she never had enough milk for her babies.

My grandparents had heard of the government project in Washington. Grandpa was advancing in years and wanted to give up painting. He applied for a job at the Hanford Project and he was hired on as a guard. This government project, first set up along the banks of the Columbia River in 1943, had one main purpose –to build atomic bombs and other war weapons.

Grandfather ended up retiring after a few years of working at Hanford. He built Dolly the home of her dreams with five acres for him to farm in Pasco, Washington. It was just a few miles from Richland, and they spent the remainder of their lives there.

As we continued to prepare for the move, Ruth and I exhausted Mother with our many questions concerning what we would take and where we would live. Would we see Mr. Bain and Mr. Touris again? They were elderly gentlemen who were good friends to our family, and they always delighted Ruth and me when they came. I never knew how my parents met them, but they usually came bearing treats and would sing songs with us and tell stories.

One day Ruth was playing in the yard alone, and Mr. Bain came and took her to the store around the corner to get an ice-cream cone. When Mother discovered Ruth missing, she was so upset. Then she saw them a few houses away, walking toward her. They were licking their ice-cream cones and having a wonderful time. Mother ran and scolded Mr. Bain for not telling her he was taking my sister, and how much it frightened her. She told him that he was never to do that again. She saw the hurt in his eyes, and he apologized and said, "I didn't think I was doing anything wrong." I never saw my mother so angry, but she did forgive him.

I had no idea at that time that moving would become a large part of my life. At the age of five, I had lived in three towns. (At this writing at the age of 75, I have moved 23 times.) Concord, California, where I was born, was my first home. Dad had gone there to be an independent paint contractor. Things were still economically slow after the Great Depression, but business went well for him until the United States joined World War II in 1941. We then moved to Brentwood, California, and he drove for the Greyhound Bus Company.

Eventually, we ended up in Antiock, California, and that is the home I remember most up to that time. There were hardwood floors in the bedroom, and I did not like them. Someone had told me that when people die, they turned into dust balls. Sometimes I would look under my bed, and if I saw any dust under it, I would wonder what dead person was under there.

On my fifth birthday, Mother planned a surprise birthday party for me. When all the girls got there, they were all wearing dresses. I was wearing bib pants, and I pleaded with mother to let me put on a dress. She said I could have just as much fun in what I was wearing. I got upset with her and spent a lot of time in my bedroom while the others enjoyed fun and games.

Our moving trip from California to Washington was long, but not too hot since it was early spring. Ruth and I sat in the backseat of the car and sang songs and chewed gum. Prince sat with us and chewed as much gum as we did. When we crossed the Blue Mountains, we saw some dirty white stuff on the side of the road. It was the first time Ruth and I had seen snow, and Dad stopped so we could play in it. As we looked higher up on the mountains, we could see the undisturbed, white snow shining and glimmering through the sun rays. Dad told us that soon it would melt and then the beautiful pine trees that covered the mountainside would be visible.

Arriving at our grandparent's home seemed strange. We met Aunt LaVon, who I thought was one of the most beautiful women I had ever seen. I thought she could be a movie star. Aunt Betty was a few years younger and also very pretty, and Uncle George was only seventeen and seemed to sleep a lot. Uncle Paul was in the Navy and not due to be discharged for another year. Aunt Thelma and Aunt Naomi still lived in Salt Lake City with their husbands and children.

When Uncle Paul got home from the Navy, he met his wife to be, Ethlyn Spencer. They were to be married in a small community church. It was time for the wedding to start and everyone was there except Uncle Paul. My dad went to find him, checking the house where they were to live, his parent's home, and everywhere else he could think of. He came back to the church hoping to see Paul there, but he was not.

Aunt Ethlyn was agitated and could not be calmed. A few minutes later, Uncle Paul walked in with a bandage around his head. On his way driving to the church, there had been a big dog in the road. He said he had swerved to avoid hitting it and ran right into a large tree. He had been at the hospital and had gotten several stitches in his head. He had tried to call the church, but the only phone there was in a room that was locked, and we did not hear the phone ringing. Aunt Ethlyn just cried and then they proceeded with the wedding. Some still question Paul's big dog story.

Many of the homes looked alike in Richland because it was a town built on government money. Some were larger than others; my grandparents had one of the smaller ones. We lived with our grandparent's neighbors for a short time while waiting for a government home to be finished for us. Dad had gotten a job with the project as a painter. We had lived there for a little over a year when Dad once again decided he wanted to be an independent paint contractor.

While we lived in Richland, we witnessed one of the floods in 1948. It was one of the biggest floods that the area had ever recorded in the history of the Columbia River. Many roads were shut down and businesses flooded out. It stopped only a few blocks from our home.

The following year, our family took a trip to Salt Lake City. Mother wanted to see her two aunts who had helped raise her after her mother's death. Dad's grandmother still lived there and was in her eighties by this time.

When we arrived at her home, an indoor bathroom and all indoor plumbing had just been installed. There was also much excitement because Dad's grandmother had also just bought her first electric stove. She had cooked on her coal stove all those years. When we visited my father's sister, Aunt Thelma, we watched television for the first time. It was a 13-inch black and white television in a large console cabinet, combined with a radio and record player. It was very modern for its day. It must have seemed very funny to see ten or twelve people gathered around this square box to see this little moving picture. Not long after we got home, Dad bought our first television set.

Back in Washington, Dad found a small home in a neighboring town called Kennewick. The three towns – Richland, Pasco, and Kennewick – made up the area that was, and is still, called the Tri Cities, with only the Columbia River separating them. The home needed to be remodeled, and the family came to help. The women provided food, and we put a piece of sheet rock over two saw horses to make a table. We used a paint cloth for a tablecloth and would really have a feast.

It was just before I started third grade that we moved into the home. Everything except the bathroom was complete, so we still had to use the original one off the back porch. Oh, how I hated going out there, especially to bathe. I always found spiders and other crawly things in it, and it was cold. It took five long years for Dad to finish the bathroom inside, despite my nagging along the way.

In the few years after moving into the Kennewick home, Dad built a large double garage and workshop for his business. Mother took the opportunity to go to nursing school and became a Licensed Practical Nurse, a dream she had had for a long time. I was very proud of her when she graduated, but I did not like going home from school to an empty house. It was like I was coming to see my best friend, only she was not there. She usually worked the swing shift and would come home long after I had gone to bed. I never told her how much I missed her because I did not want her to feel bad.

One of my family's favorite things to do was to go camping and fishing. One weekend, we went with our friend Earl Dewey and his wife. The four adults went night fishing. Mother was reluctant to go, although she was always a good sport. Ruth and I had just gone to bed when we heard a lot of commotion down by the lake. We were curious and walked down to see a lot of people hovering around our parents and the Dewey's.

The four of them were shivering and soaking wet. Their boat had started to leak, and they all ended up on the same end of the boat as they tried to stop the leak while coming to shore. All the weight was too much, and the boat started to go under water. They were all grasping the same side of the boat, which made it tip over, forcing them all underneath the capsized boat. This happened three times. Finally, some other fisherman heard them and came to their rescue. Mother could not swim, and Dad had his arm under her the whole time to keep her from going under the water. When they got to shore, Earl was given a shot of whiskey to bring him out of a heart attack he was experiencing.

When everything had settled down for the night and our parents were safely in the tent with us, warm and dry, I thanked God, whoever he was, for saving my parents. I was convinced He had heard my prayer, and that He knew Ruth had her scriptures with her and had opened her Bible that night.

The subject of religion was not spoken of in our home. Mother had been baptized into the Church of Jesus Christ of Latter-day Saints, but had not attended for many years. I later found out she was very close to the Savior and considered Him to be her best friend.

The few family members who remained of my mother's family lived in Salt Lake. When my young mother was nine years old, her mother was getting off of a street car in front of their home. The driver must have not seen her and ran over her; she died instantly. Mother was watching out the window of their home waiting for her to come in the house and witnessed the whole thing happen. This loss affected her for the rest of her life.

There were two aunts with whom my mother was quite close with and had lived with from time to time while growing up. One was Aunt Millie, who was a sister to her mother, and the other was Aunt Helen, who was a sister to her father. I had the privilege of meeting these two wonderful women when I was older, and they were as gracious and loving as my mother always said they were.

Mother's father died when she was eighteen years old from stomach cancer. He was very active in the Church of Jesus Christ of Latter-day Saints. He was led a small congregation near Portland, Oregon, where he lived for a time. My mother would tell stories of when they lived in Oregon and entertained church leaders who visited in their home. It seemed the shifting around that happened to my mother in her young life somehow pulled her farther and farther from the church she was raised in. By the time she met my dad, it was not a big part of her life.

My father had no use for any church. He often took God and Jesus Christ's name in vain, and that always made me feel bad. Most of my father's family did not like the Mormons either, so leaving Salt Lake was not a great loss to them. Even though he had been raised in a Mormon culture, he had little good to say about them. Though, I do remember him saying that during the Depression he never saw any of them standing in the food line, especially the line for sugar. He knew they took care of their own.

A very sad and unfortunate thing had happened a few generations back in my father's family. It affected not only the immediate family then, but many of their posterity to come. It had such an impact that generations later, and even now, many of them still turn a deaf ear to the true gospel of Jesus Christ.

When I was about nine, religion became a very curious subject to me. I read some of the Bible. While I could not understand a lot, I did believe in Jesus Christ and that he must have really lived on the earth and done good things. Because going to church was not a thing our family did together on Sunday mornings, I would ride my bicycle and hide with it behind the tall bushes as I watched the people go in and out of the Christian church a few blocks from our home. It was then that I decided that when I grew up, I wanted my family to go to church together. I knew God had to be a supreme being and wondered if he was just one giant power that lived in everyone's heart. I knew nothing of the Holy Ghost.

Ruth and I started to attend Sunday school at this Christian church and went off and on for a few years. I began attending the meeting held in their chapel where everyone met together. I always felt something was missing, and it was not just my family. My question was, "Is there something more? Something that would answer more questions about God?" I only knew I was not fulfilled.

I thought I should always look my best when I went to church. One year, as Easter time approached, I fell in love with a dress in a store window downtown. It cost $9.00. That was so much money. I told Mother about the dress, and she told me if I could earn one half of the money, she would give me the other half. I don't remember what all I did to earn $4.50. I checked on that dress every other day to see if it was still there. When I had my half of the money, Mother took me down to buy it. I wore it on Easter Sunday to the Christian church, and I felt so good in it.

In the spring of 1954, I had just turned thirteen and I wrote something on a piece of paper. I forgot all about it until 30 years later – in the summer of 1984.

That summer, I visited my parents, who then lived in Clarkston, Washington. I had been married for over 25 years and had nine children. Mother and I went down into the cellar of her home to look at some things in her trunk. It was always fun to reminisce.

We had enjoyed looking at several things when she reached into the trunk and pulled out a paper. "Here LaVelle, this belongs to you," she said. I unfolded the paper, looked at it, and recognized my handwriting. I had not remembered writing the paper, but I did remember the feeling that I had when I was prompted to write it down. I had written:

> *For I have thought for many a given live days that somewhere, someplace, there is a place more glorious than any words can describe. A place that denies all the destruction, hatred, and darkness that dwells on the earth and there is a great light that dwells in every soul. I feel that soon I will find this great light and my mind will be put at ease. After this I will find a great mission that I am to perform and a great bit of knowledge to gain, for whatever will be God's will, I will strive with all my soul and any given knowledge that I receive to accomplish these things. With my earthly strength and ways and the great power and hand of God it will be put in my mind what I have to do, to go forth. I am about to discover a marvelous work and it will change my life forever.*

Truly a wonderful, marvelous gift did await me and **yes**, it did change my life forever.

$$\sim\!\!\textit{m}\!\!\sim$$

If any of you lack wisdom, let him ask of God, that giveth to all men liberally, and upbraideth not; and it shall be given him.

James 1:5
Bible

And when ye shall receive these things, I would exhort you that ye would ask God, the Eternal Father, in the name of Christ, if these things were not true, and if ye shall ask with a sincere heart, with real intent, having faith in Christ, he will manifest the truth to you, by the power of the Holy Ghost. And by the power of the Holy Ghost ye may know the truth of all things.

Moroni 10: 4&5
Book of Mormon

Chapter 2

Experiencing Pure Joy

I was often told that I was too reserved and sober—that I took life too serious and never took time to be a teenager and do the things most of my peers would do. I was very serious. However, that was the way I wanted it and had no desire to change. My friends weren't doing bad things, just things I did not wish to engage in.

They would get together and swoon over music of the current rock stars. When they saw those stars on television, they would go wild. When their movies came out, my friends couldn't see them enough. They were so silly over them, and I felt they were very foolish. Their giggling sessions would drive me crazy. When I think back on it, I suppose I must have been pretty boring.

I seemed to have more "boyfriends" than girlfriends. Sometimes I was sad about that. My dad said the girls were jealous of me, but for what reason, I don't know. I will never forget Scott LaValle. We were both eleven years old, and he insisted on walking me home from school and carrying any books I had. Sometimes I would write his name and think if I married him someday my name would be LaVelle LaValle, which would have been too funny. For my twelfth birthday, he gave me a box of 24 Snicker candy bars, which I thought that was a wonderful gift. Can you imagine the dilemma he put his mother in when he asked her what he should give this twelve-year-old girl for her birthday? Maybe it wasn't so hard after all, because later I learned that his father worked for a candy distributing company.

When I was thirteen, we were living in our Kennewick home. It was just after I had written the paper Mother had preserved for me. Ruth started going to a church on a week night with her friend, Carol. Carol and her mother were meeting with missionaries from this church. I was excited when they told me that on one weeknight each week, a meeting for both boys and girls was held. They would meet in the chapel to pray, sing, and read scriptures before separating into classes of their age group. Girls had women as their teachers, and men taught the boys. This was followed with dancing and refreshments. I was interested in going and asked if I could go with Ruth and Carol. My sister, knowing the tagalong I still was, said I could.

From the very first time I stepped into the church, I felt different. I did not know what it was, only that I had a warm feeling and could not get enough. I almost felt that I was coming home. It was all so new, yet so comfortable. Each song we sang had a special message, and I was learning new names and stories from their Book of Mormon as well as the Bible.

The dancing was fun; a young couple gave us ball room and modern dance instruction. Sometimes we would just do the hokey pokey, but that was fun too. It seemed we just had a good time and always went home feeling edified in every way.

The person I remember most from these weeknight gatherings was Sister Sharp. She had a great impact on me, and probably never knew what she did for this young girl who came to class reeking of cigarette smoke and coffee fumes. My parents and all their friends used these things, and I did not even realize that I carried these odors. I had never been without them.

My parents would give me a sip of beer upon my request when they would have friends over. One day, when I was about seven, they were drinking. I asked for some, and they gave me a whole can. I drank every drop and then decided to go over to our neighbor's and swing.

Our neighbors had a very high swing hanging from their large tree in the front yard, and Ruth and I were always invited to use it. After I drank the can of beer, and I was going very fast in it and higher than I ever had. The next thing I knew, I was on the ground. Looking around and seeing there was no one to feel sorry for me, I picked myself up and limped home. I never drank another sip, let alone another can, after I heard of the Word of Wisdom this new church taught.

Sister Sharp was about 40 years old and a mother of five children. She was quite plain looking, but there was something very beautiful about her. I later learned it was the spirit of the Holy Ghost that made her just glow. I could not wait for her lessons.

She taught me things no one had talked about. Her lessons included not just Jesus Christ, but other principles of the gospel. She talked to us about dating and how Heavenly Father wanted us to conduct ourselves when we were dating. (This was before the Prophet counseled youth not to date until the age of sixteen). She taught me the sacred nature of the human body, and that obedience is the price of having power.

She taught me that the more obedient we are, the greater our faith becomes, and that the two are vitally connected. She encouraged me to have the power and strength to continue to do the right things, especially while dating. I learned of the sacredness of marriage and relationships between a boy and girl. I have often wondered if she came into my life to save me from self-destruction. She was teaching me about faith, not only in God, but also in myself.

One of the most important things I have learned about faith since then is that it is like a gentle young tree that has been planted. It must be nourished and protected from the winds of life. If it is, its roots will grow and mature. The tree will become sturdy and unshakable. Faith can grow with the test of life if we remain obedient. True faith and obedience will be eternally connected, and we will have eternal blessings for being valiant in these two principles.

Up to this point, I had the notion that if a man and woman loved each other, it would be all right to do the things that should only be engaged in after they were married. I was sure that if they were really in love, it would be all right with God. Where I got this deadly idea, I do not know; I only know that what Sister Sharp taught me saved me from a horrible trap that I may have found myself in.

I had gone to a few movies with boys, which I suppose was considered dating. My parents did not object, my friends were doing it, and my dad wanted me to be popular. This seemed to be important to him. However, I don't recall any guidelines from my parents. Mother just always said she thought I was a good girl, and she trusted me. I appreciated that, but even good girls can get some wacky ideas and feelings.

Even at this young age, there were times I had to defend myself to save my chastity. A handsome young man who attended another church had always been nice to me and invited me to Sunday dinner with him and his family. I said yes because I thought if he went to church, he would be a gentleman. The dinner was very nice, and his mother made me feel welcome. The next Friday night, he walked me home after a football game. We were cutting through a park when he suddenly bent my arm around me and tried to pin me to the ground. I am not sure how I got away, because he was much stronger than me. I was quite familiar with the park, and I ran to a huge tree and circled slowly around it. He got closer to me, calling my name, and he was just a few feet away when he gave up and walked out to the road next to the park to go the other direction. I made my way home by way of the park and the canal that flowed by it. We saw each other at school, but I never did talk to him again.

Another time, my father hired a painter who had recently moved to town. He had a son who was just a few years older than me. I was going to a drive-in theater with some friends one night, which was a very popular thing to do in those days. My father wanted me to invite the man's son to go with us. I was reluctant and didn't have a good feeling about it. Dad finally talked me into it, saying, "It is a good way to help the boy get acquainted and feel welcome." His father told my dad that his son was having a hard time adjusting to the move. So I finally checked with my friends, and they agreed to let him come.

He and I were in the back seat, and he was doing everything except watching the movie. He was like an octopus with as many hands. Finally, a good elbow in the ribs gave him the message. During the intermission while we were at the concession stand, I told my friends that I did not want to stay for the second feature movie. We went home. My dad could not figure out why I didn't want to be around this boy anymore, and I didn't tell him why.

It was not long after I had sat through many of Sister Sharp's lessons and started to attend Sunday School and Sacrament meeting when I asked my parents if I could have the missionaries come to our home to teach me the lessons so I could be baptized. I was sure that Mother would agree, but my father was a different story because of the bad feelings he had about the church. To my surprise, he said, "Well, if you are going to join any of those churches, it may as well be that one." My father did not know that this was the greatest gift he ever gave me – his consent to join the Church of Jesus Christ of Latter-day Saints.

It was September of 1954 when the missionaries came and gave the first lesson. Ruth and Jerry, the man she was engaged to, sat in on the discussions. However, they eventually stopped attending. I never figured out if Jerry had been offended or if something had happened, but they suddenly showed no interest. Jerry had been raised Catholic, and they were married in the Catholic Church.

As I heard each lesson, I had chills go through me. I not only understood what they were teaching, but knew without a doubt the things they said were true. The plan of salvation made so much sense to me as I gained knowledge about it, and I felt a purpose of life that I never had known before. To learn where I had come from, why I was here, and to learn that there were options when I died was sobering. This knowledge brought me great peace and joy. Being told my spirit would not be dead at the time of my mortal death was overwhelming. Because of Jesus Christ, I would only be separated from my body for a short time.

The teachings of the Savior Jesus Christ were just plain sweet, and they brought me pure joy. Up until then, I still did not know He was a real person. The missionaries gave me challenges to read about Him in the Bible and the Book of Mormon, and I knew He had lived and sacrificed his life for us. I didn't fully understand the atonement and why it was necessary, but I knew it had happened.

Learning about the Godhead and how they were three separate beings cleared so many things up in my young mind. Like many in the world at that time, I thought Heavenly Father, Jesus Christ, and the Holy Ghost were one, but I knew what the missionaries were teaching me was true. As they talked about the Holy Ghost, I realized He had been preparing me to find this wonderful church. He was also preparing me with further light to recognize the truth. Then, in a very short time, I knew with every fiber of my being this was the true church of Jesus Christ.

I can still see in my mind the first time I saw a picture of the First Vision. It was a painting of the prophet Joseph Smith kneeling in the sacred grove, and of Heavenly Father and Jesus Christ, His son, appearing to Joseph and talking to him. I read Joseph's own testimony in the front of the Book of Mormon. I had the same question that Joseph and so many others have had. Which church was true? There have been a few times in my life I have felt my heart taking a leap, and that was one of those times. Again, it was confirmed to me that the things I was hearing were true.

My mind was racing. Joseph actually saw and spoke to our Father and His Son, Jesus Christ, but how could this be? But it had happened – I knew it had – and something so powerful was burning within me. I wanted to cry when the missionaries had me read it. Joseph had been called by Heavenly Father to be the prophet of this dispensation. The tears came later that night when I was alone.

When I learned there was a prophet on earth today, I was so excited. Like many, I supposed that the days of prophets on the earth were over, but why would God restore His church and then leave us without a leader? I wanted so much to see him, but was sure that would never happen. He lived in Salt Lake City.

Upon my asking the missionaries why the church had to be put back on the earth again even though Jesus Christ had organized it when He was here, one asked me to get a jar or something glass that could be broken. I thought it was a strange request, but went to the kitchen and got one. He told me to think of the jar as the Lord's true gospel. He had a bag in his brief case, and put the jar in it. Then he stood up and threw the bag as hard as he could onto the floor. I sure did wonder what he was doing. He opened the bag, and we saw many pieces of glass. He said that after the Savior had died, was resurrected, and then later told his apostles he had sheep not of this fold, he left them to teach His gospel. After their deaths, men slowly changed parts of the gospel to better suit themselves. Much of our Savior's teachings were omitted or changed, and eventually the priesthood of God was taken from the earth, and much of the original teachings became the philosophy of men.

Each piece of the glass in the bag represented a new church that was started from the original and true church. None of these churches had the complete truth. The Lord knew that would happen, and the day would come that the gospel of Jesus Christ would need to be restored, never to be taken away again. Joseph Smith had been preordained in the spirit world to be the one instrumental in restoring the church under the direction of Jesus Christ.

After a few months, I completed all the lessons. My parents took me to Richland, where the stake center was, as it had the only baptismal font in any of the churches. I was pleased that my father came.

After my baptism, Dad wanted to go to a drive-in movie. I certainly do not remember what the movie was. I do remember wondering how I could ever get my father to accept the gospel, and especially the Joseph Smith story. As I said before, I was beginning to know of Mother's thoughts of the Savior, but circumstances in her life then did not allow her to act upon them.

There was a standing statement about me when I was baptized: That when I came out of the baptism water, they handed me a towel in one hand and a Primary (the organization provided for the young children to learn about Jesus) manual in the other. By the next time the Primary met, I was the Sunbeam teacher, teaching the youngest of the children. Little did I know then that I would spend twenty-seven years teaching Primary, and hold every position in it except pianist.

I was so impressed with the Jackson family and how devoted they were to the church. Their daughter Rhonda became my best friend. As the second oldest of six, I thought she came from a large family. They lived in Finley, a small town outside of Kennewick, and had to drive through Kennewick by way of a road just a few blocks from my house. I would either meet them on the roadside or at my house, and then we drove over the Columbia River bridge to the church in Pasco.

The Jacksons were in the process of building a nice new home and had been for a few years. Meanwhile, they lived in a small, two-room house which included two sets of bunk beds just a few feet from the large dining table. The table was a few feet from the kitchen sink, stove, and refrigerator. Four of the children slept in the two sets of bunk beds, and the two smaller children slept in a bed next to their parents in the other room. There was one small bathroom.

I wondered how they could be happy in such crowded conditions, but they were, and you could always feel a wonderful spirit in their home.

They would often invite me to sleep over. When I did, two of the kids doubled up to allow space for me. I loved having family prayer with them, and I could talk to Rhonda's father about the church anytime. He would always go out to do his chores early in the morning so that we girls could have our privacy.

There was a small group of the church's teenagers who hung around together. I was the youngest, but some of them were old enough to drive, and that really helped me out. Those who could drive would pick up the rest of us for seminary at 5:30 am so we could be to the church by six and be done by seven to get to school by 7:30. Sometimes we would have adult instructors, and sometimes the older boys or Rhonda's older sister, Sandra, would teach.

In February of 1956, I attended my first church conference. A visiting apostle was the main speaker. He had come from Salt Lake, and I was intrigued by him. He spoke of so many gospel principles that I had been taught, and gave me further enlightenment on them. He said the Prophet sent his love to each one of us, and again I had a desire to see him in person and hear him speak. Some of my friends had the same desire.

It was not long after this that my friends invited me to go to Salt Lake City with them to attend General Conference. This was a dream come true. At 15 years old, I was sure my parents would not allow it. The oldest driver was 19 and investigating the church. The next oldest driver was seventeen. When I asked my parents if I could go, they said they would "talk about it." Once again, I was shocked, but elated and grateful when my father said I could go. The only stipulation they made was that I try to see my father's sister Aunt Thelma and her husband, Uncle Barr, and try to contact Mother's stepmother.

We left on Thursday before the three-day conference started on Friday. It was a 700-mile drive. We stayed in a motel the first night, but once my Aunt Thelma and Uncle Barr knew we were in town, they insisted that all seven of us stay with them. They had a large home and could accommodate us, so we were able to save a lot of motel money.

When I made my first visit to the Salt Lake Temple Square grounds, the whole square was breathtaking. Looking up at that beautiful, majestic temple was a sight I will always remember. It looked so magnificent, and I felt so small and insignificant. I had been told that it was the Lord's temple and that He walked in the halls. I was in awe and wondered if I would ever be able to go inside. Again, that seemed to be so out of reach for me. I determined I would someday be married in this building, the house of the Lord, and I would be sealed for time and eternity to my husband and any children we might have.

On Friday, we arrived on Temple Square about 7:30 a.m. to get a seat in the tabernacle. We had seats in the balcony. Everyone stood up when the prophet walked in, and I felt such a warm and exciting spirit. I don't know what I expected; he looked like a loving grandfather with his beautiful white, wavy hair. I felt very humble and very blessed to be in the presence of a living prophet of God. I never thought it would be possible, but between my parents and my good friends, I was there. My prayers had been answered. As he spoke so kindly and wisely, I knew he was indeed God's prophet. We only got to four of the six sessions as some of our party had to contact other family members, and there was one car to be shared.

On Saturday night, Uncle Barr took the boys to the Priesthood session of conference and I had the opportunity to get acquainted with Aunt Thelma. She was very involved in the church, serving in the Young Women's Organization most of her life. One of her legs had been crippled. She told me that when she was a little girl, she had fallen off the porch at their home, and her leg had never been the same. A short time later, she got polio in it. She was ill for a long time and had to be carried everywhere. Finally, she got well enough with the help of a metal brace that she could walk on her own.

I asked her if there were other members of the family that were members of the church. She said her sister, my Aunt LaVon, was. There had been several of the ancestors who were, but not any of the direct line. I asked if she knew why my father was so bitter about the church.

She told me that my great, great grandfather and his wife were the first to join the church. They were born in England and came to the United States in the mid-1800s with four children. She died at 64 and he married again; his second wife died eight years later at 73. He died when he was 83.

Their oldest son Ben and his wife had four children, and two died in infancy. Ben's wife died shortly after and he married Aunt Winifred. She worked for the prophet in Salt Lake City, and he liked the way she made his stockings. She had contacted poison ivy as she crossed the plains to Utah from Indiana and had to have her leg amputated.

They moved to a small town in Utah, and she found life very hard there, especially with only one leg. She resented Ben and the Church because he wanted to serve the church and pay tithing. Eventually, she divorced him and turned most of the children against the gospel. My grandfather was the eighth child born, and lived with these resentful, bad feelings. This deeply affected my grandfather, and it was passed on to my father and many of my grandfather's seven children. I remember my father saying that he would not give a dime to that or any church.

The things I was hearing made me very sad, but at least I now had an idea why Dad never listened to anything positive, and why he had the feelings he did. I was beginning to understand why he only found fault with the church members. Winifred had come to Utah with her father, because he was very devoted to the church and wanted to be with the members. He had sold a lot of land he had inherited in Indiana, and most of the money was given to the church. Many of his family members disowned him for doing that and wanted nothing to do with this new church.

As for my great-grandmother, Winifred, I have always had a special place in my heart for her. Life can be difficult today raising a big family. I can't imagine doing it with only one leg and no modern appliances like we have.

While in Salt Lake during that conference trip, I did get to visit with mother's step-mother. She was a gracious lady, but I could see immediately why she and Mother did not get along well, even though they were always cordial to each other. Mother never could relax around her. She would always say, "they have to take me as I am," and it seemed everybody loved mother because she was so genuine.

The seven of us left early Sunday afternoon and drove all night so we could go to school the next day. We felt our testimonies had grown so much, and we were so grateful for the experience. I felt so close to my friends, and though we each came from different backgrounds, we all shared in one thing in common – the Gospel of Jesus Christ. I truly did experience pure joy. I did not know that there was much, much more to come.

These things have I spoken unto you, that my joy might remain in you, that your joy might be full.

John 15:11
Bible

Looking forward to that day, thus retaining a remission of their sins; being filled with great joy because of the resurrection of the dead, according to the will and power and deliverance of Jesus Christ from the bands of death.

Alma 4:14
Book of Mormon

Chapter 3

Feeling the Arms of His Love

There is an old saying, "When one window or door closes, another one will open for you." The first time I heard this was in the movie *The Sound of Music*.

What Mother was about to tell me was going to close and open many doors and windows in our lives.

Mother sat trying to regain her composure. But now the tears were coming, and then she said, "LaVelle, we have to move."

"Move? Where? When? Why?" I asked.

As she dried her tears, she told me that Daddy had lost his business and we would lose our home and furniture to the bank. She said that tomorrow, they were coming to take her car. I knew Dad's income had been a lot less the past few months, but I didn't know it had been this bad. His paint trucks would be repossessed except for one that he could keep for means of transportation to work.

She explained to me that the general contractor of the new subdivision of thirty new homes had lost all of his money, and the homes would not be finished at this time. (To this day, I do not know the whole story.) My father was not the only one affected by this. The plumbers, electricians, and all the other sub-contractors were losing thousands of dollars, and some were losing their businesses also. The project had gone well for several months, but suddenly there were no more draws of money, so no one could pay for their material or employees. The contractor tried several ways to raise money, but many people still went bankrupt, including my father.

I had been so wrapped up in my own life that I did not see this coming. As Mother explained, I cried, and I felt so bad for my parents. She told me that we could stay in the house until school was out at the end of May. I was sick, heartbroken, and somewhat in disbelief. The next day reality hit me when I watched the tow truck come and take mother's 1953 Ford away. She had driven old cars for so long, and had been so happy to get that new car.

Some years later, as a parent, I realized the sacrifice my parents had made for me by letting me go to Utah with my friends. It didn't take a lot of money for the trip, but I am sure they could have used it elsewhere. Perhaps they knew that I would soon have to leave this group of friends, so they allowed me to spend as much time with them as possible.

My father took the one work truck left and went to Soap Lake, Washington, a small resort town about 80 miles away. He had found work there. Mother still had her nursing job until we left, so that provided some income. It was decided that I would live with my Aunt LaVon and Uncle Bob and help take care of their three children while Aunt LaVon worked. I only spent about three weeks there before school was out.

Mother had left with Dad, and they found a small trailer for us to live in. Before we left the tri-city area, we went over to see our neighbors at our former home. I had not been able to find a favorite blouse since I had moved, and wondered if it was still in the house. I went over to the house, found the door open, and ran into my bedroom. I flung the door open and it was so empty—oh so empty! I backed up against the wall and slid down onto the floor to cry. Reality was terribly painful that day. It was the emptiest feeling I had ever experienced. Dad told me later the only things he was able to salvage were the sewing machine he had bought for Ruth and me, Mother's trunk, her cedar chest, and some of his work tools. That is why we had gone to visit our neighbors. He had stored these items at their home.

I had said goodbye to my friends. I was so sad to leave them, especially those who were members of the church. Mother said there was not a Church of Jesus Christ of Latter-day Saints where we were going, which made the move even harder. I later found out that most of my family thought I would get over this church that had come to mean so much to me, and probably go to another one or none at all. However, I knew that what I had found and been taught was the true church of God I knew it then, and I know it now. I was determined that nothing would change my thinking. I would never be happy with another religion. Furthermore, I did feel the arms of my Savior around me, and though I was sad, I knew I would be okay. I mostly worried about my parents, and especially my mother.

When we arrived at the trailer court, I was shocked and not prepared for what I saw. The trailer was about eight feet by sixteen feet. There was one bed at one end for my parents to sleep on and a couch on the other end. The trailer had no bathroom, and we had to share a big community bathroom a few trailers down from us with twenty-seven other families. The men had one side, and the woman had the other. There were eight showers, sinks, and toilets on each side. The shower stalls had curtains, but they did not provide much privacy.

There was only one vehicle, and Dad had to take to work. He got home after the only store was closed, so Mother and I were somewhat stranded. We were about a mile from the resort town, so she and I would walk through the fields and cow pastures to get groceries and sometimes just hang out by the lake. I can't tell you what we laughed about, but we had the best time walking and laughing. My little mother always seemed to be happy, no matter what was going on in her life. She was only five feet tall and never weighted over 110 pounds, and what a sense of humor she had. She could take any lemon and turn it into lemonade. There were some large tumble weeds in the fields we walked through, and we would pretend they were beautiful rose bushes, and the little weeds were pansies. She will never know how much she helped me through this time. I only hope that I helped her.

My father was having a hard time, too, but he would not talk about it. He told me much later that he felt like a failure. During this time of duress, he lost his hair. (It did grow back.) He was only in his early forties; the whole ordeal took its toll on him. He got the hiccups for twenty-five days. He couldn't eat, sleep, or do much of anything. Nothing he did would stop them, until one day they randomly stopped. I would see him just sit and be so depressed. I prayed our situation would get better.

Finding a place to pray while we lived in this trailer was difficult for me. I did not want to kneel in the trailer when my father was there, as I was afraid he would wake up and make fun of me. I decided to wait until I was sure all the ladies and girls we shared the bathhouse with were done. Then I would kneel by one of the wash basins and talk to Heavenly Father.

It was about three or four weeks later when my father came home with some good news about our housing. He had found a little resort cabin we could rent. It only had one bedroom, so I slept on a couch in the kitchen. I didn't know where I would attend school, which was starting in about three weeks.

We were only in the cabin for a few weeks when Dad came home with more good news concerning our housing situation. He had found a house in a town called Electric City. It was a few miles from Grand Coulee, Washington, where he was now working. The Grand Coulee Dam was down river from Grand Coulee. The town of Coulee Dam was below the dam. It, too, was a government town where most of the workers on the dam lived.

The Grand Coulee Dam was considered then to be the largest dam in the world, and it was quite a site to see. It is truly a modern marvel; some have called it the eighth wonder of the world. The sheer magnitude of the structure created many unique problems in need of inventive solutions. When they found exposed bedrock, clay came forward and threatened to swallow up the foundation. After frantic deliberation, the engineers froze the clay and saved the dam.

I was taken on a tour under the dam, and I was amazed at how big the structure was underneath. It had millions of gallons of water going over the top per minute. The manpower it took to not only build it, but also to keep it running, was tremendous.

When we drove up to the house, neither mother nor I showed our disappointment. But we both felt it. As usual, she made the best of it. The house was filthy. I didn't want to touch anything, let alone live there, but we were determined to make it home. Dad said it wasn't much, but that he knew that Mother and I could fix it up.

For days, we scrubbed and scrubbed, and then we scrubbed some more. It began to look like something and smell better. Mother offered to tackle the bathroom, something I was so grateful for because my stomach was not very strong.

It had been my responsibility to do the laundry when we lived in Kennewick. Ruth and I shared the job before she married, and I solely inherited it when she left. There was an old, wringer-type washer in the Electric City house. I wondered how something that old and rusty could work, let alone get clothes clean. I scrubbed out the old machine until it looked pretty good, and when I plugged it in, it even worked! Hurray! I went out back and cleaned the old clothes lines and chopped the weeds down under them so the clothes wouldn't get tangled up in them.

Our next-door neighbors, the Bowman's, had a daughter my age. Her name was Carolyn, and I was glad to know her even if we were very different in personality. She introduced me to most of the kids in our school class who lived in Electric City. Most of my classmates lived in Grand Coulee, three miles away. The community included three small towns and the Nez Pierce Indian Reservation.

No one there had heard of the Church of Jesus Christ of Latter- Day Saints, or if they did, they did not want to admit it. There was a Baptist church, and most people attended it if they went to church at all. There were also a Catholic, Assembly of God, and Community church in the area. I was invited to most of them, but I didn't feel comfortable attending. I knew I had found the only church that I wanted to be affiliated with, and I could wait.

I prayed that something would work out so I could attend it again. The thing I missed most was not being able to renew the covenants that I had made at baptism. Not being able to take the sacrament left a void in my life. Even then, I felt that there had been a reason my father had been directed to come to this community, and that things would work out.

I missed my friends from church. Rhonda wrote that they were having another road show that fall, and I remembered how much fun the last road show had been. I even missed picking rows and rows of grapes that were to be shipped to Welfare Square in Salt Lake City and made into grape jam and juice.

My junior year of high school at Grand Coulee High was filled with many things. My father wanted me to be a cheerleader. I tried out and lost by four votes. I was never so relieved in all my life. Dad just didn't know how uncoordinated I was. I was the class secretary and was in the school play. I loved singing in the school choir, and was selected to sing with a special group of girls called "The Non-Nettes." I suppose that was the name because every year there were nine girls chosen for the group.

I was required to take U.S. history our junior year. Our assignment at the end of the semester was to pick anything that had been written in the two-inch thick textbook and write a six-page essay. I couldn't decide what to write my report on, and then an idea popped into my head. I checked with the teacher again if it was all right to write about anything that pertained to the history of the United States if it was mentioned in the book. He said that was what the assignment was, so it was pretty much open field.

I went to my book and re-read the two short paragraphs that told about the westward Mormon migration and the origin of the church. While my classmates wrote about the Civil War, the Constitution, slavery, the Boston Tea Party, and many other subjects, I wrote about Joseph Smith.

We did not have the modern technology that we have today, and the encyclopedias did not offer much on the subject. I turned to the Book of Mormon itself and Joseph Smith's own testimony and story. I also used material from pamphlets I had saved. I concluded my paper by writing that I believed the things I had written, and that these things had really happened to him. Although he had been martyred by evil men, I knew he lived because this church taught eternal life. I had some reservations in the things I had written as far as what the teacher would think, but felt prompted to hand it in and deal with any consequences.

The class was anxious to receive our graded papers back. I was pleased to see that I got a B+. Word got out that I had written about a young boy who said he had seen God. I told my peers the same thing I had written: I knew that it had happened, and if they wanted to know more, I would tell them. They just walked off laughing.

This was a real beginning for me in learning about myself. I realized I could and would always stand by our Heavenly Father's prophet, Joseph, and would testify that the things he said happened did take place.

I have had numerous opportunities since then to proclaim my testimony of him and how he was instrumental in restoring the complete gospel of Jesus Christ to the earth, under the direction of the Savior himself. I have known great joy as I have seen the prophecy of the Angel Moroni to Joseph come to pass. Joseph wrote in his own history, "He called me by my name and said unto me that he was a messenger sent from the presence of God to me, and that his name was Moroni, that God had a work for me to do and that my name should be had for good and evil among all nations, kindred's and tongues, and that it would be spoken of among all people."

In the April 2018 General Conference, many of the talks included the prophet Joseph Smith's name, and his name was known all over the world in over one hundred languages. Truly, I have seen this and other prophecies come to pass.

I don't know what may have been said about it, or me, if anything. I am sure there are some who had a heyday with it, especially the fact about a young boy talking to God. However, my principal was very nice to me afterward. I'm not even sure he knew my name before I wrote that report. I am sure the teacher told him some things about me. Perhaps, he, too, thought I was weird, or maybe just curious.

A wonderful thing happened early in my junior year of high school. I was visiting my good friend Carolyn. We were talking when her older brother came in the room. I had never met him before as he had been working out of town for the summer, but I had heard a lot about him. He was a tall blond, and nice looking. However, the person who interested me more was his friend, Harold Olsen.

Harold and I became friends and started to date. He was religious and went to his own church and believed in God. I told him of my desire to find others of my faith, and he did some inquiring around the area for me. One night he came over and said, "I think I know a man who is a member of your church. He owns the service station at the foot of the dam, right next to the bridge in Coulee Dam."

His name was Howard Tolman, and he was the branch president of the church's small branch there in Coulee Dam. A branch is what our church called a small congregation. He told me there were about 35 members in the branch, and they met in a small, two-bedroom house. The branch was mainly comprised of women and children, and there were only four Priesthood members. (This is what the men in a congregation are called, because men can be ordained to hold the power and authority of God, which we call the Priesthood.) I was so excited and told him I would be there on Sunday.

I started going, and it was not long before I was teaching junior Sunday school. The living room of the house served as the chapel and a meeting place for the adult Sunday school. The small kitchen was used to prepare the sacrament, and the bedrooms and garage had been converted into classrooms. I was so grateful to Harold for finding President Tolman for me to be back with members of my own faith, even if we were few in number. Once again, I felt the arms of Heavenly Fathers love.

Harold was preparing to go to college, and the last night that he was in town we went out. He wanted to go over to the community hospital that also served as a rest home for some of our senior citizens. He had worked there and became quite good friends with some of the residents. As we drove into the parking lot of the hospital, he said, "Oh, there is old John!" I honestly thought he was referring to one of the residents who lived in the rest home because he had said "Old John." I did wonder why a nursing home resident would be emptying the garbage, as that is what the man was doing.

We talked to the nurses at their stations. My mother, who was working that night, introduced me to some of the other nurses. After a few minutes, we had started down the hall toward the rest home portion of the building when a young man came in. Harold introduced him as John Holmes. He worked as an orderly, and had been the one emptying the garbage when we drove up. We talked for a moment before Harold turned and started walking down the hall. He asked if I was coming with him, but I told him I would rather stay and visit with Mother and the nurses.

I learned later that Harold had told John he was to keep his eyes off me as he had found me first. When he came back from his visits, we told Mother goodbye and left to enjoy the rest of the evening.

When mother got home about 10:30, I was still up. She asked, "Do you remember that young man Harold introduced you to at the hospital?" I said, "Kind of, I don't remember his name or even what he looked like, so what about him?" She said, "Are you ready for a good laugh?" I said, "Sure." She reminded me that his name was John Holmes. She went on to tell me that he came up to her after Harold and I left and said, "I just met your daughter, and I am going to marry her."

Mother and I both started laughing. I said something like, "I bet I'm even going to have a bunch of kids with him, too."

The more we talked and said silly things, the harder we laughed. Soon our hysterical laughter turned into tears. This time we were laughing because this John Holmes had said he was going to marry me.

In that I command thee this day to love the Lord, thy God, to walk in his ways, and to keep his commandments and his statutes and his judgements, that thou mayest live and multiply: and the Lord thy God shall bless thee in the land whither thou goest to possess it.

Deuteronomy 30:16
Bible

For whoso receiveth you, there will I be also, for I will go before your face. I will be on your right hand and on your left, and my spirit will be in your hearts, and my angels round about you, to bear you up.

Doctrine and Covenants 84: 88

Chapter 4

I Loved You Before I Knew You

Mother had told me that John would be calling me for a date when he had his next night off. I asked her what her opinion was of him and if she would feel good about me dating him.

"I feel like he is a nice young man. He's good with the patients and doctors, and is funny and witty at the nurse's station," she said. "He also seems mature and a gentleman."

The next day on the school bus, I told Carolyn what my mother had told me. When she asked what his name was, she got very excited and said, "I don't know him personally. I hear he dates only the popular girls and is quite a Casanova."

I didn't know if this was a good thing or a bad thing. She told me she had a yearbook from his school the year he had graduated, and would bring it over after school. I would be able to see his picture – because I couldn't remember what he looked like – and we could see if he had been involved in any school activities.

She brought the book over after school and showed me his picture. I thought he was quite handsome even though I didn't look at him the night before. As for his school activities, he had done them all. He had lettered in all four years in football and basketball, and was picked for all-state in these two sports. He also lettered in baseball, track, and tennis. He was in the school choir, and played the sousaphone in the band, and was the drum major in the marching band. He served as class vice president in his junior and senior years, and graduated with honors.

This was quite impressive to me, and to tell the truth, I was somewhat intimidated by all of it. That night, he did call and ask me out on his day off. I accepted, not sure if it was the right thing to do. He told me that Mother had told him that I had just bought a green sweater. "You wear your green sweater, and I will mine," he said.

Well, when I opened the door that night, I was wearing a purple sweater, since no guy was going to tell me what to wear, especially on our first date! He asked me where my green sweater was, and I told him I felt like wearing purple.

Did we have a nice time? I am not quite sure; he sure did talk a lot. We went to a movie at the only theater in town. I don't recall the name of the movie, only that it was a true document story and it showed some African women walking around their village with nothing on their tops in a few scenes. I wanted to vanish; I was so embarrassed. He looked at me for a second and I stared straight at the movie screen. He did apologize to me afterward, and said he had no idea those scenes were in the movie. He took me home, thanked me for going out with him and said he would call again.

About our fifth date in, I started to talk more. I had learned a lot about him by that time. I let him know how much my faith meant to me and sometimes he asked me questions concerning the gospel. We were feeling quite a connection, and there was something special about our relationship. I was wondering if he was *ever* going to kiss me. On our sixth date, it was about nine in the evening and neither one of us wanted to go home yet, so he drove to a place called Crown Point. It had a huge gazebo where you could picnic, dance, and have small parties, and it looked over all the small towns below and had a beautiful view of the dam. We were sitting in the car when he said to me, "Would I be too bold to kiss you?" I was going to say it would be all right when he gently turned my face to his and gave me the gentlest, sweetest kiss. Even today, over 60 years later, I can close my eyes and remember that kiss.

A few days later, he took me to meet his family. Their home was a government home like the one where my grandparents lived. These homes were built for temporary purposes. They were basic, with a living room, kitchen, bath, and either one, two or three bedrooms. A few years later, his parents were able to buy the home for $2,500. They fixed it up quite nice.

His mother was a very talkative, take-charge woman. When I got to know more about her background, it was easy to figure out why she was that way. She had a hard life. She had been left at an orphanage in Lincoln, Nebraska, while very young. I don't believe she was able to talk to anyone about her true feelings as she grew up. Much of the time she needed to survive, and kept a lot of things pent up inside. There were times that she talked with gratitude, and times when she spoke with much bitterness in regard to her family. I do know that both her birth and adopted family meant a lot to her. She had so much deep emotional hurt and anger in her, and it was a release for her to have someone to tell her story to, as I was a good listener.

It seemed all the years I knew her, she had to have the last word on every subject and discussion. I am not sure if I ever finished a sentence before she interrupted me. Anytime anyone had any opinion other than hers, she became contentious and wouldn't give up on the subject until everyone around was upset. I found it very hard to have a close relationship with her. However, as I grew older, I did acquire more of an understanding of her and her feelings.

I wished I had paid more attention to her as she talked about her family, both about her birth and her adoptive family. I would get confused when she started talking, and sometimes I would just tune her out. She had a wealth of information concerning genealogy, which at that time I had very little interest in. I wish I had taken notes; I truly regret that.

John's father told us that he had come to the United States from Sweden at the age of seventeen to join his father who had come to America some years earlier. His father had changed their original name from Grandholm to Holmes. Both Gunner and his brother Fred, who later joined him, took the new name. We thought that John's father had been born in Sweden because everyone called him "Swede." We tried to get information from him about his ancestors, and he always said, "You leave the dead alone." There are many memories he did not want to discuss.

John and I continued to date while he lived down his reputation that he was a lady's man. He kept his true feelings to himself, and I became the only person who he would talk to about them. This remained true throughout his life. We were building a spiritual connection as we would talk about things we both believed in, and how we thought our lives should be as adults.

In the fall, John left for airline school in Spokane, Washington, about 90 miles from Coulee Dam. The school had come well recommended to both John and his mother. He was to be taught the airline business, and then they would help him find a job. However, this did not ever happen because the school turned out to be a fraud. Many people had invested a lot of money in it. No one was reimbursed.

One weekend, when John wanted his parents to come to Spokane to get him, they invited me to go with them. As we drove, we hit a bad snow and ice storm. His father was driving very slowly and carefully. This was pre-seat belt days, and I was in the front seat between his parents. I heard his father say, "Here we go!" The car slid and rolled over several times. When it finally stopped rolling, we were upside down. His parents managed to get the passenger door open, and we got out. I had taken my shoes off and his mother crawled back in to find them. We all seemed okay, except for being shook up. I had blood all over my face and was spitting blood.

We had just driven through a small town. John's mother saw a light and managed to get to a home where they let her use the phone to call the police and John. She told him to have someone come who could take us all back to Coulee Dam because the car was not drivable. The first thing he asked her was if I was all right. That hurt her very much because he did not ask how her condition was. But because she was calling, he assumed that she was all right. We later learned that she had some cracked ribs and was in quite a bit of pain herself.

John and his friend got to us, and the police came. The small town did not have a hospital, but the police called the doctor who had a clinic there. I was still bleeding, and a lot of blood was coming through my mouth. After he examined me at his office, he found that it was only a cut in my upper lip caused by my own teeth going through the inside of my lip. John had to hold my mouth open for the doctor to put stitches in it. I was black and blue for several days. John's friend drove us back to Coulee Dam, and we spent a lost weekend. The boys would come over to my house and we would just watch television and play board games. Carolyn came over and made a foursome. I was grateful to her for that. I didn't want to go anywhere because I was such a mess. John had told his friend that he had a pretty girlfriend, and I am sure he thought, "Oh yeah, right!"

Several months later, his friend got married. John was his best man, and I was the maid of honor. I had not met the bride until the day before the wedding. We had become good friends through letters and phone calls.

A few weeks before Christmas that year, I was at John's home visiting his family when he called from Spokane. He asked Margaret something about a size, and she told him she thought six and a half would be about right. I thought she might be referring to my shoe size. My foot was much larger than that, but I didn't say anything. I thought he might be referring to my shoe size because the last time he had been home, the three of us had gone ice skating. It was the first time I had been on ice skates, and I could hardly keep upright. It was quite different from roller skating. John had been clowning around on his skates and fell and let out the loudest bellow of pain. I made my way to him, hoping that I could stand upright. He said, "Oh, oh the pain is so bad, I think I have broken my ankle." I told Margaret to stay with him and I would go for help then he jumped up, threw his arms around me and said, "Gotcha!" I was so angry with him, but relieved that he was not hurt. Then we all had a good laugh.

At Christmas time, I found out what it was he wanted a size for, and it definitely was not a shoe. He gave me a beautiful diamond ring and asked me to marry him. I was almost sixteen, and wondered if he was crazy. I still had a year and a half of school left. The one thing I did know was that I loved him, and he loved me, but we were so young. I accepted the ring and told him that I needed to pray and think about it. One of the main things that I was told in my patriarchal blessing was that I should make the choice of my eternal companion a matter of prayer, as it would make a great deal of difference in my advancement in the kingdom of God.

My father would not talk to us about getting married. Mother told me later that he was too hurt, and he couldn't let me go. I prayed earnestly about it, and it seemed so right. I knew we were too young and that we would wait quite a while before we were married, or so I thought.

My main concern was how John felt about the church. He had studied a lot, and he loved history. As he read the Book of Mormon the first time, he read it as a historical account of an ancient people who came to the western continent 600 years prior to the birth of the Savior. He believed it, but he struggled with some other things. His testimony did not come as easily as mine, and that was all right. I felt in time he would figure it out. He knew of my desire to be married in the temple of the Lord for all time and eternity.

He promised me that would happen. Mine was a simple, deep faith, and he had questions that he had to prove by the scriptures. We spent many hours talking about the gospel of Jesus Christ. Sometimes he would ask me questions I couldn't answer, and between the two of us we would find and figure out the answer. It was a wonderful learning experience for both of us. There were no missionaries in our area.

After the airline school adventure did not work out, he came home from Spokane one day and announced to his family and me that he had joined the Marine Corp. I was shocked and upset, sincehe had not said a word about it. He had been thinking about it for quite a while and decided to do it. He said he would leave for boot camp in April, be there for four months, and have leave to come home. He then would be stationed somewhere, and I could join him after I finished school.

I was furious. He didn't know how close he came to getting his ring back. He certainly didn't know much about marriage – that these big decisions should be made together. However, unknown to the two of us, there was a plan that we feel Heavenly Father interjected that would bring us closer together than ever.

John left early in April for boot camp in San Diego, California. I received a letter from him almost every day. I lost those letters for several years, and have just recently have found them. I am enclosing a copy of one. I just want the readers of this book to know what a sentimental, deep-thinking, and God-loving person he is. This is the John that he only let a few people know. This letter was one written while he was in airline school. All his letters that followed, no matter where he was, were of the same loving and spiritual nature.

My dearest love,   *Dec. 16, 1956 6:30pm*

Today has been a strange day for me. I've read in the Bible four or five times. I am hunting for something. I am not sure where it will be found. I know that the Bible is where I am to look. I need God's help more than ever before for I'm about to make a decision that is going to affect the life of both of us now, and when you are my beloved wife and mother to our children. I have prayed for you and me, our love and future. LaVelle, since last night you have been the only thing that has been on my mind. You, my love, are the most wonderful person, the purest person in the world. You, LaVelle, have reached the farthest possible place in your love for our Father (Heavenly). My love, God knows this, and you are going to be blessed as very few of us have had or ever hope to be. Over and over I thank the Lord for bringing us together, for we were meant for each other and no one else.

My love, my heart cries for your closeness, there are many words that I want to tell you, not by writing to you but by having you at my side. My love, will you send me your ring—the one with the red stones in it. I promise to not only bring it back, but something else. You might say that I am about to make man's boldest move.

Believe me, I have prayed and meditated over this thing, and today on the bus the answer came to me and my love, I know that I am right for I know that all things work together for good for them that love God, to them who are called according to our wonderful Father's purpose.

Love me as I love you and may God bless you in everything you do.

LaVelle, my love, read these following lines with most care and full heart for they are meant for you this very moment that you read them. The light of the body is the eye, if therefore thine eye be single, thy whole body shall be full of light and pureness.

But seek ye first the kingdom of God and his righteousness, and these things shall be added unto you.

LaVelle, this is my way of telling you the things that have come to me. That I believe they were meant for not only me, but for you also. Ponder them.

Well my love, I must get some rest. Be good and write soon. Always remember that I love you very, very much.

All my love, Johnnie, dream of me and may God bless you. Bye bye

In his letters, he would always tell me how much he loved me. He would address the letters with "My dearest love," or "My dearest darling," and he would express his deep feelings for me and his feelings concerning Jesus Christ and Heavenly Father. Over the years, I have learned how precious it is to be told how much you are loved. I know women who may have been told only once by their husbands that they are loved. Perhaps their husbands felt that if they told them once, they should know it. These are words any woman longs to hear. Others of my friends have not had the opportunity yet to have that blessing.

After he left for training, John would tell me how things were going for him. He'd tell me how tough it was, as well as the crudeness of those who did the training, but he knew it would be this way. By the end of the first month, he was writing me a lot about being in the infirmary. He was there more and more. He kept getting boils on his legs and hips. Then his letters were coming from the hospital. They had admitted him because he had dozens of boils on him, and they could not find the cause. At one point, he had sixty-five boils below his waistline that each had to be lanced and drained. This was a very painful procedure.

One day after he had several of them lanced, he was drowsy from the ordeal. A man came up to where he was lying, took his dog tags, and said to him, "Are you one of those lousy Mormons?" John had put the Church of Jesus Christ of Latter-Day Saints down as his religious affiliation. His first impulse was to sit up and give the man a good punch on the chin. But because he lacked the strength, and because the man was a sergeant, he knew this was not a good idea. Instead he said, "I am, so what about it?" (Though he had not really joined the church yet.) The man extended his hand out and said, "Put it there, brother, so am I."

I never met this man, nor do I know his name, but I am eternally grateful to him because he had a tremendous influence on John. One of the things John was struggling with concerning the church was accepting the book of The Doctrine and Covenants. This sergeant was able to explain many things in it, as well as some other principles of the gospel he was studying. They became good friends as John continued to be hospital-bound and fight the boils that persisted.

On July 11, 1957, he was called in to the Captain's office and told he would be given an honorable medical discharge because they could not find a cure for his boils. His parents received a call from John, and the next day we once again found ourselves at the Spokane airport to greet him when he arrived on the plane.

He had changed, and whether he thought I had, I do not know. One of my biggest concerns about him joining the Marines was that he would change. That he would take more to the ways of the world because of the actions of some of those around him. He was different coming back, but in a way that I had not expected. The trial that he had physically endured had much to do with it, and the spiritual change was one of the greatest that I had ever seen. I was praying that the Lord would help him and that he would still have the beliefs and habits that he took with him. My prayers were answered to my utmost satisfaction. He had been captured by the spirit of the Lord, and the Holy Ghost had testified to him of the truthfulness of the gospel.

After we had been together for a month or so, we both felt it would be better if we married. Again, my father struggled with our plans. John's father counseled him not to marry me because he believed I would never be faithful to him. Despite this, we still wanted to be married.

John and I felt that he was supposed to come home. We have maintained that feeling and belief for all these years. We felt that Heavenly Father allowed the things that transpired in my parents' lives so that we could find each other.

Whether or not this is just a romantic fantasy, I cannot say. We have felt that way for over fifty-five years. As for the boils, he had one or two small ones after he came home that soon went away, and he has never had any since.

One day, John and a couple of friends from high school who were home from college were over at the high school playing basketball. They were taking a break and sitting on the bottom bleacher several feet apart from one another. They were the only ones in the school when the gym door opened, and a well-dressed man came in. He walked past John's friends, came up to John, stopped, and said, "John, join the church," before leaving through the other door. John turned to his friends and said, "Who was that man?" His friends looked at him somewhat puzzled and said, "What man?" Only John had seen and heard him. John did not share this incident very much in his early years. We have talked about it often. He held it very sacred.

He was baptized on September 29, 1957, in the Columbia River in an area behind the Coulee Dam. He promised me that we would go to Salt Lake City to have our marriage solemnized in the Salt Lake temple for time and eternity as soon as we could. I did not doubt that he would keep that promise. He needed to become an elder in the church, and we had to save enough money to make the trip.

His becoming an elder happened quite quickly. In the church, we believe that faithful men are granted power and authority from God, called the priesthood. There are different classes that young men generally attend as they grow up—they start at twelve as a deacon, become a teacher at fourteen, and then a priest from eighteen on. If men are faithful to the covenants that they have made and are called to a higher calling, they are ordained an elder. Many times, men are ordained as elders before they serve missions, but of course John had not grown up in the church or served a mission.

The branch president, who led our congregation, wanted to ordain John immediately. John told him he wanted the experience of being a deacon, teacher, and priest in the Aaronic Priesthood, and they let him be each class for about a month. His first calling in the church was to teach Sunday school to all the teenage girls that belonged to the branch. This was quite educational for him because they wanted to spend the class time talking about their Saturday night dates.

John found employment at the local sawmill, and it was me who told him we should marry soon. He agreed. The plan was to marry, and while I attended my senior year of high school and graduated in the spring, he would work at the sawmill. Then we would move to Cheney, Washington. There we would both find jobs, and he would attend Eastern State College of Washington. We did not know what our future held for us; no young couple does. What we did know was that we loved each other and that we wanted to be together. It seemed to me that we had been together before, and as my love grew for him, *I felt I loved him before I knew him.*

Nevertheless neither is the man without the woman, neither the woman without the man, in the Lord.

Corinthians 11:11
Bible

Thou shalt love thy wife with all thy heart, and shalt cleave unto her and none else.

Doctrine and Covenants 42:22

Chapter 5

Marriage 101

Both of our mothers were excited about the wedding. Mother and I talked about some ideas. I could tell by the telephone conversations that Mabel wanted to be involved. After about a week, we set up a time to go see her. I hadn't realized how enthused she was. As we talked, she told us that she would make the arrangements to have the wedding at the community church. She had asked a friend of hers to make the cake, others to take care of the gifts, and had investigated where the invitations should be made. She had also asked a friend of hers to sing, and another to play the organ. When I saw Mother cross her legs with her foot swinging back and forth, I knew what it meant. She was not one bit happy. When we got in the car, she let it all out. Who was the bride's mother, anyway? Why did she do all this planning without discussing it with us first? I was upset, but mostly bewildered.

I guess I did not realize how assertive my future mother-in-law was. She and John had locked horns several times when I had been there, as she was always telling him what and how to do things. "Oh great," I thought, "how am I going to handle this one?"

Eventually, things did work out. I chose the colors I wanted and the style of the cake. The wedding was held in the Community Church because there were not many other options in the area. Mabel's friend did sing one song – "I Love You Truly." The women she had asked to be "in charge of" gifts were her best friends. I didn't know that being "in charge" also meant opening them. The gift table was around the corner from where we received our guests, and I was shocked when I saw them all opened and displayed. This was something that I thought John and I could do together. Oh well!

Mother and I budgeted only so much money for the dress, and I had decided I would make it. We went into Spokane one Saturday to get the material. We parked by the fabric store, but saw a bridal shop a few doors down. It seemed to have a magnet on it, and soon we found ourselves going inside to just get some ideas. After I tried on several dresses and saw the price tags on them, we thought it would be best if we left. Just as we were approaching the door to leave, the lady who had been helping us asked, "Do either of you sew? I said that I did. She asked us to wait a moment. She went into the back and brought out the most beautiful dress with a long train and bow on the back. It had lace on the bodice and long sleeves. She told us the dress was no longer being made and was on a closeout. The problem with it was that it was a size 16. I was a size 8, so it would need to be altered. The dress was so beautiful, I was sure it would still be out of our price range. The lady then said it was on sale for $35.00. I looked at Mother; had this woman peeked into Mother's purse and saw that this was exactly what we had allotted for the dress fabric? I looked at the inside seams and decided I could make it fit, though I had never taken on a project like this before. I had enough money for the veil. We chose one, made our purchase, and left the store feeling very happy about our find.

Ruth and Jerry were now living in Grand Coulee, and she was able to help me with the sewing of bridesmaid's dresses and with other details. I was able to work on my dress, and was pleased with the way it turned out. Ruth was my matron of honor, and Rhonda came from Kennewick for the wedding. She and Margaret were my bridesmaids.

The wedding plans were simple, and the weeks passed quickly. I kept busy with school and helping mother with her new business. She had quit the hospital and opened a pet shop. Being on her feet in the nursing profession was too hard, and her legs ached constantly. Mother had a pet monkey, Annie. She was quite an attraction at the pet shop, and brought in a lot of business. One day, some people from out-of-town came in and ordered a baby skunk. Mother had to bring it in from a large pet store. The little skunk arrived a day before the people could pick it up. When it came time to close the store for the night, mother did not know what to do with him, so we decided to take our little baby home. He was restless and lonely, so I put him in bed with me and he snuggled up and settled right down. (Yes, he was de-scented.) When I told John that I had slept with a skunk, he wondered what other creatures I would bring into our bed.

John had bought his first car by now. It was a little Metropolitan Nash. When I say "little," that is an understatement. It wasn't just small; it was a gutless wonder. One day while I was driving it, I had both Mothers and his sister in the car. We were going up the heights of Grand Coulee, as the town was divided in an upper and lower part. Climbing the big hill was the only way to get to the upper part where we lived. I thought we were going to roll backward as there was no power in the car. His mother kept saying, "Floor board it, floor board it." I told her, "If I put my foot any harder on the gas pedal, we would be walking, but still in the car." It just could not pull all the weight in it. We did have a lot of fun in that car, but never had to worry about speeding.

The day of the wedding, John didn't know what to do with himself. So that morning, he took my dad to a favorite canyon where he had done a lot of hunting with his dad while he was growing up. The canyon was very steep and had a very narrow road. As they were going up the road, two elderly women were coming down it in their vehicle. Usually in a situation like this, each driver will pull to the right as far as possible so they can pass each other. This time, the other driver did not pull to the right. The lady just kept coming right down the middle of the road. John was as far to the right as he could go. One tire had slipped off the road and was hanging over the cliff. My dad managed to get out, but John dared not move. He looked in the rear-view mirror, and the other driver never looked back. He did not know if they had realized what happened. She just kept driving down the mountain. Then two men came down the road in a truck. Seeing the situation, they stopped, got their rope, and pulled the car to safety. John did not tell me this until after the wedding. I was almost a widow before I was a bride.

On Friday, November 8, 1957, I arrived at the church about an hour before anyone else. The building seemed so big and quiet, the flowers looked so nice, and I sat and took it all in. It wasn't the temple – that would come later. Soon, Mother, Ruth, and Rhonda were there to help me get into my gown. They all looked so nice. I was pleased with how things had turned out. Now, I just had to not trip as Dad walked me down the aisle. John looked so handsome—or "dashing," as Mother would say—in his white tux coat, dark pants, and bow tie.

Our new branch president, President Barker, performed the marriage ceremony. Then we went into the hall adjacent to the church for our reception. My grandparents and aunts had come from Kennewick, and we had a nice turnout of the local people.

We left town about 9:15 and headed toward Omak, Washington, about forty miles from Coulee Dam. John said, "Well, here we are all signed, delivered, and two married people." I broke in and said, "Oh my gosh, we didn't sign the marriage license! You've got to turn around and go back." He was reluctant, saying we could do it when we got back. I insisted, and he could see I was serious. I wasn't going another mile down that road without doing it. He turned the car around and we went back.

After we got the marriage license signed, we left for Omak again. He drove to the resort where he had made the reservations for the honeymoon suite. To our surprise, all that was there was a pile of ashes and a lopsided bird bath. The resort had burned down the week before, and they had no way of contacting us because all their records had been destroyed. We found a motel that had one room left and we took it.

The next day, we traveled to Penticton, in British Columbia, Canada. It is a pretty country. We had heard a lot about the movie *The Ten Commandments* and wanted to see it. The film turned out to be a huge box office success. The special effects, especially the parting of the Red Sea, were the most sensational in a movie up to that time. Before we sat down, we decided to get some popcorn. It was so crowded and noisy, that John told the girl who waited on him to keep the change. The crowd silenced and looked at him. He wondered what he did wrong. Didn't our neighbors, the Canadians, tip? We just quickly found our way to our seats.

When we got back to our hotel, John had a high fever and was shaking very hard and sick to his stomach. He remained that way all night, and I was one scared bride. Here we were, far from home, not knowing anyone in a strange country, and my new husband was sick. We wondered if the popcorn had made him sick. His fever broke at about dawn, and we were able to enjoy the rest of our stay.

We got home on Monday, and we went right to the Coulee Dam High and Grand Coulee High School's annual Veteran's Day football game. These two teams were bitter rivals, and just a few years before, John had been in the thick of it as a player for Coulee Dam High. I was still a student at Grand Coulee High, so now we wondered who should we cheer for – his school or mine? We did a little of both – or at least I did! I felt like a traitor.

We had found an apartment to rent. It had no doors on the cupboards, so I made curtains for them. The apartment had a very interesting layout, especially the bathroom. There were two bedrooms, and in between them was the toilet and shower. You could then step into one of the bedrooms for the wash basin. The place was furnished, and we made it home. All this, including utilities, cost us $35.00 a month.

We learned after we got home that there was a salesman staying at the Coulee Dam Motel right across from the church where we married. He had a car exactly like ours, and when he went to leave the next morning, he was quite surprised to see ribbons, tin cans, and a "just married" sign attached to his car. It was also put on blocks as our wonderful friends had taken off his tires. What a way to be welcomed into a town. I wonder if he ever came back.

I graduated from high school in June. The school choir did a lot of traveling at the end of the school year. Once again, I was in Omak. This time, I was on stage singing with the choir. Our choir robes were very hot. As we were finishing our last song, I got dizzy and struggled to stay standing. I got hotter and hotter, and the next thing I knew, some of the kids were holding me on the bleachers we were standing on. I didn't know what the matter was until the next week when I went to the doctor, and he confirmed that we were going to have our first baby. He would be born in January of 1959.

My patriarchal blessing (a personal individual blessing that is given to each member by a man who holds the priesthood and called by God, to this position) had said nothing about me being a mother and this had greatly concerned me, even to the point that I went back to the Patriarch and asked him if something could have been left out when it was typed. He assured me nothing was left out when he transcribed it from the recording machine. Most women and girls I knew who had received their blessing found mention in them about motherhood, so why not mine? Would there be no children? I certainly didn't have to worry, because after our baby was born in January, eight more would come.

We moved into a small house on the heights of Grand Coulee that summer and got a little dog called Mornie. The little dog had some mental challenges and never did seem quite right. We left him home one night with our kitten, and that was a mistake. We had done a lot of Christmas decorating, and he and the cat had a great time tearing them down. The living room was in shambles when we got home. He ran away one day, and we never saw him again.

It seemed we went through a lot of pets that first year. Next, we got a little female miniature collie. She was so sweet and a nice companion. One day when John had come for lunch, she was sitting by the table when she fell backward. Her eyes rolled up in her head, and she started foaming at the mouth. John grabbed his 22-rifle and shot her right there in the kitchen. I was several months pregnant, and all he could think of was that she had rabies and she would turn on me and the baby.

John brought home a hawk one night, too. He was working at a gas station, and a customer did not have any money and asked if he could trade the hawk for gas. The hawk lived with us for a few weeks and was eating us out of house and home. He was noisy and dirty, and his cage took up half of a room. We finally took him up in the mountains and let him go. We stayed until he found his wings and watched him fly off. He was a beautiful bird, and now he was where he needed to be.

With all the children that would come to our home, pets became a large part of our lives. I can't remember too many years without one. I am a firm believer that pets can add so much to a family. Not only can they teach children responsibility, they also teach them many other things. The miracle of the birthing process is one. Pets can also be such a great friend when sometimes friends aren't all we hoped they would be.

Yes, pets are great, but what we were soon to experience when our little David was born was the greatest joy yet. Heavenly Father just kept sending me these wonderful blessings. The gospel of Jesus Christ, my husband, and a baby son.

What a responsibility was coming to me; this is what I had dreamed of. Suddenly, I was nervous, scared, and wondered if I could do what was expected of me. It wasn't the physical part of the baby that concerned me. I was sure I could do that; it was the nurturing and teaching that I felt was my job that worried me. Long before our first son was born, I had long talks with him. I did so again with all his brothers and sisters who followed. I had no idea so many were to follow. With each one, I told them they were loved and wanted in our home and family. (Sometimes I had physical problems with my pregnancies, mostly morning sickness that lasted up till the seventh month. I have never until this day figured out why they call it "morning sickness," when you wake up with it and it sometimes lasts all day and night.) I would talk to them, and sometimes plead with them that if he or she had any say in this, then if I did my part, and they would do theirs, together we would get them here. I wondered if all mothers talk to their unborn children.

A mother's influence has eternal consequences. I believe there is a season for all things in our lives. I knew as a young mother that to neglect this eternal assignment in any way would be a mistake. Mothering is so much more than giving birth. We need to rear these spirit children God sends to us in all righteousness so that they will one day return to Him. I had to constantly be learning, and use most of my energy for this calling. Although I was excited to be a mother, it was often overwhelming. Furthermore, I learned that what I did one day was not necessarily what I would need to do the next day. Each dawn brought a new adventure, sometimes large, and quite often very perplexing.

...For this cause shall a man leave father and mother, and cleave to his wife: and they twain shall be one flesh.

Matthew 19:5
Bible

Wherefore, be not weary in well-doing, for ye are laying the foundation of a great work. And out of small things proceedeth that which is great.

Doctrine and Covenants 64: 33

Chapter 6

Moving to Utah

Mother gripped the steering wheel tightly as we drove between the two towns. She did not like the winding drive. She always said she felt like she was driving down a slide with the big mountain to the left, the drop-off to the river on the right, and the huge dam below. This morning, it was worse than usual because it had snowed lightly, and blustery winds were now following.

She was taking me to the hospital to induce labor as my baby was two weeks over due. John had to go to work early that morning and would join us later. This was before the days the father could go in and be with the mother while she gave birth. The doctor said, "It would be a long process."

It was late that afternoon when I heard a lot of screaming and moaning coming from the labor room adjacent to mine. This went on for hours, and it got to the point that I was more concerned for the other new mother than for myself. I kept asking myself "Can't they help her?" One of the nurses told me that she was a 15-year-old unwed girl whose baby was breach, and they could not get it turned. She was from out of town, alone, and so frightened. She was placing the baby for adoption the next day.

I was so sad for her. Here I was with my mother, and my husband and I were greatly anticipating the birth of our baby. Finally, two hours before our little one came, the screaming stopped. When I inquired about her, I was told the baby had been born and the girl was now resting.

Finally, it was our big moment. David Lynn Holmes made his grand entrance late on the night of January 22, 1959. He was quite red, and had thick black hair. David means "Beloved." I thought he was beautiful, and certainly he was loved long before I set eyes on him. When his daddy and grandparents came in, both grandmothers were so happy that he was here and so perfect. Grandpa Holmes just said, "Oh golly!" That was what we heard from him every time a new baby was born, or it was announced another was coming. I never did figure out what my dad was thinking; he just stood there with a big grin on his face.

It was all new to me. I realized later all the mistakes I made as a new mother. In fact, it took me three babies to figure that I should forget the book schedule. I had heard it all my life and I believed it, but it was so far from the truth. It was like saying all babies and children are the same. When I realized babies were as different as adults were, (after all, they were just a miniature person that came with their own personalities), then everything became much easier for me, and I had much happier babies.

Later that summer, we moved to Cheney, Washington. John had been accepted at the Eastern State College of Washington. We both got hired on at Lakeland Village, an institution for mentally challenged children who had their permanent residence there. I took the early shift, and John took the afternoon shift to work with his school schedule. We had to have a babysitter about fifteen hours a week. I didn't like having a babysitter at all, but it seemed to be the best that we could work out.

We hired Mrs. Badget, who came under good recommendation. She was a lady in her seventies and she came to the apartment. She was good with David and always good natured. She brought a small bottle with her and said it was cough syrup. We were sure it was not cough syrup, but the bottle was so small we knew she couldn't get drunk on it. I have since wondered how many small bottles she had in her bag. I was trying to figure out how to kindly dismiss her, but that problem seemed to fix itself. She wasn't with us long before she came one day and announced it would be her last day. She was going to elope that night and wouldn't need to work anymore. I hope her plan worked out. We thought we could have that problem with someone our own age or younger, not with a 70-year-old grandma. Our neighbor, who was expecting her second child, became our next babysitter.

In August of 1960, we had finally saved enough money to make our trip to Utah to be sealed in the Salt Lake Temple. I wanted to have Aunt Thelma and Uncle Barr go through the temple with us. Uncle Barr was one of the witnesses, and Thelma was my escort.

On August 25, 1960, we set out for the temple. Their home was in Holiday and quite a distance from the temple. Aunt Thelma was notoriously late for most occasions. I didn't know this at the time, but I realized it when I got to know her better. We were scheduled for the 5:30 session and supposed to be there by 4. Uncle Barr was meeting us at the temple. We left her house at 3:30. We were late, she was driving, and I think we hit every stop light there was. She kept saying old scratch (Satan) did not want this marriage to take place. I missed out on the bride's talk, which I really had been looking forward to, and did not get it until I was the escort for our oldest daughter Cindy when she got married.

After we left the Temple, we went to the first Kentucky Fried Chicken restaurant that was ever opened. Aunt Thelma said it was the best chicken that we had ever tasted, and she was right. Little did we know that it would grow into a huge franchise and become famous worldwide.

We liked Utah and talked about how it would be to live there. I never thought it would come about, or even considered whether I wanted it. But John was doing a lot of thinking. The night that we were sealed in the temple, we stayed up talking about what had transpired earlier that evening and about our future. Most of all, we were grateful to our Heavenly Father that the desire we had had come to pass. I gave thanks that once more, my prayers were answered.

When we returned home, we talked a lot about moving to Utah. The more we talked about it, the more it seemed that it was the right thing to do. Explaining it to our parents was not an easy task. They were very upset with us. It would not be easy to leave them; however, our reasons were not something they could completely understand. One of the reasons was that we were getting too much interference from my father and his mother. They both wanted to run our lives, and we were both much too independent to let them do that. Much of our thinking centered on teachings of the gospel. Perhaps I felt they would have too much negative influence on our children. Dad disliked the members so much, and Mom Holmes was such an argumentative person. I did not like the contention, and I could see that John had already inherited some of this trait. I wanted our children to be independent thinkers. My belief was, and always will be, that they could find a more civilized way to communicate.

Perhaps I seem harsh on my father and John's mother. I loved my father very much, even if he frustrated me a great deal. I was eventually able to build a relationship with Mother Holmes, and she found great joy in her grandchildren and their accomplishments. I somehow felt that the only way to hold on to my family was to be separated from our parents at this time in our journey of life.

Another reason we wanted to move to Utah was that John wanted to attend Brigham Young University. He applied and was accepted. He was to start in the fall of 1961. We sent money for our deposit on student married housing. He then made a trip to Salt Lake to find employment, and was hired by Hy-Land Dairy. He was told that he would be in the Provo area, but it did not quite work out that way.

We were not able to leave exactly when we wanted, so he did not get registered for the fall quarter. Our cash flow was not as we planned, so we remained in Cheney. It was during this time we experienced what we recognized to be a wonderful blessing from paying tithing. We had received our paychecks and paid our rent, car payment, and other bills. Extra doctor bills had come, and we paid them and our tithing. We had debated whether to pay tithing or save the money for food. We had a full tank of gas in our car, and about $5 to last four weeks. I did not know how I was going to stretch what little food we had in the apartment until the next payday. A few days later, I went to the mailbox and saw an envelope from the B.Y.U. Housing Department. We had thought the deposit money for the housing was non-refundable, but the amount in the envelope was a few dollars more than we had paid in tithing.

In the late spring of 1961, we were finally prepared to leave. We went to Coulee Dam and then to the tri-cities to tell our families goodbye. It was hard for all of us. We promised to come back as often as we could, a promise that we kept. We went to see them every year, sometimes more often, and they would come see us when they could. We knew it was important for them to see their grandson and other children who may come, and we thought it felt like the right thing for us to do. We did miss them. I especially missed my sister and my mother.

When we arrived in Utah, we went straight to Aunt Thelma and Uncle Barr's home. John checked in with Hy-Land Dairy the following day for orientation and to see where his route would be. To our surprise, he was to work in Brigham City, which was quite opposite of what he had originally been told. He had been promised a route near Provo so that he could attend school there. We had to take the job, at least temporarily, as we had a small amount of cash on us.

As we were going through the small town of Willard, Utah, we saw a small white house sitting on the right side of the road, hidden by some large trees. It looked like it might be empty. We turned around to see it again, saw that it was empty, and found out the last residents had just moved out the day before. We inquired as to who owned it, and were told the landlord lived two houses away. We knocked on the door, and a lovely lady answered. Her name was Marion Pinnion. We asked about the house, and she rented it to us.

Marion and her husband Wallace became very good friends to us, especially Marion. All she knew was being a farmer's wife. Of course, raising ten children was quite an education itself. She was one of the hardest working women I had ever met. She was a beautiful woman, though she did not think so. Her skin was prematurely aged, and her hair was graying. Her hands indicated that she had done farm work all her life. She had striking eyes that were captivating when she smiled. From the first time that I saw her, I thought she emulated what a beautiful daughter of God should look like.

She taught me many things about being a good homemaker— things mother had probably tried to teach me, but that I was too busy with other things to understand. We had long talks about the gospel. Having come from outside of Utah, I had never met another woman who understood me and my thoughts concerning religion. We had lived so far from the members in Washington that I was unable to establish many relationships. She also helped me because I missed mother more than I'd expected to. She had adult daughters who had moved out of state, and she really missed them. We were good for each other.

I had been desirous to have another baby, so when I learned I was pregnant in August of 1961, I was happy. I once again found myself very sick, even worse than I had been with David. By early fall, I had lost ten pounds and was so weak. One day I was so hungry and dizzy that I sat down on the couch, thinking I would just sit there a moment and watch David play in the living room. I fell asleep and was awakened by someone pounding on the front door. I realized David was not in the room with me. I went to the door, and there stood a man holding David. He asked if this was my little boy. David had unlocked the door and was riding his tricycle in the middle of the highway in front of our house. I was so thankful to our Heavenly Father, though upset with myself that I had fallen asleep and let my little one get away.

My condition worsened, and I got weaker. My doctor said I would need to go to the hospital to get hydrated and see if I could gain some strength. After a few days, there had not been any improvement. The doctor said that if there was no change in the next twenty-four hours, he would strongly consider interrupting my pregnancy. I was not sure what he meant. When he said the word "abort," I was horrified; no way was that going to happen. I was at a spiritual, mental, and physical low point.

I prayed to Heavenly Father about my unborn baby and made a promise to Him at that time. I was sure that I was having another son and knew he would serve Him all the days of his life, if I could keep him. It was as if I was dedicating his life to the Lord. I, too, committed to serve Heavenly Father in any way that I should be asked to the best of my ability.

I had prayed and cried so hard that I finally fell asleep from exhaustion. John was so worried about me, and he was praying for me as he sat by my bedside as much as he could. Our prayers were answered. The next day, there was some slight improvement. By the following day, the doctor told me I could go home if I stayed quiet and worked hard to keep food down. I wanted to ask the doctor how he expected me to do that?

Marion helped us out with David. John had called Mother, and she was coming to help. I had been home a few days when I went to the bus stop in Willard to meet her. Never was I so glad to see her. She stayed about a week, and during that time I rested and regained strength. I was so grateful to have her and sad to see her go. But I knew it was a sacrifice for her and Daddy to have her come.

On March 30, 1962, our son Eric Bryan Holmes (which means "eternal ruler") was born. He looked much like his older brother with much less hair. He was such a good baby and slept a lot. I had to wake him up to feed him. He ate well and did not have any problems. I am also sure that being an experienced mother helped both of us.

It was shortly after this that we moved to Salt Lake City, and John's sister Margaret came to live with us and attend the L.D.S. Business College. She was so good with the boys. She would have Eric giggling so hard he would almost lose his breath. John baptized Margaret into our church during this time. After one year of school, she went back home and soon married Roger Wert.

It was during these years that I learned about leadership in the church, and the correct way to conduct meetings. I had some wonderful role models. The women I was around were poised, polished, and educated, with mature testimonies. I did not know then that I would preside and conduct many Primary, Young Women, and Relief Society meetings in the years to come. As these opportunities came, I was glad for their prior examples.

In the summer of 1963, I realized we were going to have another baby. This time, things went better. I felt good most of the pregnancy.

On Feb. 19, 1964, Mother Holmes came so she could help with the boys while I was in the hospital. The next morning, John and I left for the hospital and labor was induced. Our third baby boy, Craig Leonard Holmes ("firm like a rock") arrived.

Unlike his brothers, Craig had no hair and the brightest blue eyes. He was a joy to us and I felt so grateful that I had three sons who would be bearers of the Priesthood. I felt this was a great honor. Craig was a happy baby. As he grew, he was always busy, didn't require much sleep, and had the most curious mind. I could tell he was very determined to do what he set out to do, a trait that has stayed with him all his life.

In May of that year, we bought two small homes— one to live in and one to rent. They were at 232 and 236 Browning Avenue in Salt Lake City (14th South). The houses were connected by the water and sewer pipes, but otherwise were two separate dwellings. We knew we would not stay there too many years, but it was a start. John was now working for Carpenter Paper Company, first in the warehouse, then on the order desk, and then he started his career as a salesman for them.

One afternoon, I was cutting out a dress on the kitchen floor while David and Eric were at school and Craig was napping— or at least, I thought he was. It was almost time to go to Primary that afternoon, and I went in to wake him up. Much to my surprise, he was not in his bed nor anywhere else in the house. I looked all over the yard and checked with some neighbors. I don't know how he got past me because I could see the hallway from where I was working. Looking up and down the streets, I saw something lying under a tree about a block and a half away. I ran to the tree, and there he was—holding his blanket and sound asleep. I woke him, and he told me he had come to get "Erky," which is what he called Eric. I knew I really had to stay on my toes to keep up with these active little boys.

The house we were living in was the older of the two, and needed some tender, loving care. I liked being able to fix it up and decorate. I had watched my father turn rooms that had previously been plain into lovely, warm, inviting ones where you felt comfortable. As a paint contractor's daughter, I had inherited some talent in this area. I found great satisfaction in taking on these kinds of projects.

John enjoyed yard work and turned our yard into a place of sanctuary. We had large trees and lots of rose bushes. Inside, we had a strange four-by-four box in the corner of the living room. At first, we planned to remove it. We soon found it was there to stay as it had many permanent pipes under it that were built right up into the box. We bought small white rocks to cover it and filled it with plants. It was not only very pretty, but made quite a conversation piece.

Larry and Sally Butler, our neighbors behind us, were deaf. Larry had some hearing and Sally could not hear at all. She and I got to be pretty good friends, and we used a lot of paper to converse. I wish now that I had taken the time to learn how to sign. They had three children. One day, when all our children were gone except for her baby, I had opened a can of tomato soup for lunch and had scorched it. I opened the window to get the odor out, and I heard her baby screaming. This went on for a few minutes. It concerned me. I saw that Sally, too, was working in her kitchen, but the screams were coming from the bedroom. I knew that he was in trouble. I ran into her house, went into the kitchen, grabbed her, and pointed her to the bedroom. His cries were getting more and more pleading. When we got to him, his little head was stuck between the bars in the crib. We had to break the bars off to get him released. He had started to turn blue and was so frightened. Sally just sat down, held him close, and cried. I can't imagine the frustration and heartbreak she must have felt not to hear her baby's cry for help. As for me, I was just glad for burned soup or I may have never heard her little one's plea.

In 1966, I decided to do some child-care in our home. I was caring for two little children when our ward Relief Society president came and asked me if I would consider taking care of a newborn. Her neighbor, Janet, was going to have her baby soon and would need to return to work after six weeks. I told her that I would. When I met Janet, there seemed to be an instant bond. I looked forward to tending her baby.

When baby Derek was six weeks old, I became his daycare provider. He was a beautiful baby with his round little cheeks and big eyes. His mother always had a curl on the top of his dark, thick hair. The boys loved him and told me we should get another baby of our own.

I will never forget one day in May 1967. It started out as a normal, beautiful day, but it did not end that way. John had stopped at the house in the late morning to get something he needed. We talked for a while before he headed back to work. I started to prepare lunch for the children while little Derek slept on our bed. I heard him wake up, so I went in to turn him over and change his diaper. Our doctors always told us to have a newborn sleep on their tummy then. He seemed quite content, so I put him in his infant chair and returned to the kitchen. I planned to feed him as soon as the other children were fed. When I went in to get him a few minutes later, his little face was white. He seemed lifeless, and there was spit up on his face and mouth. I grabbed Derek and gave him mouth to mouth resuscitation, but nothing I did revived him. Again, I found myself running to a neighbor's home. I literally threw the baby in her arms and screamed, "Carol, Carol! Is this baby dead?"

Be pleased, O Lord, to deliver me: O Lord, make haste to help me.

Psalms 40:13
Bible

And when [Jesus] had said these words, he wept, and the multitude bare record of it, and he took their little children, one by one, and blessed them, and prayed unto the Father for them.

3 Nephi 17:21
Book of Mormon

Chapter 7

Knowing His Tender Mercies

The ambulance ride to the hospital seemed so long, and traffic seemed extra heavy. Why wasn't the driver going faster? I held little Derek ever so tightly in my arms. I kept asking the paramedic if there was something we could do, and was the baby really dead? He was very quiet and patient with me and told me that they would do all that could be done. I asked myself over and over what happened because it all happened so fast. One moment, he was a happy, content baby... and now... what had I done wrong? In my heart, I knew he was dead, but prayed for a miracle that he might be revived.

At the hospital, they took him from my arms and someone asked me some questions. I could not tell them any more than what I have written here, there was so little to say. They had me sit in the waiting room. When I saw Janet come through the door, I ran to her and threw my arms around her saying, "Oh Janet, I am sorry, so very, very sorry!" When the attendant told her that her baby was dead, she wilted in my arms. We were both trembling so hard that we both had to be helped to be seated. She asked me what had happened. I told her what I could, and then they took her to baby Derek.

Both John and Lance, Derek's father, arrived shortly after. I went over with each of them what had happened. I knew I was not making much sense. I was too upset and in shock. I felt my soul had been jerked out from under me. My heart was breaking for Lance and Janet. John was so caring and understanding to me, but I did not feel deserving of it. I felt every emotion, yet I felt nothing.

We were told we could leave and that Lance and Janet would get with us later. When they arrived home, they called us on the phone and we went right over. I could not believe how loving and caring they were to me. Right from the moment of the news, they did not blame me. We sat and talked, trying to console each other. We cried, and there seemed so little we could do. I went over the story many times, trying to remember if there was something I forgot or had done wrong.

The cause of death was diagnosed as SIDS, or Sudden Infant Death Syndrome. It's a condition that is far too common in infants, especially little boys. Usually the baby would be on its tummy sleeping peacefully one moment, and the next would not be breathing at all. They knew little about what caused it then. Much research has been done in the last 50 years, yet there are no concrete answers.

Janet had taken Derek to the doctor for his three-month checkup just a few days before his death, and he was in every way a beautiful, healthy baby boy.

The next few days are a blur. The morning of the funeral, I was at the mortuary. When I walked up to his little casket, seeing him for the first time since I had held him so tightly in the ambulance, I looked down at his sweet little body and then collapsed into John's arms. I was almost hysterical, and everything flashed through my mind again. Janet said that I took his death harder than she did. Of course, that could not be true. No pain can replace that of a mother's broken heart, yearning empty arms, and indescribable emptiness.

I felt so accountable, so responsible, and so at fault. The guilt of not being in that room when he needed me was unbearable. If only I had brought him in the kitchen with me, or had listened more carefully. The guilt and the questions consumed me. For days and weeks after that, I just existed. I went through the motions of caring for my family, and I could not tell you one thing that went on with the children and John. What did I feel? Nothing—only complete emptiness. I pled with the Lord for His mercy and help, so that somehow, I would be able to raise my own beautiful sons and be a wife here on this earth. I felt I had let the unthinkable come upon me, though it was not intentional, and I felt my mortal and spiritual life would be taken from me.

All I could do was to cry out to the Lord and go to him in secret prayer to find consolation and solace. I had never known such despair. If I had to go on living, I needed some peace. I needed sleep so badly. The nights seemed endless, and the days so long.

During this time, Lance and Janet became good friends to John and me. Their attitude and love were the only comfort I found. They had not been attending church and had not been married in the temple. They started coming to church, and Lance was ordained an Elder. Janet had a wonderful testimony of the gospel. I knew the plan of salvation gave her strength.

One morning, I received a phone call from her. She had just talked to her grandfather, a Patriarch in the Shelly, Idaho Stake. He told her he had a dream the previous night about little Derek. In the dream, he was told it was Heavenly Father's will that Derek should come back to Him now, that he had come to Earth to receive his body and completed his mortal mission. This gave Janet great comfort. In the dream, he was told she should tell me to go on with my life, that what had happened was not my fault. I found some solace in this. Relief would come for a few days at a time, but then the feelings would start all over again. The despair would again build, and I would slip back to the state I was in just after his death.

I realized, too, that I was not just mourning the death of Derek. I was mourning for myself and for the separation I thought I would eventually have from my own children and John. I was sure I would not be with them. I already had missed so much of their lives, especially that of Craig, now three-years-old. I had been so stifled by the death of Derek.

John was traveling for the company he worked for and spent every other week out of town. One sleepless night while he was away, the anxiety and anguish built until I crawled out of bed and went to my knees. I stayed there for what seemed to be many hours in prayer, pleading to the Lord for peace to accept Derek's grandfather's dream as my answer. I asked the Lord to allow me to forgive myself and return to some kind of normal life. At about 5 a.m., I went back to bed, knowing that in a few hours I needed to be up to take care of my three sons. I still did not sleep. When it was time to start the day, I was exhausted. A repeat of so many days.

The following Saturday night, I received a phone call from the second counselor in our ward bishopric asking if John and I could meet with him and our bishop on Sunday morning before Sunday School. I had talked to the bishop several times in the prior months.

When we went into his office, we talked for a few minutes. He then asked me to be the ward's new Primary president. I looked at him with a blank look on my face, and then an overwhelming feeling of love from the Lord came over me. I was being asked to be the leader of the children of the ward—which is another name for our congregation. I was being entrusted with their spiritual welfare, along with their parents. There was close to one hundred of them. A great burden then lifted from my shoulders. I knew for sure the Lord had not only answered my prayers, but that I was forgiven in any fault I may have had in Derek's passing. Never had I felt such tender mercies from our Heavenly Father.

The bishop then said he felt very impressed to tell me how they came up with my name and knew I was the one that Heavenly Father wanted to fill this position now. He said the bishopric had met on the previous Wednesday night (The night that I had prayed so hard and long). They had been discussing for several weeks who the next primary president should be, but no answer had come to them. As they parted that night, their assignment was to pray and fast the next day about the matter before meeting again Thursday with a name to submit. The name that had come to each of them was mine. I knew Heavenly Father had heard my prayers and pleas. I had never felt so humble.

I felt like I had returned home, that I had been in a terrible, grim darkness, and now I was stepping out of a huge, dark cloud and back into light. I never lost any of my testimony through the experience of little Derek, but I did lose much of my self-worth. That is something that we can never let happen. Once we do, Satan can take control, because one of his greatest tools is discouragement. Feeling there is no use to try to do what is right can take us down so quickly. Oh, how that must make him rejoice.

Sometimes when we pray, we think no one is listening, and feel separated from the truths that will help us. We feel we are carrying a crushing weight, and no matter what we do, we cannot shake it. We feel emotions that give us temporary relief, then we have relapses and we feel abandoned again. Our Father in Heaven and the Savior will never abandon us. My faith in God had been tested, and so had my faith in myself.

If we ever experience the feeling that we are losing our faith and self-worth, we must fight with all our might, mind, and strength. Like the pioneers of the Willie and Martin Handcart companies, who needed to be rescued with food, blankets, clothing, wagons, and the help of good men, we too must turn to our Heavenly Father and plead for His help. Then, after we have done all that we can to help ourselves to make that rescue come to pass, light and knowledge will come to us. We can be confident again knowing that we are His son or daughter. He loves us so much, and wants us to overcome the things that come into our lives that bring us down spiritually, physically and mentally. He wants us to succeed. There is a special assignment and mission for each of his children to do, and we must do our part to help bring the gospel of Jesus Christ to the world. We must always remain optimistic, knowing that help will come if we are patient and don't succumb to the enticements of the cunning one. We, too, can be rescued.

From this experience in my life as a young woman, I learned more of the atonement and gained a greater understanding of its purpose. He who walked on water, raised the dead, healed the sick, and whose blood had been shed for each of us gives us great healing power. Truly, the Savior does ease our burdens. He does visit us in our afflictions.

Over the years since the experience of little Derek, I have gained a deep assurance that our Heavenly Father has a perfect love for each of us. We must sense the value He has for all His children. We must ponder the great principles of the gospel and the eternal nature of our own identity to feel His infinite love. I thank my Heavenly Father for the challenges that have come to me, for each one has taught me so much. I will always thank Him for His "Tender Mercies."

The Lord is good to all: and his tender mercies are over all his works.

Psalm 145:9
Bible

...But behold, I, Nephi will show unto you that the tender mercies of the Lord are over all those whom he has chosen, because of their faith, to make them mighty even unto the power of deliverance.

1 Nephi 1:20
Book of Mormon

Chapter 8

Taylorsville Years

I had the privilege of working with some fine women in the church's Primary program who taught me a lot. We submitted names for the bishop to call some sisters that had not been active for quite a while, and they accepted their callings. It was a thrill for me to not only see them teach the gospel to the children, but to witness them building their own testimonies.

Fourteen months had passed since the passing of Derek. Life was busy with the boys and serving in Primary. In those days, we had to raise the money we needed for the budget, and do the Primary Penny drive. There were always fundraisers to do.

John and I were expecting our fourth child, and we were also having a house built in Taylorsvillle. Many young families were moving into the area, and houses were going up all along the west side of town. With another baby on the way, we needed more room.

Our little Cynthia LaVelle ("brings much light") came before the house was finished. She came a little earlier than expected. The day before she was born, I went to Farmington with my neighbor to pick cherries to can. My back started hurting. The next day I did a lot of washing, canned thirty-five quarts of cherries, and then decided to go to the doctor as I was sure she was on her way. The doctor said I could go to the hospital or go home and wait, as it would be a while. I chose to go home because John was working in Wyoming and had to be contacted by his company. I made arrangements for the boys and folded and ironed some clothes. I scrubbed the kitchen floor as it was sticky from the cherries, but ran out of energy and was too tired to wax. Aunt Thelma came to stay with the boys.

Our neighbor, Bill Jackson, said he would take me to the hospital. All I wanted him to do was to drop me off, knowing I would be fine and John was on his way. Bill insisted on staying with me. It was a little confusing to the nurse when she wanted to check me because I said, "He is not my husband." John finally arrived minutes before Cynthia did. I was so happy to have a girl. I was sure she would be another boy, which would have been okay, but I didn't know how much it would mean to have a baby girl. When she was placed in my arms, I laid there and cried. The doctor asked me what was wrong, and I blubbered through my tears and said, "I am so happy."

John's mother and dad came to stay with us, but a sad thing happened. His mother kept saying she could do anything except hold the baby. I should not have taken her so literal. They were there for four days, and she still had not held Cindy. There was a pioneer program being put on by the Primary, and I wanted to attend it even though I had one of my counselors in charge. Eric had quite a large part in it and had worked hard to learn it, and I wanted to be there for him. I nursed the baby and told mom I was sure she would sleep till I got back, which she did.

The next morning, I was in the bedroom nursing Cindy. David came in and told me Grandma and Grandpa were leaving. I thought they were going to the store, but he said no, they have their bags in the car and they told him they were going home. I went out to the car as they were about to drive off and asked what was wrong and why were they leaving. Not a word was spoken, and they just drove off. I stood there stunned.

The only thing I could figure out was the fact that she had not held the baby. I should have just put her in her arms at some point. We called them when they got home, and she would not talk to me. I wrote her a letter and apologized for whatever I had done wrong. She did not answer. About six weeks later, she called and asked how we were all doing and acted like nothing had happened. The whole thing was strange. I am sure I hurt her.

Two weeks after Cindy was born, we moved to Taylorsville. We settled in and the children did not lack for others to play with. One day, I looked out my kitchen window. I could see down to the end of the street and counted how many children lived on our block. There were 72.

Craig had made friends with a boy named Tommy Westley. They were both quite adventurous. While hanging clothes on the clothesline one morning, the thought came to me: "Go find Craig." Craig and Tommy were always migrating back and forth to each other's houses. I was sure they were at Tommy's, but decided I'd better make sure. Again, the feeling came to me saying, "Go find Craig!" The third time it came, I went into the house and called Tommy's mom, who said she was sure they were at our house. David and Eric were both at school, and I grabbed Cindy in her carrier and jumped into the truck without a clue where I was going. At the end of one of the streets, I saw a dirt road and turned down it. It led me to a canal that I did not know existed. There I saw two little boys about to take their bikes into the swift-running water. I got to them just as Tommy had put his front wheels in the canal. I was very upset with the boys, but mostly I was so grateful that I had been warned by the Holy Ghost to go find them.

When Cindy was four months old, I was nauseated again. Yes, another baby was on her way. I had placenta separation with my pregnancy early in July. I woke up in the middle of the night and realized I was heavily bleeding. I went into the kitchen, and large clots started to come. I called out to John. When he came from the bedroom, he found me laying on the floor in the kitchen. I told him to call an ambulance and to call our neighbor, Marvin Schmid, to help him give me a blessing. Marvin and his wife, Jessie, came right over even though it was 3 a.m. He and John gave me a Priesthood blessing and the ambulance got there and took me up to the LDS Hospital. I was still giving directions for the boys and Cindy as the ambulance prepared to drive off. They got the bleeding stopped. The doctor told me that a few more minutes and they would have lost both me and the baby.

I needed to be on bed rest until she was born. Mother came to help. She was about to go home after two weeks, but on Sunday Aug. 3, 1969, Kimberly Marie ("ruler, leader") was born. I had the name Kimberly picked out if we had a little girl, but did not know what to give her for a middle name. A nurse named Marie had been so kind to me both times I had been in the hospital with Kim, so we gave her the middle name Marie.

She was a happy baby, and it was fun to have two little girls. She slept with her eyes open, and every time I saw that I went into an inner-panic mode and could not leave her alone. She finally outgrew this. The doctor told me it was a quite a common thing in babies.

Little league football came into our lives at about this time. David seemed to be a natural. Later, Eric and Craig started playing. After a few years, Eric said he would rather not play football, and that was alright with me. Getting them to all their practices and games was a full-time job. The practices were clear across the valley. It turned out that basketball was the sport for Eric. His dad would tell me that he was as "smooth as a jet" when it came to handling the basketball.

Both Dave and Craig went on to play football in high school. Dave was picked as an all-state all-star in his senior year and awarded a scholarship to Snow College in Ephraim, Utah.

Dave was involved with the school play "Annie, Get your Gun" in his senior year as one of the back-stage people. One day during the rehearsal, the girl playing the part of Annie lost her pet snake.

It was spotted up in the high rafters in the auditorium. He was telling me his story and said, "Guess who got to go up and get it?" Yes, my son. I have never liked snakes, and do not like heights! It was a good thing this mother was not there to see this.

Eric was our gentle and serious one. When he did play football—and then later in basketball— if someone fell, he would stop, help them, and then continue the game. With him, people were his priority. I could always depend on him to be there for me, and he was such a big help as more babies came along. He was a very deep thinker for a young boy and so inquisitive about many things. He had a great love for the animal kingdom and had a desire to learn about so many things. This helped him so much in his high school years as he joined the debate team and had great experiences.

Craig never ceased to amaze me. He had so much energy, and seemed to be one step ahead of everyone. He was bigger physically as a young boy, and this was sometimes a disadvantage to him. In football, he was always put with the older boys because of his size and weight. It was a challenge, but he realized he just had to think smarter. This could have been discouraging to some, even to the point of quitting, but somehow, he made it all balance out. His den mother was always calling me to get ideas to challenge him. She would have projects, and he would breeze right through them and be done while other boys were still struggling.

When Craig was in sixth-grade, he participated in a school program. He told me he was singing the song, "Dixie." For some reason, I thought he was singing with a group. But no, when the time came, he marched up front by himself and boomed out the words of "Oh I Wish I Were in the Land of Dixie" so powerfully in a fine voice. I was one proud mother.

Scouting was another activity in which the boys were engaged. They all three achieved their Eagle Scout award. It seemed if we were not at ball games on the weekends, we were getting them off to Scout camp or an activity. All three held leadership positions in the Priesthood, and often at the same time. I am so grateful for good Priesthood and Scout leaders who taught our boys so much. I know that the skills and the role models taught by these men have helped them through their missions and adult lives. They have passed them on to their sons and the youth they have served.

Would I have our sons do it all again if we had to live that time over? Absolutely. These activities taught them so much about themselves and others. They learned how to work on a team. Individually, it helped them gain self-confidence and learn early on that life was not always easy. They learned to take the bitter with the sweet. They learned early that when something seemed impossible, you just do it and you don't give up.

Cindy was the quieter of the two girls. She was my little helper and always by my side, quiet and domestic. I was concerned because she didn't seem to reach out to friends, though I believe she wanted to. She had a bad experience with one girl in our neighborhood that affected her for several years. In third grade, her teacher Miss Waylen took her under her wing, and they became friends. She would take Cindy out for pizza, share books with her, and come to our house and join in with our family. Cindy learned during these years to be very compassionate. Her fifth-grade teacher, Mr. Porter, was in a wheelchair due to diabetes. She seemed to struggle with math that year, but the lessons of life she learned were far more important. Cindy was class president one year, and was chosen to be queen of her sixth-grade dance.

Kim was very outgoing and always on the go. She always brought a lot of little friends home with her. I would hope they knew where they belonged at the end of the day because I often did not. She would do whatever she was asked to, and off she would go again. One thing we learned early was not to tell her big family secrets, because if she knew one, I would have a neighbor calling to get the details. She had a gift of gab. She put up with a lot of teasing from her brothers, no matter what we did to stop them.

She held her own, especially verbally. Her quick wit and thinking came in very handy and would frustrate them.

In 1970, John went into his first business adventure. His main products were paper and paper supplies. I took the two little ones and ran the office. Robert Turner, a business man from Kansas City, Missouri, introduced some new lines to us. He worked with us for quite a while. When John went to Kansas City to see his company layout, he was highly disappointed. He wanted to check on some accounts and other concerns, but he found that we were the only account Mr. Turner had. Much of his story of how he had gotten these products was fabricated. He was to pay John a large sum of money, and in turn, he would become a silent partner in our company. As it turned out, I had to wire John money to get a flight home. He and Robert were going to drive back, so he only had a one-way ticket. The only other time that he saw Robert after that was at the Salt Lake airport. When Robert saw John, he turned and went the other direction. We were grateful we had not invested more money. When the subject came up in later years, John would say, "He was a man with a dream, and I can't blame him for that."

John still wanted to have his own business, so we bought a fabric store in Tooele, Utah. I would go out there a few days a week and work. One night as I was preparing to come home, it was getting very foggy. I could not even see the lights across the street. I left the store, and as I got out of town, the fog was so thick I could not see ten feet in front of me. I was a little nervous, but knew I had to keep going. I approached a car and saw its dim lights and thought, "Oh good, I can follow that car." As I got closer, I realized the car was not moving. I stopped for a few seconds and realized they were waiting for me to pass them, so they could follow me. I slowly got around them and took the lead. As I did, I saw two elderly ladies peering at me as I walked ahead. I had felt smug to think I could just follow them. Now I knew I was not only to get myself safely out of this, but others as well. This was one of the greatest lessons I ever had experienced in always being prepared to lead as well as to follow.

There was a women's movement going on in our country in the 1970s (that I am sure has never settled) as the role of women took on other meanings— especially in the work place. It was also the time of a decline in family values that we had never witnessed before. There was a demand for equality from women all over the world. I don't think most women paid attention to it, but some did. It became a confusing issue to some, and I got caught up in it. It was a time that women hardly knew their place. If we chose to stay home with our children, we were asked, "What is wrong with you, don't you have any talents?" If we chose to go to work, we were criticized for not staying home with our children.

Our heavenly pattern was being turned topsy-turvy. For months, although I went about my daily work in the usual way, something was off – way off. I was so grumpy that I did not want John to come near me. At times, I was so belligerent I wondered how he could stand me. There was a sadness I could not explain, and I felt a very dark countenance around me. This went on for weeks. I knew I was not in a good place.

It came down to my thinking that Heavenly Father loved his sons more than his daughters. I could not understand this. I loved Him and Jesus Christ so much and began to believe that love was not returned. I would pray and read. Nothing seemed to help; a bad spirit was with me, and I could not shake it. There were times I did not care and other times I wanted desperately for it to leave. One day I started down the stairway with a basket of clothes to wash, and **he was there!** I literally saw the dark spirit that had been my companion, turning my thoughts from all that I held sacred, making me feel small, angry, and resentful toward all men. I was confused and helpless, and yet wanted to strike out with all the force that I had. He was there standing right before me. I stood there frozen, and then felt a surge of help come to me. With all the conviction I had, I said, **"Get away from me. By the power of** the Holy Ghost, I command you to get away from me and leave me alone!" I sat down on the stairs and put my face in the clothes in the laundry basket and cried. I was shaking so badly. **I looked down the stairs and he was gone, but I screamed out again! "By the power of the Holy Ghost stay away from me!"**

But the fruit of the Spirit is love, joy, peace, longsuffering, gentleness, goodness, faith.

Galatians 5:22
Bible

...Ye shall teach them to walk in the ways of truth and soberness; ye will teach them to love one another, and serve one another.

Book of Mormon Mosiah 4:15

Chapter 9

From Darkness into Light– Our Errand for the Lord

I was still trembling as I got up, walked into the bedroom, and knelt by the bed to plead for help from Heavenly Father. I knew I had encountered something evil and needed help. I could not fight this by myself. Why was this happening to me? I wanted to be happy as I had known happiness. I knew I was going to find the help needed. Maybe now that I had commanded the evil to leave, it would be enough. I didn't want to get priesthood help. That was part of the problem. Only His sons held the Holy Priesthood. I was wise enough to know, however, that the devil is well organized. He had powerful emissaries working for him.

I told John what had happened. A few nights later, I woke up at 2:30 a.m. and there it was again. I woke John, and he immediately gave me a priesthood blessing and commanded it to leave. I laid there in his arms and we talked. He, too, had felt it. He knew then, if he had not before, that it was real. We were both relieved that by priesthood power it had to leave.

I talked to our bishop and read everything I could get my hands on. My feelings about women being inferior to men and the sadness I felt started to subside. I studied and tried to live closer to the spirit. I felt the darkness leave and the light coming into my life again. I want to share with you some of my findings that helped to bring everything back into perspective again.

In 1973, I wrote this on a few pieces of notebook paper:

> *I have come to realize that my biggest problem was that I was so sad because I truly was thinking that because God gave his sons the Priesthood, his daughters were subservient to them. It made me sad, and so I have studied much on the matter.*
>
> *I thought I knew what the priesthood was, and I have had a basic understanding, but know now just how powerful it is. It is the power that controls the whole universe, and it was from the beginning. It was through the Priesthood that the universe was formed, and [it] created the worlds without end.*
>
> *Its institution was prior to the foundation of this earth and is after the order of the Son of God. It is the eternal power and authority of Deity by which all things exist, were created, controlled, and are governed. The great plan of creation, redemption, and exaltation operates and was put in place by the priesthood.*
>
> *Worthy men on this earth who hold the priesthood receive the power and authority from God and are delegated to do all things required for the salvation of man. They are to perform ordinances that are binding here on earth and in heaven, ordinances by which men and woman are sealed up through eternal life and [assured] of the fullness of the Father's Kingdom hereafter. By due course, the Lord will govern all nations with the Priesthood.*

It is a wonderment to me as I discover more about the Priesthood. I know there is much more to learn. Reading more of ancient times, as well as the pre-existence, has brought me new perspective. How it was used by mankind is inspiring. How it was abused by man made me angry that men would step out of the sacred boundaries that they have been given and try to give power unto themselves.

The Priesthood was given to Adam and every prophet after him. When I speak of worthy men, I mean a man who truly honors his priesthood and bends his will to the will of our Heavenly Father's.

Shortly after Joseph Smith and Oliver Cowdery received the keys of the Priesthood and were ordained by Peter, James and John, [Joseph] was instructed to give it to his twelve apostles so that it would not be taken from the earth again, even upon his death.

I have learned much more and know with all my heart that the Priesthood is here, functioning as it was designed to be. To have this knowledge and reassurance is one of the greatest blessings that I possess.

I also have learned how important it is for his daughters to honor the Priesthood, [in order to] reach our potential and fulfill our errand. If we have trouble with the fact that our husband is the head of the home because of his position of husband and father because perhaps he is not a member of the church, or he is not honoring the Priesthood, we should not rationalize that we are not required to honor him. If you cannot submit to him, then submit yourself to the Lord and His will, and you will become the kind of daughter you are meant to be. Always be your husband's most trusted companion and partner. However, as Brigham Young stated, "I have counseled every woman to let her husband be her file leader; he leads her, and those above him in the Priesthood leads him. But I never instructed a woman to follow her husband to hell." (Relief Society Magazine, Nov. 1933, page 669.)

Most of all, I have studied and learned about the calling of His daughters. We were His daughters from the beginning. I have read about women in the scriptures— Mother Eve and many of the other daughters that we read about in the Bible and Book of Mormon. I have such a great love and respect for them.

The nature of woman has not changed that much from their time to ours, although we live in different times, with a different culture. These women were women of great nobility and they bring strength, hope, and courage to us as we now go through our probation on earth in this dispensation. I think we are living in the best and worst of times. We are living with the complete gospel— truth having been restored. We have many comforts. Will our potential become greater? I do not know. What I do know is that opposition against righteousness is great, and with that it brings much confusion.

I have learned how much our heavenly Father loves his daughters and is depending on us to do the work that we only can and are meant to do. I [envision] our Father taking groups of us, or perhaps individually, and giving instruction on how He would depend on us as we came to this earth. He had a great errand for us to do, and only we could accomplish that errand. Oh, there was so much instruction, and we were so excited to come to complete the plan, for without our part, the whole eternal plan would be defeated, [and] the plan of salvation would be frustrated. The earth would be barren. The instruction that we received included far more than bringing forth His spirit children. Each would be given talents and abilities to not only teach [their] children, but to comfort and nourish all his children. Yes, even his sons. We were to bring the softer side to life—tenderness—[and] make it more reverent [and] more enjoyable, for the world will have great need for those things. We would be the heart of a Celestial home—a spiritual influence for good and righteous living in our homes, church, and community. We would not know the strength of our errand, [and we also learned] that we should accomplish all that we could complete before He calls us home. He told us that if we were lost or unsure, we could call upon Him for further help and direction. As Latter-Day Saint Women, we would be an example to the world to bring others to Him and receive the plan of salvation.

Our most important work would be within the walls of our own homes, teaching our children to be noble, prayerful, and to love God and to serve him with all their hearts. President David O. McKay has said, "No other success will compensate for failure in the home." We are to lead his spirit children back to him through our righteous teaching and example. Oh, what a responsibility.

Sometimes we feel alone, and uncharted waters await us. We are so overwhelmed and have so much to do, [and] so much depends on us. We must plead with Heavenly Father for His help to face the unknown. We must always know that He sent us here with his Priesthood blessing to get us through and stay on course.

I am grateful for the Relief Society organization. It makes me feel like I am at home away from our heavenly home, associating with the women who have the beliefs and values that I have. When it was organized by the Prophet Joseph, he said, "The church is not fully organized until the sisters are organized after the pattern of the Priesthood." How wonderful that the prophet told the sisters that, and his words could be passed on through the generations.

I, too, am grateful to mother Eve for what she did so that we could accomplish our errand and do our part to bring to pass the purposes of God, our Father. He released us when the time came so that we could come and have these experiences, and above all, receive a mortal body. She is Adam's queen as we can be queens unto our husbands throughout eternity. The whole plan is so beautiful, and we must live to keep the adversary out of our lives, so the plan can roll forth. Does it take effort? Yes, we must always, I mean always, stay close to Jesus Christ [and] Heavenly Father, and seek the spirit of the Holy Ghost to always be with us to lead us back to their presence.

The sons of man have been given strong and direct instruction on honoring God's daughters and womanhood in general. It is required of men to honor their wives and daughters for [our] womanhood is as equally important as their calling in the priesthood.

Men should always respect and not defile His daughter in body or in spirit, as she should respect him. Recognizing that man was not intended to be alone, a righteous woman compliments what he is lacking in, and he compliments her. She is an elect daughter because we have chosen God, and he has appointed us to do a certain work for the salvation of the eternal family.

When we apply the principles taught by the gospel, we can live and work in harmony, and see the great plan for his sons and his daughters come to pass as it was meant to be. Of course, we live in an imperfect world. To see the good works come to pass, we must continue each day to work at it, [and do] whatever we see that needs to be done, in our own sphere of where we live, whatever our circumstances are.

We are his daughters. May we celebrate it often. We may think of ourselves in the kitchen, a diaper in our hand, or trying to fit things into an already tight budget that are needed for our children, but we are so much more. In our hands lies the future of the church, and our posterity.

It has now been over 50 years since I have had this experience. Only one other time have I had the throngs of Satan try to overcome me. He is real, and this is his last attempt before the Lord comes. He will try in every cunning way to trip up his daughters, sons, and the families that are good and trying to succeed in a world that has changed so much in the last several decades.

His daughters have much depending on them, and he has saved his most valiant spirits to come now. We must be strong and hold on to the iron rod. Most of us have been taken out of our homes to help provide for our family's most basic needs. Through this, we have developed more talents and different talents than our sisters who came before us and those who will come after us. We have been given more opportunities than ever before in the history of the world. The thing that I would encourage all my daughters, granddaughters, and all who read this is to get an education and prepare yourselves for the uncharted waters that lay ahead of you. Yes, our husbands must help us in our assignment more than ever. We can do this. Remember, He sends us here with His blessing and the Power of the Priesthood to call upon if we are in trouble. Call upon it and submit yourselves to Heavenly Father. By doing so, you will be put back on course. If we get off track, we can still say, "I am back on course, and I can continue my errand."

The understanding I came to that day as I wrote about our errand for the Lord has never left me. I hold it dear to me and always will. I feel a great need to share it. I have never again doubted who I was and what I was to do with my life. It wasn't all about mothering children that we had been blessed with and assigned to do, but much, much more. We must magnify and develop as many of the gifts and talents that each of his daughters have been blessed with as much as we can. By doing so, we will grow, progress, and help our fellow beings—if we do it in righteousness.

There is a scripture that I have learned to love and emulate, and I know my daughters are passing it on to their children. It is found in 2 Timothy 1:5 in a letter that Paul wrote to him. Timothy had found himself in troubled times, questioning his own faith. Paul reminds him of his mother and grandmother's faith: "When I call to remembrance the unfeigned faith that is in thee, which dwelt first in thy grandmother Lois, and thy mother Eunice; I am persuaded that it is in thee also." May we always be the example that Lois and Eunice were.

In the fall of 1974, we received on another Saturday night telephone call from our ward clerk asking if John and I would meet with our bishop on Sunday morning. I assumed it was another calling for John. However, when I was taking something off the fireplace on Sunday morning, the thought came to me like a bolt of lightning: "You are going to be called to be the Relief Society president." That is ludicrous, I thought to myself. I still don't know how to quilt and have so many children to care for. I am working part-time out of the home, and I am too young and too inexperienced. I tried to dismiss the thought from my mind, but it would not go away.

And all thy children shall be taught of the Lord; and great shall be the peace of thy children.

Isaiah 54:13
Bible

...Open your ears that ye may hear, and your hearts that ye may understand, and your minds that the mysteries of God may be unfolded to your view.

Mosiah 2:9
Book of Mormon

Chapter 10

First Call to Relief Society President

"But Bishop, I still don't quilt," I calmly said after he had extended the call to me to be the ward Relief Society president. Once again, he said with a smile, "You find someone else to help with that. There are some sisters in the ward that only want to serve in that capacity."

I looked at John and asked what he thought. I really had no idea what I was about to say yes to. He said he would support me in my accepting it. Was the bishop being presumptuous to think I could handle this? I felt very humble and had a lump in my stomach as big as a baseball. I was already so busy. Sometimes I felt I could not adequately take care of my own family, let alone a ward of sisters. There were 217 sisters on the roll. I did know, however, that the Lord does not ask anything of you without providing a way for you to do it.

I asked for Fran Kelsey to be my first counselor. It was a process of prayer and fasting. She and her husband had just moved into the ward. She was thirty years my senior and had a lot of experience in working in a presidency. I did not know this when I submitted her name to the bishop, and she was a wonderful counselor in every sense of the word. My second counselor seemed to round out and balance the presidency quite well. Jeanetta, our secretary, knew almost every sister in the ward and something about them. I think this was helpful. For me, sometimes not knowing things about sisters was better. She did keep wonderful records, as keeping track of those moving in and out was a full-time job itself. I so appreciated her.

During those years, we were asked to report our compassionate service hours. This was a real bug-a-boo to me. I felt any service we rendered was between the giver, the one being served, and the Lord. However, I am glad that I did keep some of my own records. I took twenty-seven full dinners to ward members and numerous single items to ward members. We had a lot of babies born, and the presidency took a dinner to the new mother on top of other assigned sisters doing what they could. In 1975-1976, 537 compassionate service hours were reported, and these were just the ones I knew about. I got a better appreciation of the visiting teaching program. I had always enjoyed visiting the sisters, but now I was looking at it from a whole different perspective. No presidency can function without that program.

One of the things that I found out as I visited the sisters was that I was not the only one who had struggled with the women's movement issue. Several sisters were having feelings and thoughts that I had experienced. Some of their testimonies were firm and solid, with conviction of gospel principles. Others, tender and shaky. I asked myself, "Is that why I had that experience in my life, so that I could help others?" One of my goals while I served in that capacity was to increase the knowledge that we were daughters of our Heavenly Father and He needed us to honor our own womanhood. We should come to understand ourselves and just how much our Heavenly Father was depending on us to do all in our power to help the kingdom of God roll forward. The next few years, the Relief Society lesson manuals were heavy on the subject.

A new sister moved into the ward from California, and her car broke down on the way. It took all her money to repair it, except that used to get a rental house. When our bishop learned of her plight, he tried to persuade her to let him help her. She refused him because she had issues with the priesthood. He wanted to respect her wishes, but she had two young children. He asked me to go over and see if I could get her to accept a food order. She refused. I saw the children's faces when she said she would be okay. She admitted to me that all they had was some cereal and a little bread. I wanted to just drop off a few bags of food. I reported this to the bishop, and he asked me to fast and pray that night that her heart might be softened. The next afternoon, I went back to her house. She asked me for a food order. I quickly made the order out under her direction, and got to welfare square minutes before it closed for the day. I don't know what her issues were, but she eventually returned to California. We saw many come and go.

I am sure that one of the main concerns people have when called to a leadership position is that they wish they could do more and spend more time in their calling. I know it was certainly a concern of mine. I learned how important it is to prioritize and to delegate. There was always so much visiting to be done, and it was vital to listen to the spirit as I prioritized. One regret I have occurred when a young husband had lost his job. They were a very proud couple, and the bishop assured me that they were all right. I did not go to visit the sister as she was always in church and everything appeared to be good. However, I kept getting the feeling that I should go see the sister. Then I would rationalize, "no, the bishop said they are fine." Maybe they were; however, she was not. One day, the feeling was so strong to go see her. I did, but it was too late. She was so angry with me that she cried and said she did not want me to ever come into her home. "Well, you finally got here," she said. "Where were you when I really needed you?" I tried to apologize for not coming sooner, but my apology was weak and not accepted. She had little to do with me from that time on. I learned a valuable lesson to always listen to the spirit and act upon it.

A time when I did act upon a spiritual prompting has been a great blessing to me since that day. I was making some visits to some of our elderly sisters when the thought came to me to go see Judy Hickman. She and her husband Will had eight children. It was their tradition to take each child out to dinner alone on his or her birthday. One evening, while they were out with one of their sons on his birthday, their daughter, Heather, decided to go for a bicycle ride. She was hit by a motorist who did not see her and died soon after. This was not only a great lost to Will, Judy, and their family, but to the whole ward. We were all in shock. Heather was a beautiful girl; she was in her early teens and loved life and the Lord. Her bedroom was full of pictures of the Lord, temples, and writings of scriptures— this reflected what a beautiful young woman she was inside and out.

Judy was so overcome with grief she could hardly function. We provided her with a lot of help. She had a chronic back problem, and little could be done. She just laid in bed for several weeks after the passing of Heather. She worried about whether Heather was happy and cared for.

I was prompted to go see Judy, though she was not on my list. I found her in a wonderful mood. She was smiling and almost beaming as we visited. I had not seen this in her for quite some time. She was glowing as she told me of a dream that she had a few nights prior to my visit. In her dream, she was riding in a car and saw a beautiful meadow. A group of young people were coming through it. One girl looked up and saw the car and started walking, almost skipping, toward it with her scriptures in one hand and a bouquet of flowers in the other. Judy could see it was Heather. She reached the car window, smiled, and blew kisses through the bouquet of flowers. Judy tried with all her might to get the window down, but it would not move. Slowly, the car moved on and she woke up. This dream had given her the assurance that Heather was happy, learning, and being taken care of. What a gift this was to this mother. As Judy and I sat there with tears streaming down our faces I was grateful she felt she could share this wonderful dream with me. To see her relief and to see our Judy start to come to a point where she would cope with this was a miracle. Slowly, she regained her strength and was able to care for the rest of her family. I thanked my Heavenly Father for the promptings I had to visit Judy that day and hear of her dream.

Our Relief Society meetings were held in the mornings. There was one day that was not the best, or at least, it started out not to be good. I later wrote a paper about it in a class I was taking at the University of Utah. I now share this with hope that you can always find good in any situation, no matter how awful it appears at the moment.

Bad Days Can Be Good

So, they tell me you have had a bad morning. I'm sorry to hear that, but do you know what? I really think that it is okay to have a perfectly rotten, horrible, terrible, no good, day once in a while. How else could we ever appreciate all the great or even the normal days if we don't experience miserable, bad, pitiful mornings sometimes? I want to tell you about a morning I had a few years ago.

Well, the morning wasn't [so] bad that I got out of bed, slipped on skates, broke my leg, and then strangled myself in the telephone cord calling for help. It wasn't that bad, but it didn't start out so good either. It happened like this:

I woke up and heard the wind blowing the heavy rain against the brick of the house. I could visualize its heavy, cold, wet drops splattering against the small pebbles on our flat roof. I rolled over and looked at the clock. It was almost 5:30am. I reached for the covers and pulled them tight around my shoulders. I snuggled closer to my big teddy bear that I slept with - my husband. He could sleep though wind, hail, crying children, and probably a 200-gun salute going off under our bedroom window. "I could go back to sleep for about an hour," I thought to myself.

Then it hit me. My eyes opened wide, [and] I felt my whole body stiffen and a feeling of rebellion went through me. I couldn't sleep in. This was Thursday morning, one of the busiest mornings of the week! I thought of my thirteen-year-old son who had been fighting a miserable cold for several days. He had been taking aspirin and cough medicine, and I was sure I was the only one keeping the cold remedy people in business. Then I thought of the 237 newspapers, already folded and stacked in a four-foot mountain in the middle of my kitchen. He had to have those weekly papers delivered by 7:00am.

Now what mother would send her sick son out in the wet and cold to be further stricken with disease? I knew for sure he would have double pneumonia by night fall. I would need to take him by car to deliver those papers. Then I would need to get things done at home, take care of the family, and be to the church by nine. I was the Relief Society president, and this morning we needed to be there early to prepare for the visiting teachers report meeting.

I pulled back the covers; the rain seems to be coming down harder, I thought to myself. I slipped on my robe, then walked through the kitchen and *circled the mountain of newspapers. I went down the stairs and stood at the landing and my bare unsuspecting feet were suddenly covered with cold, quickly rising rain water. "I better not reach for the light switch", I told myself, "The permanent that I got in my hair last week might really go frizzy," In the dim light filtering down from the kitchen, I could see the water that had filled the window well, flowing into the bottom of the large window and into the family room. The carpet was soaked. The huge foam pillows I had the made the size of bean bag chairs had soaked up buckets of rain.*

I waded to my son's room, and woke him thinking, "He really is his father's son, to sleep through all this." I warned him of our flood and went back upstairs and broke the cheerful news to my soundly sleeping teddy bear.

We decided that I would take our son to deliver the papers and that my husband, David, and Craig would start to bail us out. I dressed and helped Eric get the newspapers in the car. We were one block from the house when we heard this rumble, rumble, and then the car was leaning to the passenger side. I knew we did not have four round tires under us. I told my son to go on foot and I would go back home and get his father's truck.

John had geared into action and was standing at the top of the ladder; David was holding it steady for him in the rain. He was hammering the rain gutters that had come loose and failed to do their duty. I shouted through the rain and wind that I was taking his truck because my car had a flat tire. His answer was, "the gas tank is nearly empty."

I got in the truck and headed for the nearest gas station, stopping only for a traffic light that seemed to be stuck on the red signal. As I sat there, I saw a man walking up the road away from me. His collar was pulled up around his chin and his head bent low to try to protect himself from the wind and rain. I could see a pack on his back, adding to the burden of the elements as he walked further and further away from me.

The light finally changed. I pulled into the service station, filled the tank, and ran the money to the window. [Then] I was off to find my son. Within a half hour, we had the newspapers delivered and returned home. By 8am, I had fed the children and they were off to school. I was trying to do something with my rain-soaked hair when the phone rang. It was the nursery leader for the 15-20 children that accompanied their mothers to Relief Society. She said she was having a bad morning and would not be able to make it. After seven phone calls, I finally found a sister who said, "Maybe." Back then, we paid sisters to take care of our nursery children. I had already decided that we would start a new trend and hold our Relief Society lesson in the nursery with the children.

As soon as I hung up the phone, it rang again. This time it was my visiting teacher leader who had awakened with laryngitis. She had worked and worked to get her voice restored, but it was of no use. Would I please give her lesson for her? I said, "Why of course, I would be delighted," not knowing what I was going to say, let alone having time to read the lesson manual.

I held another conference with John, checking if I really should leave or should I stay and help to bail out water downstairs. We both agreed that I would attend to my other duties because it would take us quite a while to dry out anyway.

I drove to the church. John had changed the flat tire by then, [and] I was the first to arrive. "Oh good," I thought to myself, "No one has had to wait for me." I stepped out of the car, and ker-plunk. The high heel of my shoe fell right off, [and] I stood there and watched in dis-belief. It floated right toward the drain, hit the curb, and was swallowed up by the rain gutter. I limped to the door of the church and told myself that I would get the doors opened and hurry back home and change my shoes. I pulled the key out of the lock, and there they went, clang, clang, clang; every key on my ring flew in a different direction. My counselors drove up, and they must have thought I was crazy as they saw me down on my hands and knees in the rain. No, I wasn't praying, only retrieving my keys. I handed them the church keys, and ran back to the car to go home to change my clothes.

When I walked into the hallway, John was standing there. I could tell by the expression on his face something else was wrong. He told me he received a phone call from Ann, the lady that worked for us at our Fabric store in Tooele, Utah. It had rained hard there also; the roof had leaked, and much of the fabric was wet.

"Why are you back?" he asked. I showed him my wet dress and heelless shoe. We just stood there and looked at each other, and then we both broke out laughing. We laughed so hard! Oh, there is

nothing like a hardy laugh when you feel so stressed.
It was 8:50am, and it already had been a terrible,
awful, no good, rotten, miserable day.

Now, let me tell you why we all need this kind
of day every once in a while. The next thing that
happened was beautiful. I quickly changed my
clothes and headed back to the church. As I was
driving, my thoughts reflected to the man I saw
while I was waiting for the traffic light to change
[earlier that morning.][The one who was] walking
in the rain, with a back pack on his back, his
head bent low [as he went] further and further
from the main road, having miles to go before he
reached another one with few houses in between. I
thought of him alone, cold, [and] perhaps hungry.
Where was he going? Did he have a destination?
What were the circumstances that led him to this
condition? I felt regret. I should have sent John to
help him.

The sounds of laughter I had moments ago
shared with my husband were now completely shut
out. All I could hear were sweet words of thanks
and rejoicing. I wondered about this man; when
he was a boy, did his mother care enough to help
him in an emergency? Did he have a home to flood?
Obviously, he did not have a car to have a flat
tire, let alone another to be low on gas. Did he
have a second pair of shoes and another change of
clothing? Was that pack on his back his sole earthly
possession? I would never know the answers to
these questions.

As I parked my car at the church, the rain had
subsided, [and] a ray of sun was coming through
the sky. I looked up and saw a lovely rainbow. It is

said that at every rainbow, there is a pot of gold at its end. I had my pot of gold; it was right here in my heart. I take it everywhere I go.

I knew exactly what my lesson would be on. I would talk about children to help, a home that needed to be bailed out, vehicles with problems, broken shoes, [and] wet hair and clothes. Most of all I would talk about the opportunity to worship in the faith of my choice with the people I have grown to love. I was grateful for a companion who could laugh, work, and cry with me. Yes, this terrible, awful pitiful, miserable, no good morning had truly proven to be a great, grand, glorious day that dipped into my buried [and] rusted sense of deepest appreciation!

It was shortly after this day I have written about that I was standing in the kitchen at the church. The bishop walked up to me and asked, "Is the rumor I hear about you true?"

I looked at him, smiled, and said, "Yes, our baby will be born in November."

"How are you feeling?" he asked. I told him I had my days, but it was getting better. He said, "Didn't John say that the doctors said there would be no more babies?"

Again, I said, "Yes, but here we are." A few weeks later, the Relief Society was required to feed the ward the annual spaghetti dinner. Each year we fed about 500. I got so sick to my stomach as we prepared the sauce that I was not able to eat spaghetti, or anything related to it, for several years.

I was attending the evening Relief Society meeting on Tuesday, Nov. 18, when I knew I was in labor. I stood at the door and greeted sisters as they came in. One time I sat down because of a contraction. I knew she was close to coming, but I stayed for the meeting and then told my counselors I didn't know if I would be there on Wednesday for the morning meeting.

Our Linda Kay ("beautiful") was born Nov. 19, 1975. She was not only the darling of our family, but also of the ward. She had so many mothers, and her brothers adored her. We would sit her in her infant seat on the portable dishwasher in the kitchen, and it seemed everyone just automatically had to kiss her on the forehead as they walked by. She loved all the attention and was such a good traveling baby. Linda went everywhere with me, and made so many elderly sisters happy when I visited them. She attended her first Relief Society meeting when she was 10 days old. She was so good; it was like she was taking it all in.

On Jan. 21, 1976, John was ordained a High Priest. A short time later, he was called to be in the stake Sunday School presidency and put in charge of organizing a regional adult fireside for the bi-centennial coming up. He had visited the church headquarters to invite the president to speak at the bi-centennial, and was told that he was to follow up with his secretary. He also was introduced to two other apostles at that time.

Late on the Friday afternoon he was to call back, John called me and asked me if I would make the call for him as he was running late and would not be home in time to do it himself. It was fifteen minutes to five, and I picked up the phone, called the church office building, and a man answered. I asked for the president's secretary, and he told me very casually to hang on. I waited for him to return and then I heard him say, "They have all flown the coop; I am the only one here. Can you call back Monday?"

"Who am I speaking to, sir?" I inquired. He identified himself has one of the twelve apostles. I almost dropped the phone; I was talking to an apostle of the Lord. Even if he had said "they have all flown the coop." I felt so privileged.

It turned out the president was not able to speak at the fireside because he was at a conference in South America. He recommended John ask a well-known member of the church and American conservative author to come speak. He did come, and it was a wonderful fireside.

One Sunday, sitting in a ward council meeting, Bishop Kane brought up a name of a family in the ward he was quite concerned about. The family had two boys who were seventeen and eight and daughter who was fourteen. The father had let it be known some years back that he did not want anything to do with the church, and not to send home or visiting teachers. Our bishop said he had such a strong feeling to try again to contact this family. He had discussed it with his counselors, and they decided to open it up to the ward council. "Do any of you have any suggestions?" he asked. Everyone sat there with blank, uneasy looks on our faces.

Finally, I said, "What about the sisters; do you think we could send visiting teachers?" All eyes were on me, and I wondered what I had done to myself.

"Who would you send, Sister Holmes?" he asked. Sisters Yeates and me, was my reply. There was silence in the room, and then he said, "I will need to think about this; will you do the same?" He asked me to consult with Sister Yeates, my new counselor, and pray about it. He then said he would get back to me on Tuesday night.

On Tuesday evening, the bishop called. He was still hesitant. I told him I felt we would be okay. Sister Yeates was one of the best bread makers in the ward, and we planned to deliver bread to some other sisters on Thursday. We planned to take a loaf to the family also.

Thursday night came, and I picked her up in my car and we had prayer. We went to see our first sister. When we were done, we asked if we could leave the car in her driveway. We planned to walk down the street a few houses. She said that would be fine, so we stopped at the car and Sister Yeates got another loaf of bread out. We started down the driveway when a lot of honking started. Cars that were going fast had almost come to a halt. I looked up and saw a big dog coming right toward us. It was a golden lab, and he was on a mission. He wanted the bread that Sister Yeates was now holding high above her head.

We picked up our pace, and I tried to shoo him away. As we approached the sister's home, the dog was on the sidewalk as were reached the door. I assumed it was safe to ring the doorbell, which I did. The door opened and "zoom" – the big dog almost knocked me down as he ran into the house.

"Is this your dog?" I inquired, as I saw him running in circles in the living room. Then I heard and saw a smaller dog come down the hall, barking with all of its might. He was chasing the bigger dog, and all I could see was the lab's tail wagging and barely missing the beautiful things on the end tables as he ran. We were headed for disaster; the chase was on. The lady started chasing her little dog, and I stepped inside and started chasing the big dog. I finally got him by the back of the neck and escorted him to the door, which Sister Yeates was still holding open with one hand while holding the bread high in the other.

I closed the door after I had pushed him out and turned to the sister, trying to collect my composure and dignity, and said, "Hi, I am Sister LaVelle Holmes and this is Natalie Yeates. We are your visiting teachers." I was sure she was going to order us out of her home. But, she didn't. Simultaneously, all three of us started to laugh.

She invited us to sit down and we visited about big dogs, little dogs, and pretty things on our end tables. The time passed very quickly, and we all had an enjoyable time. When we were leaving, I asked if we could come back next month, and she said, "I would like that."

Within six months, our ward split, and her family went into the newly developed ward. By then she was a visiting teacher and a visiting teacher supervisor, her oldest boy was preparing for a mission, her daughter loved going to young women, and her youngest son was active in primary and the Scouting program.

This is just an illustration of what can happen when a ward council pools their resources to fellowship a family or individual. First, we had a bishop in tune with the welfare of all his families in the ward. Then, we had priesthood and auxiliary leaders who followed his lead and acted upon the promptings of the spirit. It was wonderful to be a part of this. I may add here that sister Joann had never seen the big dog before, and never did again after this incident.

Shortly after this, I held a presidency meeting. The main question that came from my counselors was, "What can we do to help you?"

"You look positively green," said my counselor. I thanked her for the compliment and said that I would be okay in few months. Yes, I was expecting again. However, something was different about this pregnancy and I didn't know quite what.

As I watched myself grow, I suspected there were two babies. When I suggested this to my doctor he said, "No, I can only get one heartbeat." He did suggest that I strongly consider not having any more babies, that another one would be too hard on me. He was pretty firm about me having a tubal ligation. I did not give an answer one way or the other, it just didn't feel right to me. When he wanted to discuss it, I changed the subject. When I was in my sixth month, I had an ultrasound. Sure enough, there were twins. Two little girls. This was my first ultrasound as it was a new procedure. After he had shown me two heads, four legs, and four arms, he continued the process. Finally, I asked him what he was looking for and he said, "A third baby, because you are so big." He really knew how to make a woman feel good about herself. I already felt like a huge cow and had three months to go.

Just before I was released from my position as Relief Society president, the ward was divided. Marvin Schmid was called to be our bishop. He and his wife Jessie were our best friends.

Years earlier, Jessie had been married in the temple to another man for just a few months. He had been killed in a work accident in Monroe, Utah. This was very devastating to this young bride. She did not know if she would remarry, or if she would ever want to. She went back to college and became a school teacher and served a mission for the church. Then she met and fell in love with Marvin. She had mixed emotions concerning her first husband. She had been granted a temple annulment and felt he was being left out and that she had abandoned him. She attended the temple several times trying to come to grips with the matter. One night, she had a dream of her first husband standing by another woman. He smiled at Jessie and nodded his head, and then he was gone. She was so grateful for this dream. She felt a great burden had been lifted from her shoulders. She knew that everything was all right with her first husband.

Marvin had just got back from Europe after being in the Army for four years when they met. By his own admission, he had done everything while he was in the Army. Everything that would not allow him to go to the temple. He had come from a large family, and his parents were strong church members. His parents were heartbroken with the way he had conducted his life. When he met Jessie and fell in love, she had a good influence on him. She let him know in no uncertain terms if he wanted to marry her, he would need to repent and become temple worthy. He went through the steps, and they were married in the temple and now had four children.

The day after Marvin was set apart as our bishop, Jessie came over and said, "LaVelle, I would like to share something with you that was said last night when the Stake President set Marvin apart as bishop." I asked if it was okay with Marvin. She replied that it was. She said, "Do you remember that Marvin had to come back to the church and that he had to go through the repentance process?"

I said "Yes, you and he have told John and me that."

"Well, last night in the blessing that the President gave him, he was told that through the faith and prayers of his parents both on this side of the veil and on the other side, he had come to this point in his life." His parents were now both deceased. What a blessing and revelation to know that prayers are ongoing. I have always remembered this, and kept it close to my heart. I urge all that read this to do it also. If one of your loved ones go astray from the gospel, remember the atonement and that it is for all things, lest we deny the Holy Ghost. Remember also that our prayers and righteous desires can come to pass on both sides of the veil. Never give up on a loved one.

In the fall of 1977, I was released from Relief Society. Our new bishop asked if I wanted to stay in. I thanked him and told him no, someone else needed to have the opportunity. He told me he did have another sister in mind. When I met with her to give her the handbook and keys to the building, she told me that she had felt that this call was coming to her. She tried to prepare by painting her house both inside and out. She had just finished when she received her new calling.

David had had earned a football scholarship from Snow College in Ephraim, Utah. He had left in early August for football training. He called me two or three times stating that something just did not feel right, and he felt he needed to come home. I offered all the motherly advice as to why he should stay for the quarter and then come home to get ready for his mission, but I felt he was not listening.

One morning after we had talked about it on the phone, I was downstairs and walked by his bedroom and noticed the bed was all messed up. I thought the younger kids had been in there and had a pillow fight. I stepped back and took another look and thought, "No, there is a body in that bed." Sure enough, it was David. He had gotten a ride from a friend who had to come to Salt Lake, let himself in with his key, and just went to bed. When I asked him why, he said, "Mom I need to get ready for my mission. When I was out on the football field, it just kept coming to me, 'Holmes, what are you doing here? The Lord has other plans for you, go home and prepare.'"

How could a mother argue with that? I told him he needed to come upstairs and talk with his father, which he did. John had never had a prouder moment. Though he loved the game of football and wanted to see him play, when our sons chose the Lord over sports, we felt we had done something right in raising them.

John and I were about to make other changes in our lives. Another move was on the horizon. The house was too small for our growing family, and he now worked in Bountiful. We had looked at and put a down payment on a seven-bedroom, three-bath home, in Layton, Utah. A dream come true for me. We were buying it on contract from a man whose wife had left him. We had taken out several truckloads of items and were set to move on the last weekend of October, 1977.

The Sunday prior to that was our stake conference, and we had all attended the morning session. David was presented as a new elder. I was too tired to go to the afternoon session, and I stayed home with Linda. At about three in the afternoon, I received a phone call from the man we were buying the house from. He explained his wife wanted to come back to him under the condition that she could have her house back. He told me he would refund our money and help us move. He would do anything he could to help us, but he could not sell us his house.

I sat there in a daze wondering what had just happened. Ten minutes ago, I was lying on my bed, contemplating the new home we were moving to next weekend. Then the phone rings, and suddenly, the home is not going to be! I grabbed the newspaper and started circling homes for rent and making calls. It would be a long hour before John and the children returned home. Our home had been sold, and the new owners were moving in on the next Sunday. We had six children, two more babies on the way, and we had no house to live in!

Now the God of patience and consolation grant you to be likeminded one toward another according to Christ Jesus.

Romans 15:5
Bible

And he commanded them that there should be no contention one with another, but that they should look forward with one eye, having one faith and one baptism, having their hearts knit together in unity and in love one towards another.

Mosiah 18:21
Book of Mormon

Chapter 11

Winter Quarters

I turned to John and the man standing next to him and said, "Please follow me." I stepped into the bathroom, put the seat of the toilet down, and sat on it. There was no other place in the house to sit except the stairs, but I felt if I sat on them, I just might topple over because I was so top heavy. We had called on a home for rent in Sandy, Utah. It had five bedrooms and three bathrooms, and the man said we could move in the following weekend. We made the deal and wrote the check out right there in the bathroom.

It was a traumatic move in many ways for the children. With me not being able to function fully as a mother, much more responsibility went on John's shoulders. I had been put on bed rest until the twins were born. He did well for the most part, with some exceptions. On the first day of school for Eric, who was a sophomore at Brighton High School, John just left him to get himself registered and find his way around this 3,000-student school. Eric did well, but he did miss his bus home. He walked all the way home, and to this day I do not know how he found his way. The area was completely unfamiliar to him, and our phone had not yet been hooked up. I was so worried, because it was way past the time he should have been home. But when he told me about his day, I was so grateful for his sense of direction. I felt I had let him down in the worst way, but I was so proud of him and grateful because I knew he had help from another source. I also was very upset with John before realizing that he, too, had many challenges thrown at him – including being so far from work – and he was doing the best he could. We had several challenges coming at us at once. The rest of the school year went well for Eric. He served on the Seminary council and enjoyed that very much.

It was a different story for Craig. He had one of the most miserable years in his young life. Still big for his age, he was not accepted very well, especially when it came to sports. I think there was a lot of jealousy going on as he seemed to be a threat to some of the other athletes. As for Cindy and Kim, they seemed to take it in stride. Kim always made friends easily, and Cindy was my little homebody.

We called Mother again to see if she could come help when the twins came. She had only been there a few days when on the morning of Nov. 9, 1977, I told her I would like something to eat, but my back hurt so bad that I couldn't walk. She brought me some oatmeal and toast. When I tried to sit up in the bed, I had only moved a little bit when my water broke. She was so alarmed (my mother – the nurse) and asked, "What we should do?"

I said, "I am calling 911." We had a Volkswagen, but Mother did not know how to drive it. I made the call, and in about three minutes, a fire truck, an ambulance, and a police car were there. Six men stood in my living room while I was on the gurney. They were discussing who was taking me when I asked who had experience delivering a baby. All of them had been trained, but only one had done it. I pointed to him and said, "I want you to be in the ambulance with me."

Once we got to the hospital it was only nine minutes before Alysia Ann ("leader and helps others to bond") was born. It took Melissa Nadine ("able to calm and make stable") sixteen minutes more to come, as she was lodged under my rib cage. The babies were six weeks early.

Both were a tiny four pounds and six ounces. Melissa was put on oxygen immediately and they handed Alysia to me as soon as she was cleaned up. My doctor turned to the nurse and told her to schedule me for that afternoon to have a tubal ligation. Just as he said that, I had one of the most spiritual experiences of my life. I had just brought these two little spirts into the world, and they had received their tiny bodies. I then heard a little boy's voice say to me, *"Mama, don't forget me."* I felt like heaven itself was there with me. I asked the doctor to come over to me and I told him I could not go through with the procedure. He told me that I must because my body could not go through another pregnancy. Again I told him, "No!"

He said, "I am going to find John. I want him to talk some sense into you." John had stepped out of the room to register me, since there had not been enough time when we first arrived. When he came in, I told him what had transpired. He turned to the doctor and said, "You cannot change her mind." The doctor shook his head and walked out of the room. I am sure he was thinking, "Women!"

Melissa was rushed down to the nursery. A few minutes later, I was told she was slipping fast and was being transferred to the New Born Intensive Care Unit at the University of Utah Hospital. I was not able to see her before they took her. I held on to Alysia, thanking Heavenly Father for her and praying for Melissa to receive the help needed that she might live. I so wanted to leave that hospital and go on that ambulance with her, taking Alysia with us. I was told that was out of the question. John went to the hospital with Melissa. I was so torn. Within hours we found Alysia was having problems as well. She needed oxygen, and was turning jaundice. Later, she could not keep any food down.

On the morning of the third day, I was able to leave Cottonwood Hospital in Murray and go to Melissa. There were tubes connected to her little head, hands and chest. I was so sad and wanted to take the pain from my little baby. All they would let me do was touch her tiny hands, talk to her, and say a silent prayer. How I hoped that she knew that I was there. I stayed for several hours, and then had to get back to Alysia at the other hospital.

At Cottonwood, they told us Alysia was more stable, and that we would be able to take her home in a few days. I was somewhat relieved, but still very concerned. Early the next morning, we got a call from the University Hospital saying that Melissa was not responding to her 100% oxygen, and they had to comatose her because she was fighting the equipment. We had our coats on and were going out the door when the phone rang again. It was Cottonwood hospital telling me to come, saying that Alysia had screamed for hours, and they could not calm her. I did not know to which of my babies I should go to. John put his arms around me and told me to go to Alysia, and he and David would go to Melissa and give her another blessing.

When I got to Alysia, she calmed right down, and I nursed her. She would not take any formula; if she did, it came right back up. I had little milk to give because I was so exhausted. I was also leaving milk for Melissa, so they could give it to her through her tubes. All I wanted to do was cling to her.

John and Dave gave Melissa a blessing, and John said he had the strongest feeling she was going to live; in fact, he knew she was going to live. Later, as he and Dave were coming down the hill from the hospital, he ran a stop sign and was stopped by a policeman. He told the officer he could give him one ticket or as many as he wanted, because he had just learned that his baby daughter was going to live. The officer was very kind and told him to go on, but to be careful.

The next few days, I was able to be with both babies. Alysia was improving if she had my milk. They still had Melissa in a coma, but she was not laboring so hard to breathe. When I saw her two days later, the tubes were out, and she was awake and crying. Oh, what a blessing to hear her cry. They were about to give her a sponge bath, and I told them I wanted to do it. After her bath, I was able to hold and rock her for the first time. What a sweet time that was. The hospital staff was amazed by her remarkable improvement. We knew it was the Priesthood blessing and all the good equipment and care they had given her. After about an hour, the other hospital called and told me to come as soon as I could; Alysia was upset and getting more and more jaundiced.

On Nov. 16, we brought Alysia home. Four days later, we were able to bring Melissa home. Both babies were less than four pounds now. The doctor told me he would not normally have sent them home so tiny. But because I was an experienced mother, he believed I could handle it, and we would all be better off. I agreed. We weighed them on a meat scale until they reached five pounds. On Nov. 22, we put Alysia back in the hospital because she was turning more and more jaundiced. The doctor finally established that it was a hormone in my milk that was not agreeing with her and was causing it.

When John and I came home after taking Alysia to the hospital, the children were sitting in the living room with very sad looks on their faces, some with tears. We knew something was wrong. Together they said, "Grandpa Holmes has died." He had been in a hospital in Spokane, Washington, for bad headaches. The doctor thought the problem had been resolved, and he was going to be released to go home the next day. That morning he had gotten out of his bed, gone into the bathroom, and fell to the floor as he was returning to his bed. He died from an aneurysm. I put my arms around John and told him how sorry I was.

We called Mother Holmes, and then put a plan into action to get the boys and John to Washington as fast as we could. They left early the next morning and stayed a week. John spoke at his father's funeral, and the boys took part in offering prayers and the dedication of the grave. John spoke not only of a tribute to his father, but on the plan of salvation, which was a strange concept to many who attended. They commented to him on the principles that he had explained, and took great comfort in them.

Mom Holmes took his death hard as it was quite a shock to her. She depended on him far more than she had realized. She had never learned how to drive, and doing her own errands and shopping was a challenge. After a few months, she said she wanted to come to Salt Lake and be near us, but then changed her mind and moved to Brainard, Nebraska, where she had lived with her adoptive parents. Clara Coufal, her adoptive mother, was still alive and she wanted to be near and help her. Mom later bought the family home, where she lived the rest of her live.

I was so grateful my mother was with me when we were able to bring both baby's home. When it was time for her to go home, I really missed her. She was so good with the babies, and the children loved her. A lot of that was because of her keen sense of humor. We tried to live normally, but the first six months seemed like one long day to me with very little sleep.

In April, David left on his mission. He and Teresa had gone together for a few years now, and I don't know who it was the hardest on when it came time to say goodbye. For me as his mother, I had looked forward to this time all his life. But now it was here, and it was a different story. The Lord had given him to us for 19 years, but now it was time to give him back for two years. I will not deny that it was hard, and it did not get any easier as his three brothers left when it was their time to serve their missions. We were very pleased with our sons for their desire to serve the Lord.

We were assigned a wonderful home teacher while we lived in in the Sandy ward. He was a large man from Sweden. On one of his visits, we told him of John's father's death and that he was also from Sweden. We told him we knew very little about his ancestry. There was a picture sitting on a table of John's father. He looked at it and said, "he is not Swedish, he is Finnish." "But he was always called Swede," John said, and asked him why he thought he was Finnish. He told us that it was because of his high cheek bones, a trait of the Finnish people.

It turned out that our home teacher was very much into genealogy and family history, and asked if we would give him what little information that we had. A week later, he came to our home again. He had been correct; we had been looking in the wrong country for John's family. He did not find a lot, but it was a start, and we were able to do some of the temple work in 1979. We were so grateful for this brother who put us on the right track as the search for John's family began.

We met some wonderful people in the short time we lived in Sandy. I became good friends with a sister who served on the Relief Society general board. I still don't know how she found time to befriend me, but she did. I do believe it was because I had five daughters, and she thought they were so cute. She was always bringing me things for them.

She shared the story of when she was preparing to for a conference with the Relief Society sisters. She had felt so inadequate, and prayed for humility and for the spirit to be with her as she prepared to meet with them. When she got on the plane, she still did not have the feeling she had hoped for. She prayed again for the help she felt like she needed. Upon arriving, she was told that her luggage had been lost. Knowing she had neither time nor money to shop, she knew she would have to make do with only the few personal things in her purse.

On the third day of wearing the same clothes, she realized it did not matter what she was wearing. She knew her prayers had been answered in a way she never would have suspected them to be. This calm, beautiful spirit led her to tell the sisters what He wanted her to tell them, and she felt the great humility that she had earlier prayed for. On the end of the third day, she went to the hotel lobby and found her luggage there. She did wear different clothes on the fourth day, because they were fresh and smelled nice. She said she learned from this experience that it was not so important what she was wearing, only that she spoke to the sisters with the spirit of love and humility. Surely, this applies to all of us.

It was a good example to me that the Lord will keep us humble, and that he allows experiences to come into our lives to keep us that way so that we can do his work. With humility, we have a greater understanding of his love, understanding of one another, and the gospel.

David had written a letter telling us there was a sister who accepted the gospel, but had questions on one thing. Why didn't the women hold the priesthood? He was turning to me for help on that one. I wrote him of my findings and feelings that I shared previously in this writing, telling him that I knew Satan was on his greatest campaign to destroy the family. I always hoped that what I shared with him and her in that letter helped her to understand the great role of God's daughters.

Craig had made a good friend in our ward whose mother was ill with terminal cancer. She told me that Craig had been an answer to her prayers. She was so worried about her son, and the friendship he had found with Craig helped him so much. They had such a good time on their trip to Lagoon. Craig had the ability to make people laugh and find humor in life. I loved it when he would share his good times with me.

Eric and I talked a lot, and he always seemed to have so much wisdom, and a calm, assuring outlook on life. I felt he was wise beyond his years. He wasn't too interested in socializing, though he was a friend to everyone. On New Year's Eve that year, he volunteered to babysit the twins and Linda so that his dad and I could go out for a few hours. I so appreciated that. I told him I owed him a New Year's Eve.

When school was over that year, we found a home to rent in Woods Cross, near Bountiful. Once again, we prepared to move. I was downstairs sitting on the fireplace, looking at a big mess and wondering how we acquired so much stuff, when Linda came down and sat next to me. She asked, "Where is my Davie?" She seemed so forlorn and confused. We had told her he was telling people about Jesus. Dave and Teresa had spent a lot of time with her before he left on his mission, and she missed him.

She also felt somewhat pushed out of her spot as our little princess when the two baby sisters came. She was not quite two years old when they were born. That day, I just took her in my arms, and we sat there and felt sad together. I hope she will always know that she is still our princess, as each of her sisters also are.

We were finally going north as we had originally planned. Our "winter quarters" for 1977 and the spring of 1978 helped us all to grow and gain many life experiences, and we felt there was great purpose for us to be there, even for a short time. With another move on the horizon, I knew new friends, schools, and opportunities awaited each one of us. I worried for my children. I prayed that each one would be strong enough to meet the new challenges that lay ahead, and that I would try to be there at every corner to help them with the adjustments that were ahead of us.

There was a scripture that was becoming very dear to me. I hoped that I would remember it always, for I was finding much comfort and peace in it.

⁓

Trust in the Lord with all thine heart; and lean not unto thine own understanding. In all thy ways acknowledge him, and he shall direct thy paths.

Proverbs 3:5-6
Bible

And thus we can behold how false, and also the unsteadiness of the hearts of the children of men; yea, we can see the Lord in his great infinite goodness doth bless and prosper those who put their trust in him.

Helaman 12:1
Book of Mormon

Chapter 12

Woods Cross to Bountiful

I liked the town of Woods Cross. It was so green and had slopes and meadows with homes that just seemed to be perfectly built into them. When I looked up at the tall mountains, I could see that it was the slow release of water as it flowed down in a timely manner that kept these small valleys and peaks so green. I especially liked Val Verta, perhaps because of its big arches that welcomed you as you entered. It was so unlike Sandy, where it was exactly that – dry and sandy. Taylorsville soil was like clay, and truckloads of top soil had to be brought in to get anything to grow.

The city had gotten its name from Daniel Woods, one of the richer settlers in the mid-1800s who settled there. He later gave up some of his farmland for the railroad crossing and the depot. It was first called Woods Crossing, and later shortened to Woods Cross.

The children liked the home John had found, and Eric and Craig told me that was the home they wanted to bring my grandchildren to. From the kitchen window, we could see the Great Salt Lake, Farmington Bay, Antelope Island, Farmington, Bountiful, gorgeous sunsets, and planes coming and going from the airport. It had a lovely yard, and John would make it even more beautiful. The only thing it lacked was a basketball court, but the boys had a place for that all figured out. Life seemed a little more settled for everyone in our new home.

I was called to work in the primary. It was still held during the week in 1978. I was also in charge of the young men, young women, and the road show. I had a lot of fun writing, directing, and holding early morning practices for that. One morning at about 5:45 a.m., we were all running late and had to get the practice done and get the kids to school. I guess I was whipping around the neighborhood a little too fast as I collected kids. The next thing I knew, there was a flashing red light behind my car. I just got a warning, but I didn't think I would ever live that down.

Cindy and Kim seemed to be happy and well-adjusted. Cindy was there for me to help with the little ones, and Kim went out and found more friends to bring home. We needed more income with Dave on his mission, so I brought in more children to tend. I was a little apprehensive because of my former experience, but it went well. Both the older girls were a great help to me.

Craig was in his last year of junior high. He attended Davis Junior High, where he found wonderful friends and was readily accepted. The ward had a lot of activities that summer for the youth. We had only been there about ten days when Craig went with the young men for a week-long trip to the Snake River. The boys repaired roofs on the nearby cabins. In return for their work, they could run the river rapids for two and a half days. He was always doing something that showed his wit and humor. He had poured some liquid in a bottle for sunburn, and he told the boys he was with that it really worked well for the burn. It was light yellow in color, and the boys asked him if it was urine. He said it was and it would work for them, too, if they used their own urine. When he told me this, I was disgusted and appalled, although it really did crack me up. Later in the summer, he spent a month up in Washington with his Grandmother Holmes.

Eric chose to go to Woods Cross High, though he could have gone to Bountiful – a decision I am sure he never regretted, because there is where he met his sweetheart Heidi Briscoe. Almost every night he went running, and I could almost set the clock as to when he would be home. One night he was gone a much longer time than usual. When I asked him if he had been running all this time he said, "No, I have been making cookies." He told me he had met Heidi at school and he just happened to know where she lived. It seemed we did not see him as much anymore. He had acquired two loves: Heidi and basketball.

Linda had some little friends nearby, too. When she was not with them, she was my constant companion, which I enjoyed so much. One day, John and I were talking about me going back to school and taking classes from the University of Utah extension program that was offered in Bountiful. John said he would like to take a few days off and go fishing. Linda was listening to our conversation, and said she wanted to go to "fishing school." You could always tell she was thinking, and sometimes she was way ahead of me.

We learned our landlord was going to sell the house we were living in, and he wanted about $20,000 more than we qualified for. We began another house search again, and this time we would buy if we could find the right one. We looked at several; they were much too small. Then we drove up to one on 1100 South in Bountiful that looked even smaller than the rest of them. The realtor assured me that it was much larger than it looked. There had been a new addition put on the back a few years earlier. After looking at it, we knew we could make it work. Though, it had some strange features. I kept telling myself that they gave it character. The one that stood out the most were the two staircases going to the downstairs. There were bedrooms on both sides with no opening between the old part of the house and the new. We had to go up one flight of stairs and down the other to get to the only bathroom downstairs; it was down in the old section of the house. Sometimes it was very comical, and other times very frustrating.

It was in June of 1978, shortly after we had moved to our home in Bountiful, that the announcement of the revelation came from the First Presidency of the LDS Church concerning *all worthy* males' ability to hold the Priesthood. This included men of African descent for the first time in modern church history. The change was officially announced to the body of the church on September 30, 1978, at General Conference. It caused some stir in the church, but was such a blessing. I know that it was revelation to our prophet and the apostles after much extended meditation and prayer. Many wonderful people had joined the church and were waiting upon the Lord for further blessings to come to them and their families. The change allowed these families to obtain blessings in the temple for the first time. I can't say that there was an immediate influx with people joining the church, but eventually the gospel was opened to so many other parts of the world. Now millions more could enjoy all of God's blessings.

I have always liked what an NBA African American basketball star had to say about the manifesto after he had joined the church. When he was asked why they were not allowed to hold the priesthood from the time of the organization of the church, he only said, "No man could hold it until 1829." I have always remembered that statement, knowing that the Lord works in his own time for all things. If one considers what was going on in the world in those years, and what was about to take place, you come to know that it was for the good of all mankind and for this nation where the restoration took place. Now it was time for the work of the Lord to move to all nations.

In April of 1980, David returned home from his mission. He had grown so much spiritually, and it was so good to have him home. Though, it did not last long. The night he arrived home, it took Teresa eighteen minutes from the time he had met with the stake president to be released as a missionary to arrive from Taylorsville. There was so much excitement when she walked in. The little ones just wanted to be a part of it, and did not want to miss one word. I had to escort them out of the room so that Dave and Teresa could say a proper hello. By no means had she sat around waiting for him for two years; that is not in her nature. She worked and had a quite a life of her own. However, the wedding did take place in a very short time after that. Her mother was very well organized.

Dave had served a good mission, not only in teaching many people, and performing and witnessing many baptisms, but also in holding leadership positions—including assistant to the mission president. These experiences gave him strength to move forward with his life and continually draw from them over the years.

When Dave had been home only a short time, I was cleaning up the kitchen when I needed to get away from the smell of food and get some fresh air. I went out onto the deck off the dining room and Dave followed me.

He said, "Mom, you're not?"

I said, "Dave, I am." Being the oldest of eight, he knew the symptoms. That little boy's voice that had said, *"Mama, don't forget me,"* was on his way. I was very happy, but had become concerned because on my next birthday I would turn 40.

Eric had a great two years with basketball. He did not make the school team, though many really questioned why. He was a good player, and in those years, the church had many intense regional games and tournaments. Our ward team won the playoff and went to regional with all intent to take first place. Our bishop was such a supporter of the boys. He would arrange for buses to take the ward fans when we had to travel far. It was so exciting for everyone! On the day of the championship playoffs, I had ordered a cake saying they were the winners. On the way to the game, I wondered if I had been too premature. Would I make the boys feel even worse if they lost? It turned out okay because they were the regional champs. We were so proud of the Bountiful Fourth Ward basketball players.

John had started a new business a few years earlier called it CRS. It was a sealant business – sealing concrete, asphalt, wood, and other surfaces. Dave worked for him, sealing large parking lots and buildings. John had connections with those who maintained the buildings on Temple Square. He had won the bid to seal the outside of the Salt Lake Tabernacle.

Two days before Thanksgiving of that year, I decided to do some cleaning and cleaned out a closet that was cluttered in the dining room. There was a box in there, and it came very clear in my mind that I should put the box in another room. There was no room for it anywhere. Finally, I shoved the eight-inch-high box under our bed. It contained some family pictures, and the Finnish genealogy papers that we had received from the home teacher we had in Sandy. The only other thing I had under our bed was my journal, so I could write in it before I went to sleep.

Most Thanksgivings we had a lot of people for dinner. This year I did not feel like cooking for more than our family. I was seven months pregnant. That night, after a wonderful day, I was in the living talking on the phone to Jilleanne Hall, my cousin. Most of the family was sitting in the family room off the kitchen/dining room when I heard John cry out, "Somebody help me!" My first thought was, "Honey, can't you do it yourself?" I had been on my feet most of the day, and then I heard him again in a voice that I never had heard before. I knew he was in trouble. I got to my feet as fast as I could and started toward the kitchen. Already, the flames were so high I could not get through them. I clicked on the phone to call the fire department; I was clicking so fast I couldn't get any response. I threw the phone and ran out the front door, still hearing my husband's voice in my head, though I could no longer hear him: "SOMEBODY HELP ME!"

125

The Lord looketh from heaven; he beholdedth all the sons of men. From the place of his habitation he looketh upon all the inhabitants of the earth. He fashioneth their hearts alike; he considereth all their works.

Psalms 33:13-15
Bible

And now, because of the covenant in which you have made ye shall be called the children of Christ, his sons, and his daughters; for behold, this day he hath spiritually begotten you; for you say that your hearts are changed through faith on his name; therefore, ye are born of him and have become his sons and his daughters.

Mosiah 5:7
Book of Mormon

Chapter 13

The Fire

November 27, 1980

As I ran out the door, I did something that it took a long time to forgive myself for. I did not check on the safety of all the family. I could see them gathering in the driveway and assumed they all got out the door of the family dining room safely.

I ran to Jake and Connie Parker, our good neighbors across the street. I was banging on their door shouting, "Call the fire department. Our house is on fire!" Connie opened the door and told me to calm down, and that "John would get it out." Then she looked and saw flames shooting in every direction and quickly called the fire department.

I saw the family in front of the house and ran to them, gathering them to get them across the street to safety. John and Dave were moving vehicles. David had keys to the downstairs and could get extra keys to the cars and trucks, so I thought they were both safe, but Cindy told me John had been on fire. I got the little ones inside the Parker home and went back outside and stood there in horror as I watched our home burn.

It seemed like an eternity before the fire department got there, but it really was only about four minutes. They attempted to go through the front door, but the combustion just threw them backwards. John directed them to the back entrance. Connie was trying to get a coat on me, and our other neighbor, Maggie Sheperd, was chasing me with a chair because she was afraid I would have my baby on the spot.

I looked to find Cindy and Kim. Cindy was standing by a boy, and he had his arm around her. Then I saw Kimmy, and she was standing there with no coat or shoes. She had gone downstairs before the fire broke out. I stood there and tried to comfort her and knew I needed to get her inside a house. As I stood there amid all the commotion and the people gathering to watch our home burn, the warmest feeling came over me. I knew that everything was going to be alright. I was as calm as a summer day. I did not know how it was going to be alright, only that the Holy Ghost had given me this assurance that it would be. It was like he embraced me as I was embracing my daughter, and I felt like a pair of warm arms were around me. The feeling that I experienced then remained with me throughout this whole experience.

By now, the paramedics were on the scene and asking if we were all okay. The children were all fine, but I told them my daughter had told me my husband had been on fire. I had not had time to talk to him. They went to the driveway where he was standing, cut the leg of his pant, and down he went onto a stretcher. I ran over to see how bad he was, and realized it was far worse than any of us expected. They were calling the University of Utah Hospital Burn Unit to tell them they were bringing him for admittance.

Eric and Craig were gone for the evening, and I got to a phone to call them at their friends' homes. Craig had gone to a movie with some friends, and Eric was at the Briscoe home with Heidi. Eric was the first to arrive, and it was decided he would be the one to accompany his father to the hospital. Craig arrived a few minutes later and could hardly get down the street to us because of the emergency vehicles and spectators.

I had many offers by now where we could stay for the night. I knew the family would have to be split up for this night, but before we did, I wanted to have family prayer. I asked Connie if we could use their bedroom. I gathered the family and we knelt around the bed. I offered the prayer and gave thanks for our very lives, our many blessings, for the beautiful day that we had, then pleaded for help in our hour of need, and especially to bless John with whatever lie ahead for him. As I came out of the bedroom, the television was facing the bedroom door. I glanced at it only to see the evening news showing our burning home. It was like living the horror of it all over again.

When things settled down a bit, Connie's husband Jake, who was a building contractor, went over to the house before they roped it off to get some idea of the damages. The whole top floor had been destroyed except for our bed. We were not sure about the downstairs, mostly smoke damage. The one thing I did know was there was no insurance. Our mortgage had been sold, and we had been notified by Fannie Mae that we now would need to provide our own insurance separate from the house payment. We had talked to two insurance agents, one on Friday and one on Monday. We had decided to go with the one we talked to on Friday, and John said he would get with him on the following Friday, but as of the day of the fire, we were uninsured. I told the men as much, but they said that I had to be wrong.

The children filled me in on the escape route of the rest of the family and what had happened. John had been warming material for a job he was going to start on the next day. The chemical had to be a certain temperature. He had ordered commercial warming blankets for this purpose, but they had not yet arrived. He had warmed it in the bathtub a couple of times, but for whatever the reason, this night he decided to warm it on the kitchen stove. He put it in a double boiler and the bottom came out of one of the containers. The chemical hit the element on the stove and exploded. That is when he called for help. Cindy went to help him, and he pushed her out of the way, so she would not get burned as he was already on fire. She grabbed either Linda or Melissa, and Kim grabbed the other one. Dave was downstairs and got out that door; Teresa was in another room and had followed me out the front door and gone to another neighbor for help. They realized Alysia was not with them, and Dave went back inside and found her huddled in a corner in the family room. When he turned around, the room was so full of smoke and flames he had to feel his way out. It was then that I felt so much guilt for not making sure that everyone was out safe, but I thanked the Lord that my children were looking after each other.

We went to Dave and Teresa's apartment to try to get the children settled as much as we could, along with the family dog, Tiger, who was also traumatized. Then we took Dave, Alysia, and Cindy up to the hospital to see John and get them checked for smoke inhalation. They were found to be clear. When we saw John, all he could do was apologize over and over, but he was the one in great pain. They had not yet determined how extensive his burns were, and would know more in the morning. They were making him as comfortable as possible, and one leg was severely burned. They had him in the wrong unit and thought he had a heart attack. He told me that the ambulance had lost all power on its way from Bountiful to Salt Lake, which slowed them down. Then when they finally reached the hospital, the driver had to circle around a few times to find the emergency entrance as the building was under construction.

We were so glad to see each other and that everyone had made it out alive. I knew we would be okay, but I had no way of knowing at this point how. John would endure so much suffering in the coming weeks. His legs would not be the same the rest of his life. The next day, I would be ordered to bed by my doctor until our baby boy was born.

The next morning, after very little sleep, I went to the house. Already, ward members were there to help in any way that they could. Debris was being removed from the house. I walked through and the whole kitchen was gone – just one mass of charred ashes. The curtains had melted; everything that was in the upstairs closets was gone, including the whole closet that I had removed the box from.

The furniture was gone. The most sentimental thing that I had lost was my wedding dress as well as many important papers. A large, gold-framed mirror that John bought me when we bought our first house on Browning Avenue survived, as well as our bed. I looked under the bed to see if the box was still there, and it was undisturbed. I was assured by those with me that it would be put in a safe place. I walked out, and my nice white stove that had cooked our Thanksgiving dinner was now black as coal. The sorting went on for hours. I was amazed at how many people were there and how they kept asking me what more they could do.

Our bishop was out of town until Saturday night. His first counselor suggested we go to the church and make a long-distance call to a couple whose house was vacant while they were living on the East coast for a work assignment. The renters had moved out the week before. He wanted their permission to move us into their home until we could figure out what to do about ours. Without hesitation, they agreed to let us move in. I could not believe how generous they were.

At 4 p.m., I had a doctor appointment that had been previously scheduled. I was not going to keep it with all that had happened, but the boys and the bishopric counselor insisted. He told me the doctor had been notified of the fire and he very much wanted me to come in. I reluctantly went to see him. After he checked me he said, "LaVelle, if John wasn't in the hospital, I would put you there until your baby is born; you have acute toxemia, and you need complete bed rest until the baby comes or we may lose him and possibly we may lose you." I couldn't believe what I was hearing. I had a family to care for, a business to run, a home to rebuild, and my husband in the hospital. I had only a couch to return to, and it was not even mine. He gave me some prescriptions and I walked out of his office in a daze and was almost in disbelief in what had occurred the last 20 hours.

That night, against doctor's orders, I visited John and learned his burns were far worse than we had anticipated. They were all third-degree. He would have to undergo skin grafting, with the skin being taken from the other leg. He was in unbearable pain, and my heart ached for him. The burn was from his knee down, although the sealant was on him from his waist down. Where his temple garments covered him, he had been protected. We have the promise of protection as one of the reasons we wear the garment; never had I seen it first-hand though others had told me of other instances of its protection.

I debated about telling him of my situation, but the children thought I should. When I did, he became as concerned about me as I was about him. When I left, I was not sure when we would see each other again. I silently prayed for the Lord to give him the strength for what he was going through.

On Saturday, I stayed "in bed" (couch) at Dave and Teresa's apartment, and the Parkers came and got the younger children. Marsha Parker, one of their daughters, was so wonderful with them. They loved her. Dave, Teresa, Eric, Craig, Cindy, and Kim were at the other house, helping to get it set up so that we could move in.

My thoughts were very much on my unborn child, a little boy that I had known for three years that was to come to us. A little boy whose spirit was present right after I delivered his twin sisters. I recalled the sacred experience I had of his being there, knowing instantly that if I did not have him, someone worthier would.

Now, here we were three years later, and we were in big trouble. I remained calm, still having the calming reassurance that I felt as I watched the fire. I knew I had to do my part and bed rest was the only way that was going to get us through this. That and constant prayer and the faith that I had in our Heavenly Father and these good people who were so willing to help us. I also thought of my neighbor who had five years earlier lost her baby son because of toxemia, and the mother in town who had recently been buried, with her dead baby boy laying in her arms. Toxemia was not something to be challenged.

I talked to my baby, as I talked to all my little ones as I carried them, firmly believing that they knew me and could hear me. I always remembered as a young girl reading in the Bible about Mary, mother of our Savior, going to her cousin Elizabeth, who was pregnant with John the Baptist, to tell her that she was with child. John leaped in Elizabeth's womb when he heard the news. I firmly believed that my son could hear me, though I did not understand how. I asked my baby to do his part, if there was anything he could do, and I would do everything I could so that we could have him with us if that was Heavenly Father's will.

My doctor came to the apartment to bring me more medication and to make sure I was doing what he had told me. He was also making sure I understood how crucial it was that I stayed quiet. The phone kept ringing that day. Many friends from Taylorsville were calling to see what they could do. Jessie called several times and said, "We are determined to do something."

Finally, I said, "Well, maybe a little food. I have no idea what my food situation is."

I was not accustomed to being the receiver. I was the giver; at one point in a journal, I recorded twenty-seven dinners that I had taken to others for various reasons. Reasons listed were: "new baby", "mother had surgery", "whole family feeling ill", "maybe soup and jello will help", "so in so needs to be cheered," and so on. I never dreamed that I was about to have twenty-seven meals returned.

By 6 p.m., Mark, Janet, Ron, and Pat were at the apartment asking me to step outside. I could not believe what I saw; a truck load of food that they had gathered that afternoon. They could have not put one more box in the bed of that truck. Jesse also handed me an envelope with cash in it. One dear sister had put three $20 bills in it with a note saying that when both John and I could walk again, to go buy some shoes. I told them to take the food to the home that was being prepared for us. We hugged, and they left. Then a funny thing happened. Teresa and I went upstairs to the apartment and realized the door was locked. I waited in the 20-degree weather until she found the manager and got a key from him. I was sure grateful to get out of the cold.

At 8:30 p.m, I was taken over to the home being prepared for us. I could hardly comprehend what I saw: so many, including my own children, had worked so hard to get the home ready for us. The kitchen was stocked, linens in the closet, beds made up, furniture in the living room, even a television had been set up. All I had to do was to go to bed. For the first time since the fire, the tears came. They were tears of gratitude for the blessings that kept pouring in.

On Sunday, we had many visitors. The first one was Lynn Stokes, a neighbor. Her little girl was one of Linda's friends. She did not know it, but when she arrived, it was like an angel had been sent to me at the very moment that I needed her. Linda wanted to go to Sunday school, and Alysia and Melissa loved their class, too, but I had nothing for them to wear. Larger clothes had been donated that needed some alterations, but I did not have a needle and thread to even hem them. I told them they needed to stay home with me. I had three unhappy girls when our neighbor, Lynn, showed up and handed me three little darling dresses she had been sewing since Friday morning. We put them on the girls and they looked like three little dolls in their blue and white pin-a fore dresses with bows in their hair to match. They went to church with the rest of the family, and I went to bed.

Later that day, David, our bishop, and our High Priest Group Leader visited with an insurance agent (who checked out my story of no insurance and found that I was correct, and that there was no grace period). Jake Parker, our building contractor neighbor, met with me at my bedside. The bishop said that they were going to rebuild us.

I told them, "No, just help us until we get on our feet, and we will rebuild as we can."

He said, "No, the decision had been made, and we will start construction tomorrow." The brethren told me that we would be back in our home by Christmas day.

Jake was over construction. An electrician and plumber lived in the ward and had agreed to their assignments and were ready to roll. Paul was out of work for the winter, and I never did find out what the bishop agreed to pay him for his services. I knew he had to have something as he, too, had a large family. The bishop reminded me that was the purpose of fast offerings, and if they exhausted the ward fund, they would go to the stake. He felt this was what the Lord wanted. Then he said, "Sister Holmes, for months my counselors and I have been praying for unity in the ward. There have been members and families feuding and quarreling over things that happened so long ago they have probably forgotten why their feud was started. Yesterday, they were working side by side—enjoying each other and determined to get you rebuilt. We have witnessed the unity and blessing already." I looked at him in amazement!

I still did not have a phone, and was unable to communicate with John except through the children who were able to visit him. I knew he was in much pain, and that his first surgery was scheduled for the first of the week.

Eric returned to college. I know this was hard for him, but finals were coming up and he would lose all his credits for the term if he didn't return now. Dave and I talked about the business and what he could do, and he took over like a pro. I was so grateful to him. I was grateful, too, for my dear daughter-in-law, Teresa, and for all that she was doing for us. She did not feel that good herself, as she was in her first weeks of pregnancy. Craig helped Dave with some of the jobs when he could, but he had the busiest month of school coming. He was in the Concert Choir, and practices for their many performances were scheduled and mandatory.

On Tuesday, John had his surgery. I felt so bad that I could not be there. When skin is grafted, it is usually taken from another part of the body. In John's case it was taken from the other leg. It seemed so primitive, but that was all the technology they had then. I got permission to go visit him on Sunday, and my doctor told me that I may not be prepared for the shock of what I was going to see. That made me even more determined to go to him. The boys got me a wheelchair. When I was wheeled in, I saw both of his legs covered with blood-soaked gauze from his thighs to his ankles. It was like being skinned alive.

We just clasped hands and were so glad to see each other. He was given another blessing, and we visited for about forty-five minutes. Many times, tears ran down his face and he said many spiritual things that made my love deepen for him more than ever. My heart ached for him, but there was nothing I could do. He was so concerned for me, but there was nothing he could do for me either. We could only pray for each other and show our faith and gratitude to Heavenly Father that things had not been worse. I kissed him goodbye and would not see him until he was released from the hospital. We each had our own battles to fight. We knew with faith, determination, and love for each other, we would both win them.

Construction on the house kept moving right along. Carl would pop in on me and give me choices. Never did I see a man accomplish so much in so little time. They did away with one of the staircases, and put in an opening between the old downstairs and the new addition.

A sister was assigned to be my personal specialist, and each day she checked in on me to see what my needs were. We made lists, and she made sure we had everything for the house when we moved in. She was a very talented lady. Other sisters continued to take the three little girls. One day, Linda saw a flame when a sister turned on her gas range. She was so scared she ran out of the house and all the way home. I kept her with me the rest of the time. We read, watched television, played quiet games, and colored side by side. She would often ask me if I was thinking about the fire. I would calmly say, "no," and she would say, "I am." I tried to get her mind on other things, and later she would say, "Mama, I'm not thinking about the fire anymore." I knew she was, and I had concerns about her and how the other girls were affected by it. We would talk about it, and I tried to stay aware of their feelings. I knew it would take time to get over it. The dinners continued to come in each night, and I was so thankful for that. Cindy continued to be my other pair of hands and such a second mother to her sisters.

Kim was very busy with gymnastics. On Saturday, Dec. 6, she came in to tell me she and two of her best friends had made team tryouts. She had worked so hard and was good at it, and I was happy for her.

I had always been proud of my children, but no other mother could have been prouder of her children than I was at this time. They were doing all that they could. Eric came home on Dec. 10th and pitched right in. Craig, Cindy, and Kim all bore their testimonies on fast Sunday, and everyone who came to see me told me I had great kids, and they had shown so much faith during all this.

I went to the doctor twice a week. I was holding my own in some ways, and in others I was not. He took some fluid to determine how developed the baby's lungs were doing, but they were not far enough along to induce labor. We would have to wait at least two more weeks and I had to continue to stay down. Several times my blood pressure had risen quite high, and I had to make the decision whether to call the doctor, who I was sure would put me in the hospital, or to call on the Priesthood. It was the latter that I chose, and I knew I had made the right decision. One night it was very late, and I was having a hard time. Craig was so worried; he ran over and got our high priest group leader. He gave me a priesthood blessing. Within minutes I was resting peacefully.

When John called from the hospital and said he could come home, I called the school to have Craig released to pick him up. This was such good news. I was concerned the little girls would want to crawl on their big daddy, and we had to be so careful with his legs. They seemed to understand. He had to learn to walk again because of the nerve damage, and Eric took him for physical therapy. Our children were taking complete care of us. It was about this time that Kim landed wrong off a beam and sprained her ankle badly, so one more of us was out of commission. But we were all together again, and that was what mattered most.

On Dec. 15, all previous plans for the annual ward Christmas party were canceled, and it turned into a benefit for us. The bishop told ward members, "If you husbands don't give your wives a present this year, and if you wives do not get your husbands gifts, it is okay. Our goal is to help the Holmes family." Cindy, Kim, and Craig went over to the church as the ward gathered for stories and singing of carols and then enjoyed a potluck dinner. Later that night, the first counselor and ward clerk brought over a check for over $1,400. We were overwhelmed with the generosity of our ward members.

The Deseret News newspaper called me and wanted our story for a human-interest column. I told them no. I felt that our family had been through enough, and I wanted to protect them. It took me twenty-two years to write the story, though I had told the story many times at Relief Society and other gatherings. I kept a full account in my journal that had been under the bed with the box.

John and I had long talks, wondering if there was purpose in the things that had happened to us, other than knowing all these experiences are for our own good. Perhaps as the years passed, we would know. I did recall making a statement directed to our Heavenly Father shortly before the fire that if I were to lose all that I had except the gospel of Jesus Christ and my family, I could endure. I had not lost it all, I was just ruffled up a bit.

My testimony grew more than ever, my faith increased, knowledge increased of the restored gospel, and I again knew that nothing was forgotten when it was restored. I also had unconditional love for our ward people. Many times, I would recall the night of the fire and the feeling I had as I stood there watching our home burn; the feeling of love and comfort that came from the Holy Ghost. He is so wonderful. Many who came to visit me said they felt it when they were with me. I give full credit to Him for this feeling of peace and calmness. The feeling remained with me and gave me much comfort.

On Dec. 20, Jake told me we would be moving into our own home on the Christmas Eve. I told him it was not necessary, and that we could move in after Christmas. He said it would be ready, and he was sticking to his goal. I thought it was madness. It was Christmas and people should be with their families and other festivities, not working on our behalf. On Dec. 21, after a doctor's appointment, I went to the house. There was so much left to do. I didn't know how they possibly could be finished in three days. There was electrical work, plumbing, carpet to be laid, and cabinets and appliances to be installed. On Dec. 24, after another doctor's appointment, I was supposed to return to this house, and they would be moving our things over to it. I was sure it would take nothing short of a miracle.

I had planned for a small Christmas for each child. Some shopping had been done before the fire and had been hidden in our neighbor's garage. Teresa helped me do the rest. It wasn't much, but each child was getting something he or she needed. The boys did not ask for a thing. The older girls did not either. Cindy had seen a black dress in a catalogue and we got that for her. We got dolls and buggies for Alysia and Melissa, toys for Linda, and clothes for Kim.

On Christmas Eve, I went to the doctor. After checking me, he told me to go right home and go to bed. Eric drove me to our own home. I went in, looked around, and just gasped. It was so beautiful. My miracle had happened; everything was in place. Carpet was laid. There were appliances, beautiful oak cupboards, and lovely light fixtures. New furniture had been donated. After Eric left to go help move more things, I stood and cried, I could not believe what I saw.

Then the emotions of being a mother took over. This was Christmas Eve, and I saw no tree. I had not taken a thing to my neighbors, had not sent a card, and had done nothing that was traditional for my family. I felt so bad. I felt like I had let people down. I was the giver, not the receiver, and yet it was very apparent which end I was on this year. Then exhaustion set in—the feeling of being light headed and dizzy. I made my way to the couch and knew that this year things were the way they were, and I should feel nothing except gratitude and humility.

I fell into a deep sleep. By 1:30 p.m., was awakened by a stream of people coming in. They came in with food, a tree, and decorations for it. Soon there was a team of children putting up the tree, and sisters filling the cupboards with food and dishes. Beds were being brought in and made up. Two sisters were putting linens in the hall closet and discussing how I would like my towels folded – square or oblong. I thought, "Oh, sisters, if you knew how grateful I am to have towels, you would know that I do not care." The electrician and plumber were doing last minute things, and people were busy as bees. At about 4 p.m., people began to thin out. Then Sister Salisbury took Cindy and Kim to shop for our traditional Christmas dinner. I had told the sisters we would take care of it because Cindy was excited to do it. Sister Salisbury did not have any daughters of her own, and later told me how much she enjoyed that experience.

At about 5:30 p.m., the stream of people started again, this time on a different mission. The doorbell would ring, and the children would go and find presents of all kinds left at the doorstep. Some people did hand it to them, but most preferred to run and hide and get the joy from seeing the children come out to see who the mystery giver was. Others came to sing carols. When one family came in and sang, I felt angels were in our home. This went on for a few hours. When it was all over, there were more than 150 gifts under our tree, and Santa had not come yet. So many things were given – books, toys, clothes, small appliances, five sets of electric hair curlers, and many other items. Oh, what a Christmas this was.

On Christmas morning I woke, but before I opened my eyes, I laid there and wondered whether this was all a dream – did it really happen? I opened my eyes, saw my new bedroom, the new doors, everything so familiar and yet so different; it was not a dream, it all had really happened.

We all met in the family room around the tree, and it was such a wonderful day. We were so thankful for all that had been given to us, and for our good friends and neighbors and all who had sacrificed for us to be here this day. Most of all we were thankful for the gift of life and the birth of our Savior, Jesus Christ.

A few days later I knew, I could not hold on much longer, though the calendar said I should go another four weeks. I went to the doctor and he said, "It is time." He sent me to the hospital to induce labor. After a few days, on December 30th, our little Justin Paul Holmes ("just, lawful, fair") was born by C-section. He was a healthy, beautiful baby. When I held him for the first time I cried and told him, "We did it, thanks to all those wonderful people, our loving Heavenly Father, and our Savior, Jesus Christ, WE DID IT!"

When I went home a few days later I had some complications with my incision. It split open and drained, and I had terrible pain. John went with me to the doctor, and he gave me medication that made me sleep for four days. John, Cindy, Kim, and Craig took care of the baby, Melissa, Alysia, and Linda. For about a week, I did not know much about what was going on around me.

I had been getting my strength back and after about three weeks, I started wondering where some of the things were that had been moved back into the house. The thing I wondered the most about was the box – the one that I had put under the bed almost two months ago, the one that would have been destroyed with everything else in the dining room closet if I had not moved it. Where was it? I had not seen it since the day after the fire when I was told it would be put in a safe place. Was it downstairs? So much had been moved with all the reconstruction down there. Was it at the other home? I knew it was not upstairs. I went downstairs and looked through some things and could not find it. I felt some panic go through me, and then I looked over in a corner and saw a very smashed 8-inch tall box that looked familiar sitting underneath two other boxes. There it was. The pictures and all the papers we had searched for over ten years were there, including information about John's father's family that may not have been replaceable. It had been a miracle itself. A kind and loving Heavenly Father and Holy Ghost had prompted me to put it in a safe place.

The feeling of Christmas still lingered in me as well as the comforting arms of the Holy Ghost. Truly, this will be my most remembered Christmas. Also, over twenty-seven dinners were returned, and so much, much more!!

For I was an hungered, and you gave me meat; I was thirsty, and you gave me drink. I was a stranger, and you took me in. Naked and ye clothed me; I was sick and ye visited me. I was in prison, and ye came unto me.

Matthew 25:35-36
Bible

But charity is the pure love of Christ, and it endureth forever; and whoso is found pocessed of it at the last day; it shall be well with him.

Moroni 7:47
Book of Mormon

Chapter 14

Family Affairs

"LaVelle! LaVelle Holmes, is that you?"

I turned in the grocery store to see a familiar face. I had not seen her for over 16 years since we had moved from the Browning ward in the 1960s. It was Lenora Crain, and she looked fantastic! Then there was me. I still carried around a lot of baby weight.

We chatted a few minutes and caught up on each other's lives. Then she asked me how many children I had as she was looking at Justin sitting in his carrier inside the grocery cart. I'm sure she thought he was a grandchild. I said, "Nine; Justin is our youngest."

Her eyes widened, and she said, "Nine, you have nine? You must be so bored with life!"

I said, "Bored? I have been bewildered, confused, challenged, wondered what comes next, exhausted, exasperated, and wished each one had come with directions, but never was I bored."

I had told John that I wished the Lord had sent me to parenting school, and he said, "He did, and now you are applying what you have learned." Sometimes I felt so inadequate. I also told my friend that I also found much joy in my big family.

There was always some kind of activity going on at our house. There were times I had a house or backyard full of teenagers when I was still trying to get toddlers to bed, and other times I hoped and prayed that they all got home safe and sound.

In February of the new year, we were getting settled in our home and getting into some routine, as much as you can with a newborn. On fast Sunday, John and I bore our testimonies. He quoted the scripture from Matthew 25:35-36, for that is how he truly felt. We both thanked the Lord and the ward for all that had been done in our behalf. Justin was also blessed that day.

Early in February of 1981, my grandmother Dolly passed away. I took Justin and flew to Pasco for her funeral. She had died in Aunt Thelma's arms. At one point during the funeral, Dad grabbed my hand and would not let go of it, which was fine with me. It was the first time I had seen him show any emotion about anything except anger back when he was so depressed when he lost his business.

Eric received his mission call in February 1981. He had been called to the Montreal (Quebec) Canadian French-speaking mission. He was scheduled to leave in April. I would miss him so much; he was my brick.

Mother had been ill for so long; I was always concerned for her. There was a new procedure they could do on the arteries from the neck to the heart, and she needed to have this done. There were only two hospitals in the United States that would perform it. One was in New York and the other in San Francisco. A few years later, it became a procedure that was performed in most major hospitals around the country. Dad made arrangements to meet mother's brother, Willard, at the hospital in San Francisco. When they arrived, he was there with flowers. It was a joyful reunion.

They came to stay with us when she left the hospital (not a quiet place to recuperate from anything) and they came to Eric's setting apart prior to his leaving on his mission. In his setting apart, he was blessed that he would be creative and use his imagination in teaching the gospel and that his leadership abilities would be recognized by his leaders. He was told that much rejoicing was taking place not only by his Heavenly Parents, and by others as well. He was also told that the language would flow from his tongue and that the spirit would be with him.

While he was out, the First Presidency announced all missions would be shortened to 18 months. The policy only lasted a few years. The missions were shortened due to economic conditions throughout the world and armed services and college co-operation.

I had a dream about three days before the announcement came that he had come early, and this concerned me. I was afraid that he was going to get sick or be in an accident. When the announcement came, my fears disappeared. He said that once the announcement came, his efforts really increased and he served as district and zone leader.

Eric returned home from Canada in October 1982. After his release that evening by the stake president, John drove him a few blocks from the Bountiful Cemetery to meet Heidi. They had spent a lot of time in that same spot just to talk and walk when they were in high school. It was not too long after he came home that they announced their engagement. He and Heidi were married on December 27, 1982, and they were off to Utah State to finish their education. She had continued her studies while he was gone and did some studying in the Holy Lands for a while. Their little Emilie Ann was born on December 26, 1983.

Craig's high school years were packed with activities. He graduated with honors and was on the starting lineup for the Bountiful High football team, as well as in Concert Choir and Madrigals. He ran for senior class vice president and had so many friends. He had broken his hand during a football practice. When I tried to see him in his room at the hospital, I could hardly find him amongst all his friends – both guys and girls. The room was loaded with balloons and signs. We were told that if this had happened a couple of decades earlier, he would have been left with a club hand. The doctors had to put six screws in his hand.

Bountiful High went to the football playoffs for the state championship in 1981, and it was an exciting game. At half time, we were behind. John was trying to explain to me what he thought needed to be done to outscore the opposing team, and what plays he would use. I told him it would not help, that they were not going to win. He looked at me with a scowl and said, "How do you know?" I told him that I had a dream the night before the game. I saw the score, and I also saw some of our players walking out of the University of Utah Football Stadium very sad, with others being very angry. There were some lined up against the fence outside the stadium crying. This is exactly how it all played out. I felt so bad for Craig, the team, and coaches.

I was impressed with the group that Craig went around with. They were a great bunch of kids. At Christmas time, all the guys took flowers to the girls in the group. They took one girl whose parents did not celebrate Christmas a flower as well. They told her it was a friendship flower.

Once when he and one of his buddies were getting ready to pick up their dates for one of the formal dances, they came to our home to put on their tuxedos. I told them they looked so nice and out the door they went. A couple of minutes later they were back. They said they forgotten to brush their teeth and raced down stairs. When they came back up, they reeked of toothpaste and aftershave. I never did ask whose toothbrush his friend used. I am not sure I wanted to know.

At his seminary graduation, each mother was presented with a rose. One of the allegorical stories shared by one of the women about a family who had died really impressed me. It was a story that helped put the importance of getting sealed in the temple into perspective.

A young woman was trying to count their family members to see if they were all there. Her older brother and younger sister were, and she said to them, "Look, here comes mother carrying baby Tommy." They looked around and saw their father coming. When he joined them, he said, "I am so sorry, that car was coming so fast; it was heading right for us and there was nothing I could do. But at least we are all here."

A gatekeeper came up to them and asked if they were looking for their places to stay. The father said, "Yes but we only need one place to stay, we are all here." The gatekeeper asked if they had brought their keys. "What do you mean?" asked the father.

"Your keys to the kingdom," said the gatekeeper. "Did you go to the temple, so you can all stay in one mansion? If not, you will go to different places."

"No, we didn't get there, we always meant too, we were always so busy. They had ward excursions sometimes, but something always came up, and the temple was so far away."

We all must do what we have too, to see that we share the same mansion with our loved ones. Receiving our own temple endowment and sealings are of upmost importance.

Craig left the night of graduation for Bear Lake, Idaho. He went with a good friend whose parents owned a small farm there. The boys worked there for the summer. In the fall, we moved him to Rexburg College (now BYU-Idaho).

His mission call came in November. It came late Wednesday before Thanksgiving, and no one was home except myself. We were having a lot of family for Thanksgiving dinner, and I decided to wait until then for him to open it. He did not expect it for another week. I wrote a note to everyone who was coming to dinner, placed it on their plates, and each had to read it out loud before the blessing. When it came time for Craig to read his (and he was the last one), it said, "We want to know where you are going on your mission and we want to know now!" He said, "How can I tell you where I am going? I don't even know!"

I said, "lift up your plate." He saw the envelope, opened it and it said he would be serving in Edinburgh, Scotland, and he would leave in February. There was much excitement.

The winters of 1982 and 1983 were both hard winters. Alysia, Melissa, and Linda were sick a lot, especially Melissa, who had ear infections. It was hard to keep her well. She was not a complainer, but I could tell. She would get so pale and stop eating and lose weight. We spent so much time at the doctor's office. Also, the younger children all had chicken pox in a month's span.

Cindy was still my homebody, but she loved her music and got a superior rating on the song she sang at district competition. She also made me a plaque that said, "Mothers make the best friends." I had it for over 35 years until it got ruined when the fabric got torn. She served as the Mia Maid president. When she was a Laurel, she had to miss a lot of week night activities with the young women because of her music schedule. One leader gave her a hard time over this and said she would lose her testimony and she was not making the right decision. This really upset Cindy, and we had to tell the leader in a polite way that we were her parents and we would handle this.

I was so glad that Cindy found her music so fulfilling, was so good at it, and that she was making the right choices. As it turned out later in life, Cindy served many years as a Young Women's president herself. She also served in the stake Young Women presidency and as their camp director for thirteen years. She could understand the girls when they came to her with similar schedule problems.

Kim was always busy, too. She was in flags, had her music, and was a natural at debate. When she and her father started debating, the rest of us just wanted to leave the house. She also held the title of "Miss Blabby" for the school newspaper and wrote an all-around informative column for the school. She continued to bring new friends home. She was very ambitious. At the age of 15, she went to work for an insurance firm. She started out with just filing, and it led to other things. She was on a quest to get herself a waterbed, which were very popular in those days, and eventually saved enough to get herself a car.

The little girls took dance classes, but it did not turn out to be the best experience for Linda. The recital at the end of the year was held in a large school. Each class was to stay in their room until a parent came to get them. Somehow, she got mixed up and lost. I had sent Cindy to get her while I got Melissa and Alysia. She did not want to take dance the next year.

There was a neighbor the twins' age, and she loved to be with them. It sometimes ended up with someone crying because so many times three little people together just don't work well together.

As for Justin, he was a quiet boy and was happy if there was a basketball nearby. When he was two, he walked into my office I had at the house and said, "I see two mamas."

I said, "You see two mamas?"

He said, "Yes." I looked at him closely and could see why he could see two of me. His left eye was pulling to the right. We got him glasses, and he took such good care of them. He always put them on the nightstand, so he could get them first thing in the morning. There was one morning, however, when I was downstairs with the girls and he had still been asleep. When he woke up, he came downstairs. He came to the door of the room where we were and announced, "I cannot find my damn glasses."

I said, "What did you say?" He repeated himself, and I said, "Well, we better go find them." We could deal with the language later.

John and I were proud of our growing family, and no, I never was bored.

⟨⟩

And thou shall teach them diligently unto thy children, and shalt talk of them when thou sitteth in thine house, and when thou walkest by the way, and when thou liest down, and when thou risest up.

Deuteronomy 6:7
Bible

But ye will teach them to walk in ways of truth and soberness; ye will teach them to love one another, and to serve one another.

Mosiah 4:15
Book of Mormon

Chapter 15

Floods in the Eighties

"There sure is a lot of water on the street," I thought to myself as I was driving to Miss Laura's preschool to pick up the twins. I thought a fire hydrant or water line had broken. On the way back home, it was even worse. When I got home, I turned on the news. They were reporting there was flooding both in Bountiful and Salt Lake City.

We had several heavy snowfalls during the winter, and it had accumulated on the east bench of the cities. The weather had warmed up so fast that spring, and the snow melted quickly. Sandbagging was on everyone's mind, as well as evacuation. Watching the news, we realized how bad it was. People were sandbagging, and some of the roads were closed. It came two blocks from our house, but others were not so lucky. Homes were torn out, others filled with mud.

Three creeks had become rivers. In Salt Lake, Main and State streets were closed, and bridges were built to help people get across. This went on for days. Our ward was called out. Every able-bodied man, woman, and teen were helping sandbag.

The Salt Lake City mayor called for more help for Salt Lake, and about 100 people showed up. The church asked for more help, and over 1,000 showed up in addition to those who had already come. We worked in six-hour shifts and then rotated. Sandwiches, cake, and water were provided by the women. The response of the church members was a great part of it. The church is already organized to respond way in advance of a disaster.

One woman who lived on the east bench of Bountiful had packed extra clothes and put them in a box along with her journals. She had wrapped it in plastic and secured it with a belt and set the box on her porch while she went into grab some other valuables. She returned a minute later to get the box and run to the car just in time to see her box being swept away by the mud. They lost most of their possessions. The thing she felt the worst about was her journals. She felt horrified and thought they were gone forever. A few weeks later when we were cleaning up, a bishop on the west side of town found some books. Most of the plastic was torn off, but they were still tied securely together with a belt. He found her name and got them back to her. She was so grateful.

Craig was in Scotland by this time and heard of the flood clear back in Utah on the news there. A member had brought it to his attention.

We always tried to go visit our parents at least once a year. We would stay several days, and I saw Ruth's family, too. Sometimes John could not get away; many times I just packed up the car and kids, and off we would go. I felt it was so important for the kids to have a relationship with their grandparents. Some years they could come to us.

My parent's 50th wedding anniversary was on March 21, 1986, and Ruth and I had planned for a long time to have a family gathering and to make it a special time for them. Dad was suffering from bone cancer. He had broken both wrists two days apart due to the holes in them from the cancer, and his diabetes was taking its toll because of all the medication. He was a very sick man. As the time approached, we wondered if we should have the celebration for them. We decided to go ahead with it and are so glad that we did. They both looked forward to it as we all did. It was a joint effort on Ruth and her family's part as well as mine.

We rented a small motel there in Clarkston for all of us to have our own place to stay. At the celebration, we had a program, telling about their life. Many took part telling different parts of their journey the past 50 years. The younger grandchildren sang "We are a Happy Family." Cindy and Kim sang "You Light up My Life." I sang "It's a Great Big Wide Wonderful World." The next day, we went to Dad and Mom's, and Dad so enjoyed driving everyone around in his Model T Ford that he had restored. He was so proud of it. It was one of those times you just did not want to end.

Later that summer, John and I went to Coulee Dam for his 30th class reunion. We took a detour to Clarkston on our way and visited with my parents. Dad and I sat out on their patio for a few hours and just visited. It was the last visit I had with him.

In August, we received a phone call that he was back in the hospital and his kidneys were shutting down. I flew out and got there just a few hours before he went into a coma. He asked where John was, and I told him he could not come. Mother, Ruth, Jerry, and I were there, and eventually Dad lapsed into a coma. After several hours, the doctor told us that it was our decision to turn off the machines. He said he would never regain consciousness. We all agreed it should be done. His last words had been that he was "going on a long vacation." His neighbor, a minister, visited him in the hospital and told us Dad did tell him that he believed in Christ. That brought a lot of comfort to many of the family. John did his temple work in 1989.

Craig came home from his mission the end of 1984. He was not home long before he joined the Air National Guard Reserve. From there, he started school at the University of Utah, where he graduated. The Guard helped pay for much of his schooling.

While attending the U of U, he met and fell in love with a Cindee Shultz. The day after he proposed to Cindee, our neighbor Maggie Sheperd—who sometimes kept better track of my children than I did—saw me outside. She came over to me and said to me in a superior voice, "Do you know what time your son came home this morning?" I assured her that I did, and that he and his bride-to-be went to her home to talk to her parents after he had proposed. They were not there, and they waited for them to tell them the news. They sat up for a few more hours talking about their future and wedding plans.

I told her that he had arranged for a horse and buggy ride in downtown Salt Lake. When they got in front of the temple, he asked the driver to stop and he asked Cindee to marry him. I think I took the wind right out of Maggie's sails. Craig and Cindee were married in the Salt Lake Temple in May of 1987.

Maggie and Carl Sheperd were actually wonderful neighbors. He brought beer to kill the snails and slugs in the garden, played Santa Clause for our family Christmas parties, and always brought a hammer for the groom as a wedding present. At many of our kids' weddings, he sang as he had sung in the Tabernacle Choir for 20 years. I think Maggie's concern for our family was genuine, and we know we kept her entertained. Sometimes the kids would wave at her when they came in even if they could not see her. They knew she was watching from some window or door.

Both Cindy and Kim were in Shayla, which was an all-girl elite singing and dance group at Bountiful High. The director demanded perfection from them as much as his Madrigal group. It took a lot of time, and it certainly paid off for Cindy as she received a scholarship from Utah State. Kim did a lot of community singing with a few other women when she later lived in Eureka, Montana. She had a lot of fun with that group, and they were in high demand.

Even though our own older boys were all gone, we did not lack for young men to be at the house. They just seemed to show up. One young man would come as early as 8 or 8:30 a.m. and sit on the front porch in the summer. He did not understand that was not what a young man should do. It seemed he had his own code of normal. I told him to not come so early. He should wait until afternoon, and then call on the phone. I felt like he was somewhat like a homing pigeon. I would send him away, and he came right back. The girls were annoyed with it, but they were afraid they would hurt his feelings. First, he was madly in love with Cindy, then Kim. He finally moved on to a friend of Cindy's who lived down the street.

Cindy graduated and went to USU, and I sure did miss her. She had a great year at college, had good roommates, and dated a lot. I saw a good change in her. I felt like she really found herself. Her life was about to change, though. While she was home on break, she got a job as a hostess at a local restaurant. One of the other girls who worked there said she had a brother that was a returned missionary and going to BYU, and she would like Cindy to meet him. His name was Adam Ray Taylor. She, Adam, and friends were going tubing, and Cindy was invited. They needed to use one of our large tubes to have enough. Adam forgot to give the tube back to her that night, and so called to see if he could return it. I think he kept it on purpose.

They had gone on a few dates when he was over at the house one night. I was downstairs, and when I came up, they were sitting by the fireplace. I thought to myself, "She is going to marry him." She did in May of the following year.

Kim chose not to go to college right after she graduated, and got a job working at Carpenter Paper, in Woods Cross. She was so ambitious and always had done whatever she set her mind to. I was always proud of her. She sometimes could save and earn more money than some of her siblings who had college educations.

Our business had its ups and downs, but somehow, we seemed to survive. One of the biggest problems we had was that we had gone into it so undercapitalized. John came home one day and told me that he had met a man who wanted to invest $500,000.00. I looked at him and said, "Does he want to invest in the company, or to own our souls?"

We had town floods in the early 1980s, and now we were going to experience some personal ones.

⁓

Lo, children are an heritage of the Lord: and the fruit of the womb is his reward.

Psalm 127:3
Bible

I Nephi, having been born of goodly parents...

1 Nephi 1:1
Book of Mormon

Chapter 16

Troubles Times Turning into Blessings

The company really had its ups and downs. It was hard to grow without money. The adage that it takes money to make money is so true. We survived on what we made, and that was about all. We had a great product but needed some investment money.

When John said his associate wanted to invest half a million dollars, it seemed way too much. I was thinking maybe up to $100,000. I know an investment is just that, and is not a loan. I knew of horror stories that turned out terrible when things were going wrong. I did not want that hanging over our heads, even if the corporation was changed and the protective legal measures were taken.

John had helped this man out when he was in dire need and he was grateful to John, but this was too much. He was dealing in precious metals, which were at an all-time high in the 1980s – especially gold and silver. Inflation had really set in during the last decade. Homes had tripled in value, and food was sky rocketing. A car cost three times as much as it did only a few years earlier, and many businesses did not make it.

His friend was positive everything was going to go his way. Everything was set in place and it was only a matter time, he was arranging to buy one of the malls on the south end of Salt Lake and to build another mall further south. All this sounded wonderful for him; still, I thought that if he invested the amount of money he had offered John, he would control us. It just did not feel right to me. Perhaps I was not optimistic enough. John knew much more about this gentleman than I did. But after a while, he too began to have his reservations. As it all turned out, after months of waiting with reports and promises, he just disappeared.

John had met another man who wanted to invest in our company. He had a decorative product that was brought it by the container full, then was trucked either to our warehouse or other businesses that had purchased it from us.

We went to trade shows to promote the product, but after a few years, we were having trouble with it because of the cold winters. It had been tested to withstand the cold, but proved not to be as good as we were told it was.

We considered moving to a warmer climate and went to a warmer state to look the situation over. We put down a $1,000 earnest money on a home. The children and I were packed up and ready to move, when John walked in mid-morning with the house's "For Sale" sign in his hand. He said, "We are not moving, we are not supposed to go."

He told me that he was driving on the freeway when it just came so clear so him: "Do not move your family." I did not question it, and the kids were so relieved. Moving was certainly was not what they wanted. The nice people that we had been working with to buy their home refunded our money.

The investor was disappointed in the way things were going, as were we, and felt he did not get a fair return on his investment.

Adam did ask Cindy to marry him and the wedding was approaching. We went to the Salt Lake Temple with Cindy to receive her temple endowment prior to the wedding. Later that night, we had only been home for a few minutes when the doorbell rang. A man stood there with papers in his hand. John was being sued for a large sum of money.

We obtained a highly qualified lawyer who had come well recommended. After reviewing the papers, he said, "We could counter sue on seven counts." We did not want to sue anybody for anything; we just wanted the suit to be dropped.

The morning of the deposition, John went to an early morning temple session. At a certain point during the session when you can sit and ponder or pray, he had the rest of the day heavily on his mind and felt much anxiety. As he sat there, the calmest and most peaceful feeling came over him. The anxiety left, and he knew somehow things were going to be all right. He still had the feeling as he went into the meeting in the afternoon. The spirit of the Lord was with him.

That afternoon when the deposition convened, our attorney commenced the questioning. He did so for two hours before calling for a recess. The two attorneys were alone in the room when his counselor turned to ours and said that he wanted nothing further to do with the case and wanted to drop it. He said that everything that was testified to that day was totally opposite from what he had originally been told. When all four had returned to the room, they were told that the case was dropped, and that there were absolutely no grounds to pursue any further action. When John came home, we were both relieved and so thankful. The corporation was dissolved, and we continued to work independently.

Cindy and Adam's wedding was lovely. She was a beautiful bride, and they made a handsome couple. They lived in Provo, Utah so he could continue his education.

As it turned out, we had two weddings to pay for. Kim had met a nice man and he seemed to be very fond of our daughter. They were married in January of 1989. I told John I gave the marriage six months. We tried to talk Kim out of it. When she and I were going up the stairs to the marriage and reception center, I wanted to say, "Run girl, run, and I will run with you." However, I knew she would not listen.

It was six months less one day when Kim asked if she could move back home. When I told her later that I wanted to tell her to run on her wedding day, she asked why I didn't. I told her that I knew she would not listen, and she said, "You're right, I wouldn't have." It turned out that he preferred being with other men.

On June 19, the following year, we received a call from Adam telling us that Cindy had lost their baby. She was about nineteen weeks along and complications set in. The baby had lived eight minutes, long enough for Adam to bless and name him. They named him Seth Adam Taylor. It was the longest drive to Provo from Bountiful. When we got there, Cindy and Adam were devastated. I felt so much pain for them. We know what the gospel teaches about this. Still, when it happens, it cannot completely fill the empty arms and hearts of two young parents and a mother whose breasts will ache and yearn for her baby.

A little memorial was held for Seth there in the hospital with both Adam and Cindy bearing their testimonies of the plan of salvation and their understanding of it. I knew then that Adam would at some time hold positions of authority in the church and that he would be a leader that would comfort others.

My Cindy showed so much courage and love for her Savior and Heavenly Father. She, too, would give strength to other mothers who went through this— some who would not have the faith, conviction, and testimony that she has. Why had this happened? We only know that it was not meant for little Seth to spend time here in this mortal existence. He had come, received his body, and then it was time to return to Heavenly Father for whatever he had to do in heaven. Knowing that he was theirs for eternity and that they would see him again gave them much solace.

Arrangement were made to bury baby Seth at the Centerville Cemetery. Adam had inherited some plots from an elderly friend. I am sure he never dreamed he would need one so early in his life.

When we arrived at the cemetery, Adam carried the tiny casket to the grave with Cindy at his side. I was crying so hard; all I could do was to hold on to John. After the grave was dedicated, people started to leave.

I stood next to Cindy. No words were exchanged; I hugged her and we held on to each other. Then I knew she needed to spend a few minutes alone with her baby, so I started toward John. I looked back, and I thought my heart would break into pieces. Never had I felt so helpless as a mother. All the words had been spoken and the understanding was there, but I didn't know if the grieving would ever really go away. This was something I had never experienced. Shortly after this, Adam and Cindy moved to Las Vegas.

Later in 1989, we found the business in big trouble. John had worked so hard to save it. Most men would have given up long ago, but he was a fighter – one of the qualities that I will always love about him. There was a program set up that if the receipts were sent in for the purchase of commercial goods, there was a reimbursement due to the purchaser. The accountant and I had put everything in order and sent what had been requested from them to obtain the money. It never did come, and we learned that the funds had been intercepted and someone else received the money. It totaled over $100,000. We hired someone to find him, but that did not happen.

As a result, the company went bankrupt. We had to close the business, and eventually we lost our home. After much prayer and trying to figure out what to do, we knew we had to just hold on. John, being the good salesman that he was, picked up a few lines to sell.

I continued working at my part time job, but we knew this was all just temporary. He found a business that was for sale, and the owner only wanted $10,000 for it. We did not have $10,000. If we did, we would not be in the predicament we were in. He went back to see him a few weeks later and said, "If you can pay me $7,000 down, we will work out the rest on payments." We did not have that much either. A few weeks later John went back, and the man said, "If you can give me $1,000, the business is yours." The man was going through a divorce and wanted to get out of town. Well, we could come up with a $1,000. So, we bought a business that brought in daily revenue. It was a vehicle detail shop. Its main source of income was a protective coating put on vehicles to preserve the paint and prevent any rusting. It would shine right up again by just being wiped off with a cloth after rain or snow. Some of our accounts were the used car lots around town. It turned out to be a lucrative business for us.

Meanwhile, my job was to find us somewhere to live. We had lost the house and needed to be out soon. The problem was that there was little money to pay the first and last month rent as well as a deposit on a new place. I made this a matter of prayer. We still had four children at home. It kept coming to my mind to go to 7200 South, and about 32-something in Salt Lake. I knew that 3200 East in Salt Lake City was a very expensive part of town, so surely that would not work. I finally drove to 7200 South and 3200 West. There was nothing there but fields and some old small businesses. I looked at some other places we could not afford. I went to one in Woods Cross and took the kids. It certainly was adequate, but I did not know if the owner would work with us. This was a very humbling experience we were going through. Later, after I had taken the children home, I went back to that house because I had not remembered if I locked the screen on the sliding door. I had not. I went back in and walked through the house, and then went into the living room and knelt by the fireplace and asked Heavenly Father if this was where we needed to be. When I was done and had made sure all the doors were locked, I walked down the driveway. It came to me as clear as could be that this was not where Heavenly Father wanted us to be.

The next day, house hunting had to be put on hold as Melissa had to have tubes put in her ears. The following day, she was looking in the classified ad section under houses for rent and told me that she had found one that sounded good to her. It did not give a price or location. She begged me to call on it. I was sure if they did not list a rental price, it must be very expensive. However, she was insistent. I did call on it and got the owner, who was in the process of building a new home for him and his wife. They were living in a friend's home while their friends were on a mission. He said he was looking for a good family to rent his home which was just off 7200 South and 3200 East. I was overwhelmed when he gave me the address. He asked me a few questions. Somehow, it came up that I had been a Relief Society president, that we had sent three sons on missions, and so on. I told him some of our circumstances and he said, "Why don't you come up, and we will talk?"

Melissa and I went up to the house, which was close to the mouth of Cottonwood Canyon. He was there, and we visited for a while. I again told him of some of our circumstances, and that we could not pay him anything for a few weeks. He was so kind and said that was all right and that the house could be ours to live in if we would take good care of it. We could pay him when we had the money. The house was three levels with that many bathrooms, enough bedrooms for us, a room for John to have an office, and everything I could ask for. It had a double garage and an enormous backyard that did need some tender love and care. We knew what to do with that.

When we returned to the car, Melissa asked if this was where we were going to move to. I told her that I was pretty sure it was. We needed to talk to the rest of the family and get things packed, and then this would probably be our new home. Then I asked her if she knew what had just happened. She said, "Yes, we found a house to move to."

I said, "No, you found a house to move into, you found us that house." I gave her a squeeze and said, "Thank you, thank you so much, you are our house finder!" I also talked to her about how Heavenly Father had led us to that house. He knew what our circumstances were, and maybe for some reason he wants us to live in that house. I told her he had blessed us so much.

Lying in bed a few nights later, I was thinking of how much difference our mental attitude makes, and I realized that it makes all the difference in the world. It was a huge factor in my faith, and I believe that the two go hand in hand. We can't allow a bad attitude of complaining, whining, and blaming others for what happens to us. It helps nothing.

All I could think about was the blessings that had come to us through it all. I thought of the Prophet, Joseph Smith, when he was incarcerated in Liberty Jail. He was pleading with the Lord and he was given the revelation which is now D&C 121:7&8 - *My son, peace be unto thy soul; thine adversity and thine affliction shall be but a small moment; and then if thou endure it well, God shall exalt thee on high; thou shall triumph over thy foes.*

One thing was clear; it is not so much what our circumstances are. It doesn't matter who is rich, or who is poor, or if we were born in the United States, where things are abundant, or somewhere far away where conditions are crowded and food scarce, or if we are sick or healthy. What matters is how we respond to these things, what we do about them, and the attitude that we have toward them. That is far more significant than the circumstances themselves.

John and I closed the doors to our Bountiful home for the last time. We did so with humility in our hearts, our heads held high. We were looking forward to the future and learning from the past.

A scripture that has given me strength and comfort many times is found in the Doctrine and Covenants 136:31 – *My people must be tried in all things, that they may be prepared to receive the glory that I have for them, even glory of Zion; and he that will not bear chastisement is not worthy of my kingdom.*

When thou art in tribulation, and all these things are come upon thee, even in these latter days, if thou turn to the Lord thy God, and shall be obedient unto his voice. For the Lord thy God is a merciful God; he will not forsake thee, neither destroy thee...

Deuteronomy 4: 30-31
Bible

Nevertheless the Lord seeth fit to chasten his people; yea, he trieth their patience and their faith.

Mosiah 23:21
Book of Mormon

Chapter 17

Hidden Wedges

"Turn down the *Phantom*; the neighbors will run us out."

The music from the Broadway play, *Phantom of the Opera*, gave us the energy and incentive to lug rocks to make our own quarry. We all loved the long running musical, and we were giving the back yard of our new home the tender love and care it needed for Kim's second wedding the end of June. So, the Phantom's music was our motivator.

We had been in the home for a few months now. At first, we thought we would like to buy it, and the owner was willing to work with us. But then we realized the home had some problems, and they were not minor. The first Thanksgiving we were there, I had more pans on the floor than on the stove. The roof leaked. However, there was a second floor above where it was leaking, which meant the water was finding the beams and leaking between them. Repairs had been done, but didn't seem to help. The roof needed to be replaced, and structural damage had occurred. In the dry season, we were fine. But we lived at the mouth of the canyon, and it wasn't always dry.

John was called in by the stake president and asked to be the High Priest Leader of our new ward. He seemed to be a little surprised by this calling. The president said, "Brother Holmes, I think that you can bring to the men in your ward some humility. There seems to be lack of it."

He felt a little intimidated by some of these men because of their educations and professional successes. However, he felt strong in his knowledge and faith in the gospel, and his love for our Savior. One of the things they were lacking was their commitment to doing home teaching. It wasn't long before people were seeing their home teachers at their doors. John did not need to feel intimidated by these brethren as they gained a lot of respect for him.

I had been called into the Relief Society as the homemaking counselor. One of my committee sisters felt she should have received this calling and made it very uncomfortable for myself and others to work with her. I began to think that perhaps the bishop had made a mistake to call me to that position instead of her. He assured me that he had not. I was sure he would "fix it," but instead he said, "Sister Holmes, it is your problem and you need to fix it." That was not the answer I wanted to hear. However, he was right. I knew I was the one to fix it, or at least make it better. I had prayed about it, but I don't think I did as earnestly as I should have. I guess I thought that the bishop would handle it. Well, now I was on my own. I felt that the focus of the homemaking part of Relief Society was to help the sisters in the ward live more fully the motto of the organization—"Charity Never Faileth"—with the idea that by understanding it more fully, we would see more love among the sisters. We were to be examples of women in our Saviors Gospel, and there was not room for pettiness. We cannot be proclaiming the gospel or perfect the saints if we couldn't even feel love among one another.

I asked the Lord for His help and to know what to do so that the other sister and I would both feel more comfortable working together. I turned to the scriptures, and thought of the time I had been called into Primary because there was friction there, although theirs was of a different nature. We needed to meet the needs of the sisters. I felt like we needed to focus more on developing more spirituality in the home. This sister liked to make trinkets and do things that brought out the sister's talents. This sounds so simple to just come to a happy medium. Both were good things.

Eventually, I knew that for it to work out, I needed to change my attitude. The scripture that helped me the most was D&C 38: 27: *Be one, if ye are not one, ye are not mine.* That really brought me to my knees, and things did go smoother in our department. I knew I needed to have the spirit of the Lord with me more fully as I served him. I had to do all that I could not to have any hidden wedges. I truly came to realize that these wedges do nothing but destroy, and we cannot allow them to come into our lives. We must be humble, and we must communicate.

Another wedge that came into the family in 1990 was one between Uncle Barr and myself. Aunt Thelma was now living in a rest home because her Alzheimer's had gotten so bad. He had a terrible stroke, and we were sure he would never be able to function on his own afterward. He had a semi recovery and seemed to function quite well in his home. He even worked in the temple one day a week. My cousin, Arlene, would take him in the morning, and I would pick him up to take him home. He would spend the day witnessing baptisms for the dead.

He decided to sell his home in Holladay and move into a small apartment. He was having the home painted to prepare it to sell, and asked me if I would bring the children and move a lot of his belonging's downstairs. I was happy to do it. When the painting was completed, he called me one day and asked me where the silver tray was. It was silver and very valuable. I knew what tray he was referring too because Aunt Thelma had used it on special occasions. I had not seen the tray when we moved his things downstairs. He accused me or one of the children of taking it. I tried to convince him that we had not seen it, let alone taken it.

He did not believe me, and I was very hurt. I did not know what to do. He did not want me to come over again. This happened in 1990. At his funeral in June of 1993, his son Paul came up to me, put his arm around me, and told me that his dad was so, so sorry. I had let it go long before that, having blamed it on his illness. It turned out that Aunt Thelma had given the platter to their youngest daughter before she went into the nursing home. It was sad that a platter had created a wedge between two people that once had a beautiful relationship.

We were glad the Lord had callings for us while we lived in the Cottonwood area as we both needed them after going through a rough patch in Bountiful. Melissa and Alysia seemed to do okay with the move. I worried about the children with all the moving. Our Linda did not find it to be the best of experiences. She felt she did not fit in with the girls her age. Their parents had more money and were used to more than she had. She really missed her friends in Bountiful. On the surface, she seemed to be doing fine, but I realized what she was feeling inside was a different story. However, when she married, she found herself living in a very affluent area in Logan, Utah, and I will always feel her experience in Cottonwood helped her to adjust to her adult life. She has a very friendly personality. People love her. Because of the hard times she went through with us, she also has a very compassionate heart.

As for Justin, he started playing with a very good junior basketball team and had excellent coaches. This was going to take him a long way as he played ball in his high school years. It didn't hurt that he just kept growing, and was almost now as tall as his three older brothers.

Things were going well in our life, except for the leaky house. We had been there for over a year and a half, and John spent a lot of time patching the roof. The owner was going to replace it, but so far it had not been done.

By now we had several grandchildren. Late in September, we received a call from Adam again. Cindy was expecting another baby, and she was experiencing the very same thing she had when Seth was born. She was about to lose her second baby.

A new commandment that I give unto you, That ye love one another; as I have loved you, that ye also love one another.

John 13:34
Bible

But ye will teach them to walk in the ways of truth and soberness; ye will teach them to love one another, and to serve one another.

Mosiah 4:15
Book of Mormon

Chapter 18

Our Very Own Rising Generation

"We have done all that we can, just let him come," Cindy heard one of the doctors say. Instantly her attending physician was at her side. They bent down to her and said, "Cindy, we have done everything we know to do to save your baby; it is just not working, but I do have an idea. I have never done it before or even heard of it being done, and I do not know if it will work. Would you like me to try it?"

She said, "Yes."

The doctors proceeded to remove embryonic fluid from her, which gave them room to tuck the infants little feet back and then put in a cervical cerclage into her cervix to hold the baby in. He now did not have enough fluid for a normal pregnancy. They didn't know if the fluid would build back up on its own. Time would only tell if this procedure would work. A few days later, they put in a second stich. This would protect the cervix. She needed to stay in the hospital and be on antibiotics and steroids until he was born.

Cindy told me later she was experiencing the same thing with this baby she had with Seth. "I knew I was in big trouble," she said. She also said as she entered the doors of the delivery room a witness came to her from the Holy Ghost that she would not lose her baby. This helped her so much, as she didn't know what was ahead, but she would do everything in her power to save him. Most of all she knew she was to pray, have faith, stay optimistic, and follow doctor's orders.

Adam's mother and I made a trip to Las Vegas together to see her and Adam and be of what support we could. Cindy and I talked on the phone almost every day. She was a trooper, and I saw again how much faith and patience she had. She sat in her hospital bed and made Christmas presents for so many people. She became a favorite of the nurses as they took care of her.

She had been told that she had an incompetent cervix, meaning it was not strong enough on its own to hold the weight of a baby more than 15 to 20 weeks. Several large binders, about 4 to 5 inches thick, contained the step by step information for her and his daily progress in the pregnancy. He was born on January 14, 1991.

They named him Nathaniel Otis Taylor. We were so grateful as a family. Her name had been put on prayer rolls in five different temples. It was our prayer that the procedure used on Cindy and little Nathaniel would help other mothers keep their babies when this happened to them.

Adam had been in a car accident a week after she went into the hospital. A man had run into their car on Sierra Street, totaling their car and putting Adam out of work for a few months. His good bishop, who was also his boss, paid him his wages during the time he was unable to work. This was such a blessing to them.

I had a sweet experience during the birth of one our granddaughters. Kim was a few minutes away from delivering Kaylene, her first child. She had chosen not to have an ultrasound, so we did not know the gender ahead of time. I was sitting in the chair next to Kim when I heard this little voice say, "Grandma, I am a little girl."

I debated whether I should tell Kim or not, finally between contractions, I whispered in her ear this had happened. Yes, she was another beautiful little girl. Kaylene, Kim, and I have a special bond because of this incident.

Linda lived with Kim and John in Bountiful for a while after graduation and worked at Fred Meyer department store. She then decided to go to Logan to Utah State University. She had a good experience there. We were having a family gathering in Logan for the baptism of Katie, Eric and Heidi's second daughter, when Linda asked if she could bring a special person she had met. I asked her if he was ready to meet this many people. She said he only had one brother.

As we drove into the parking lot of the church, I saw a handsome young man and thought, "that is a lucky girl walking beside him." I looked again, and it was Linda. His name was Eric Vincent Jensen. I guess we passed the test, because they married on December 16, 1995, in the Salt Lake Temple.

Their first son was born on January 29, 1997. He too, only lived a short time. Linda experienced the same problem as Cindy; she also was told that her cervix was incompetent, something they rarely saw in sisters. They named the baby Cameron Eric Jensen. Again, standing at the cemetery in the cold and snow, I saw another daughter go through the torment of losing their baby son. My heart ached for Linda and Eric.

The day after Cameron was buried, little Daniel, Kim and John's son, was blessed. Linda didn't feel up to coming to the blessing and we understood. She did, however, come to the family dinner at Kim and John's house later in the day. She wanted to be with family, and we all hoped as she held tiny Daniel that it would help her in some way. I felt so much joy for one daughter and so much grief for another. We just had to trust in the Lord and pray to understand His ways.

Linda called about midnight that same night. We talked for about an hour. When we hung up, I remained on the couch where

I had been talking to her. I laid down and had the most wonderful dream. She was in it.

In my dream, I saw her and other women sitting around a large table. The only way I can describe the table was that it looked like a table that we see in a high council room, only much larger. I focused on Linda, who radiated so beautifully, as did all the women. At the head of the table were three men who had brought these women together. They told them that there was a special mission to perform while on earth. They said the women would perform it with sadness, but the blessings they would receive because of it would be unmeasurable, and they had been picked to perform this mission because of their faithfulness thus far in their journey of eternity. They were told that they would bring forth one or more very valiant spirits to receive their bodies, and that these spirits would be called back home soon after they received them. The looks on Linda and the other women's faces were glorious, and they seem to understand and were willing to do this because of the love they had for our Heavenly Father and the Savior. Then my dream faded, and I woke up.

When I shared this with Linda, I hoped that it helped her. Oh, the plan of salvation and the sealing power of the covenants we receive in the temple are so binding and precious. When we understand these things, we must be so grateful for the gospel of Jesus Christ. We need to know that it was His from the beginning. That it was restored upon the earth in its fullness in our dispensation by the Lord's Prophet, Joseph Smith. Both Cameron and Seth will be in our eternal family forever. Their parents will have them through eternity.

When I shared my dream with Cindy, she said, "What about me?" I assured her that she had been in a council like that prior to the birth of Seth. I was not privileged to have the dream until now, and I did feel it a privilege.

Cindy shared an experience with Linda and me that she had the night that Cameron was born. She knew Linda was having difficulty with her pregnancy, but they did not know to the extent that it was. She and Adam had gone to the temple in Las Vegas the night of Cameron's birth, and she briefly saw two personages in the large sealing room reflecting mirrors. She felt she had felt the presence of her son Seth with Cameron. Upon arriving home, they received the news that Linda and Eric had lost their baby. Cameron's death was shortly before her experience in the temple. Was Cameron with his cousin Seth? I choose to believe he was.

Linda and Eric had four more children, and she had to have cervical cerclage put in with pregnancy each time. Cindy also had the cervical cerclage with her two additional pregnancies.

Melissa seemed to look out for the ones who were less fortunate. I so admire this quality in her. She also had such a love for animals. She kept telling me about a dog she thought was starving that hung around a church and she felt so bad for it. She just picked it up one day and brought it home. She was right; I had never seen any animal so skinny and still alive. To our surprise, a few days after she brought her to our house, the dog had puppies. I did not know how a dog that malnourished could deliver live babies. We found homes for all the babies and eventually found one for Baby Girl, the name Melissa gave her. Baby Girl had seizures after that, but the lady who took her understood all about seizures as she had a son that had them.

Melissa had a beautiful singing voice and was picked to be in an all-girl show choir in high school, as well as the Acapella Choir. I loved to hear her sing solo. One time she sang in junior high for a talent show with Alysia at the piano, and I was one proud mother. She seemed a natural with electronics as well. John and I wondered what we would do when she no longer lived at home. Electronics were still foreign to us.

She was also married in 1995 to Jason Imlay. They met when she was in high school, and they were together most of the time. She, like her mother, married before she graduated. She always had honor grades and graduated with a scholarship, though she did not use it. They were married for about ten years, and she longed to have a child. She was a natural when it came to children. She loved them, and they loved her. It was always a happy and a sad time when I saw here with her nieces and nephews. Eventually, they were blessed with their little Madalyn LaVelle, born in 2005. I felt honored to have my name be her middle name. They were living in Florida at the time of her birth. It was another eight years before they were blessed with little Max Wayne in 2013. By then, they were living in South Carolina. Though they said they were coming back west, they somehow kept going farther east. I really missed not seeing them as much as the rest of the family, but we did the best we could.

Alysia was one busy gal in high school, too. She was in the Jordon High Madrigals as well as the Acapella Choir, and Future Business Leaders of America. She was president of the of the Beethoven, Dance, and Drama clubs. They did a lot of performing.

Alysia met her husband the day she went to apply for a job at Macey's grocery store in Sandy. He was already working there and was attending BYU after his mission. She had only known him a short time and invited him to join all the family at a restaurant for dinner. We all went to our house afterward. I was called outside because they were out there, and they had something to tell me. They wanted to get married! Eventually they were married in the Salt Lake Temple.

Another wonderful experience happened to me the day their son Tyler was born. Alysia was having a hard labor, and was exhausted. Times had changed in the delivery room since I had my babies. Whoever the mother invited could come in, and sometimes even some who the mother did not invite. Because of her exhaustion, everyone was asked by the nurse to leave so Alysia could rest. I was so glad the nurse did that. It was becoming a party, and my daughter needed to rest when she could. She needed her strength for the main event.

Alysia picked out a special song for each of her children that she listened to while pregnant and during delivery. We were out of the delivery room for about a half hour when I decided to go down and see if she was okay. She was resting peacefully; the door was not completely closed, and I heard this beautiful music playing. I called it "Tyler's theme." I looked at the foot of the bed, and I saw this handsome, tall young man. He was wearing a suit and standing there looking at his mother. He was only there briefly, and then he disappeared. Why was I privileged to have these experiences? I did not know.

Ye are the children of light, and the children of day: we are not of the night, nor of darkness.

1 Thessalonians 5:5
Bible

Teach them to never be weary of good works, but to be meek and lowly in heart; for such shall find rest to their souls.

Alma 37:34
Book of Mormon

Chapter 19

A Season for All Things

The house on Antler Way had been such a blessing to us from the beginning, though it had its problems. John called it the money pit. If it wasn't, it was certainly going to be. It is not the wisest thing to build a house next to a huge mountain range and then put a flat roof on it. The water and snow just built up on top of us.

Once again, it was my job to find us a house, and I was concerned for the four children more than ever. I looked in our price range all over the valley with our realtor. He was a seasoned one who knew exactly what he was doing. He showed me all these houses that he knew I would not be interested in. They were in the price range we were looking for. He could see my disappointment in all of them. Then he told me about one that he thought I would like, but that was a little bit more money. "Little bit" means different things to different people. We went to look at it, and I had found my house even before I got through the front door. There was a huge great room right off the kitchen, and all I could think of was our big family and how it was growing. I didn't know how we were going to get it. I only knew I wanted that house. John felt the same way I did, and promised he would come up with the money. We moved in right after school was out the spring of 1991.

The good thing about the move was the girls at least were not going to be switching schools again before they graduated. What I did not know was that I was about to go back to school, too.

I brought in the mail one afternoon, and there was a postcard advertising a "Back to School" for those who had been out of the work force loop for a long time. That was surely me, especially since the computer world had invaded the work world. Those things scared me to death. I was sure if I touched one, I would break it. Besides that, I didn't even know how to turn one on. Craig had tried to get me to use his before he got married, and it terrified me.

After reading the card for the second time, an overwhelming feeling came over me. Should I do this? That was my question to the Lord. I still had teenagers in my home, and my presence at the crossroads was needed. I went in my bedroom, knelt, and prayed because this feeling was so strong in me. An answer came that I should pursue taking this course. I had never had a prayer answered so quickly. Other things had frightened me, but nothing compared to this.

I signed up. There were seven different classes on computer programs used in the business world. We had to pass four out of the seven state exams to pass the course. They warned us that it would be eight intense weeks, and that we would end up hating the instructors and ourselves before we were done.

Of the twenty-two who signed up, thirteen finished. There was at least one a week who dropped out. I was certainly the grandma of the group, as the rest were in their twenties. I was fifty now and felt so out of my league. There were times I wanted to cry; I was so frustrated, and I did not have a computer at home to practice on. The younger women were kind to me, though I could feel the one instructor's frustration. Somehow, I did pass four of the seven program tests. The day we had a little celebration breakfast, the girls sang a rap that they had written about me. I wish I had the copy, because it was hilarious. The worse part of the whole thing was that almost all the computer programs were obsolete within a year or so. Quick Books was moving in.

I got a job at a local grocery store because it was close to home and the hours were good. I later got one as a receptionist for nine different companies sharing one building. Both jobs gave me computer experience.

Eventually I went to work for a company that supplied many other large companies with products. I liked what I did there, and especially the young woman I worked with and the salesmen. It paid well and had good benefits.

On Easter Sunday 1993, my mother had an episode at church that required her to go to the emergency room. The plaque had built back up in her arteries again. I flew out for the surgery. When it was complete, the doctor told Ruth and me that things had gone well. We sat there for a few minutes in the waiting room when we heard over the speaker, "Code 99, Code 99!" We were sure we knew what this code meant. She and I looked at each other, and both knew it was mother. It was; she had a stroke, and it was not a mild one. She was not paralyzed, but her nervous system was affected. It sent her into a state where she was thrashing about and had no control over any part of her body. This went on for a few days, and only when she was sedated would she calm down and be able to communicate.

Ruth and I visited some rest homes because we thought it would have been too hard for Ruth to care for Mother in her condition. The doctors told us she could get better, but that it was unlikely. A few days before I had to leave to return to Utah, we sat in the waiting room. The nurses had asked us to step out. One came out and asked, "How long has your father been gone?" We told her that it had been seven years. She then said, "I don't want to alarm you, but your mother thinks she has seen your father, and she is screaming at him to take her with him. This happens sometimes when a patient is in her state of mind. We have got her calmed down now, and if you would like to see her, you may go in one at a time." Ruth went in first. I stood at the door, feeling strongly that my father was there beside me. When I went in, Mother was calm but very upset with Dad. She said, "He was here, and I asked him to take me with him, and he told me that he couldn't take me yet because it was not time."

I had to leave for home and it was very hard. I had only taken a few days off from work, but it turned into ten. I needed to get back to the family as well. I had only been back to work for a few days when I had the feeling this was going to be the day that she would leave us. As I was walking to the bank to make a make a deposit for the company, I felt like my parents were both right beside me. They walking hand in hand, as if they were telling me hello and goodbye. It was a sweet feeling. I got home a few minutes later. The phone rang, and Ruth told me Mother had passed away about a half hour earlier. It was May 3, 1993.

Kim and I left immediately, and John and the other children came as soon as he could. Linda did not come, as she had just returned from Washington, DC, from a music competition. She had already missed a lot of school.

Mother was to be buried in Clarkston next to Dad. Someone in Ruth's family had a new truck. We got permission to transport her from Richland in the truck to the cemetery. It wasn't against state law because we were staying in the state. It was quite a caravan going to Clarkston. It was windy that day. Once at the cemetery the wind started to blow the top of the casket off. I reached for it and about fell in the grave.

When we got back to Ruth's that evening, we realized we had left some flower arrangements at the church. A church rule was to not to have water in a particular area. We had spilled water in that exact area. It struck us both so funny, all we could do was put the flowers down and start laughing. We were both so tired and stressed that we laughed until we cried. It was the best moment we had together since this whole thing began. We knew that if mother was there, she would be laughing the hardest because she knew we had to clean it up.

Mother gave me a special plate before she passed away. It was my last gift from her. The plate says, "I Sing in The Kitchen When There Is Someone to Praise My Cooking."

Justin was doing well in school, and he had a very pleasing, witty disposition. He had a very serious side of him, too, and to me seemed to be way beyond his years with wisdom. He would listen to adults' conversations and give wise advice. We knew this was a special gift he had been blessed with. He had been raised in adult world.

Basketball was so much of his world. He stayed with the team he had played on when we lived up in Cottonwood. Within a few years, they were in a super league. He was chosen to be on it with kids from a large region. Then he played on a regional super league. It was there that he met a player from Central Utah. This young man was an excellent player, especially his three pointers. When he was hot, he could not miss.

Justin grew to be six-foot-five, and he was a very good player. His dad would say about him the same as he had said about Eric; "He is as smooth as a jet and really knows how to handle the ball." In his sophomore year of high school, Justin played on the JV and Varsity teams.

Things were good in our lives. In 1996, John had now sold the auto detail business for a good profit. We had become distributers for another company. He was making good money each week, and seemed to be happier. He had the gift of gab and was always good at sales. I had known for quite a while that he did not feel well, but he prided himself on not going to a doctor many times since the fire in 1980. I think he thought he was Superman.

He was still doing quite a bit of traveling, and was in other sales, too. One day he stopped at my office. We visited for a few minutes and then he said to me, "Guess where I have been all day?"

I wouldn't even begin to guess. He could have been anywhere. Then he said, "I have been in Gunnison, Utah."

I said, "Where?"

"You know, Gunnison, where the Hale family live." We stopped there one night about midnight to get gas after the Manti Pageant. He went on to say, "I want to move there."

My response was: "YOU WANT TO WHAT? Why would you want to move there?"

We talked for a few minutes, and he said, "I really want to move there." I saw no rhyme or reason to his thinking. He said, "We can talk more of it tonight," and then he left. I shook my head when he left and thought, "He has completely lost his mind, and this too, shall pass." We did talk about it when I got home, and every minute we were together for the next week. I was against it as much as he wanted to do it.

At one point, he even said, "I am going, with or without you." He regretted it the minute it came out of his mouth, and apologized for a long time afterward. I wasn't so quick to forgive because he had really hurt me by saying that. We had never even talked about the word divorce, and this was the closest we ever came to it.

He begged me to just go to Gunnison and look the town over. I finally agreed to go. Once I was there, I realized even more why I did not want to move there. The tour of the town took five minutes. "Now, what do we do?" I thought.

"What in the world do the women do here?" I asked. "What are **we** going to do here?"

He seemed to have it all figured out. With our weekly income from our business and him finding another job—even opening his own distributing business again—we could have a good life. I would never have to work again, could pick any house I wanted, and get a new car. "Boy, what a dreamer," I thought. Nothing he could say would make me change my mind.

There was a church, city hall, Subway restaurant, Chinese restaurant, bridal shop, three gas stations, post office, bank, car dealership, large farm equipment sales place, a small high school, a middle and grade school, pharmacy, hospital, and state prison.

The next thing we did was find a realtor. She met us, lined up some houses for us to look at, and I was not impressed. I loved our home in Sandy, and hadn't we moved enough?

I was concerned about Justin moving schools again. He was headed for the varsity basketball team at Jordon High for his junior and senior years.

I hadn't seen John so passionate about anything for a long time as he was about this. He asked me to come with him for just two years, and if I still felt the same way, we would come back to Salt Lake. I gave in, and we proceeded to put our home up for sale. We found a very small, nine hundred-square-foot, one-hundred-year-old home in Gunnison. Our home in Sandy was over three thousand-square feet. I did find a new home that I liked, but it did not have a finished basement, so we went with the smaller house. Later I was so grateful for the smaller home and especially for its location in the town. I was about to meet a lady who would have a major effect on the rest of my life. Had we bought the other home we may never had met.

Justin was such a good sport. He looked at it as an adventure – or at least, that is what he said. Maybe he was just used to his crazy parents moving every few years.

While waiting for our home to sell and for school to get out, we made three trips to Nebraska as John's mother was not doing well. On April 12, she had a severe stroke and we had to move her into a nursing home. Her heart was rapidly failing, her diabetes was not in control, and many organs were shutting down. The doctor told us that he would be surprised if she lived six months. John's sister Margaret, who he had not seen for over 19 years, had come and all the funeral arrangements were made. Mom had made a lot herself. She did not want to leave Nebraska, and I totally understood her desires. We were called on June 3. She had suffered another stroke, and we went again. She did not open her eyes the whole time we were there. When we said our goodbyes, as we knew it was the last time we would see her alive in this mortal life. We took comfort in the fact that we would do her temple work and be together again as an eternal family.

On Sunday, June 22, 1997, we received a phone call from her doctors telling us she had passed away. Our home in Sandy had sold, and we were going to sign all the closing papers on both the house in Sandy and the one we were buying in Gunnison on the 26th. We got the closings moved up to the 24th so we could leave for the funeral. Linda was the only one who could go with us. We were grateful to have her with us as we made the long 18-hour trip one more time.

Even though I was sad about the move and Mom Holmes death, I did feel in my heart that perhaps John was being directed in our move. I tried to look at it as a new chapter in our lives. He had been spiritually in tune with most things that had happened in our lives. I had no idea what awaited me, starting the night before we buried Mother Holmes.

To every thing there is a season, and a time to every purpose under the heaven.

Ecclesiastes: 3:1
Bible

Now, there is a death which is called a temporal death; and the death of Christ shall loose the bands of this temporal death, that all shall be raised from this temporal death.

Alma 11:42
Book of Mormon

Chapter 20

Second Birth

We arrived in Brainard, Nebraska at about 4 p.m. We went right to the mortuary to view Mom's body and to see what last minute preparations needed to be handled. It was so good to know she was out of the pain and no longer suffering, as she had been the last few months.

That evening, we visited with Stan and Ellie, Mom Holmes' good neighbors. We talked of death and how individuals handle it differently. We talked to them about our beliefs and gave the glove demonstration of the body and spirit separating. It's a very simple demonstration in which someone removes a glove from their hand, as if it were spirit going up to heaven. Their hand remains here as if it were the body being laid to rest here in the casket. They had never thought of it in that way.

We had decided to stay at Mom's home. We had opened it up because of the heat and it had been closed for several months. We each took separate bedrooms. Linda and I were in the bedrooms upstairs, and John took his mother's room downstairs. We retired at about 11 p.m. knowing we had a long day ahead of us. We were also so tired from traveling and from the events of the previous days.

We each had a fan. As I lay in bed, I thought I should roll over and fix my fan because it was clicking. Suddenly, I had an awareness I was not alone in my room. It was the same feeling I had when my mother had suffered a stroke and I stood outside the door and felt my father's presence.

I rolled over in the bed and was no longer aware of the clicking fan. I looked up and saw John's mother standing beside me. It was so natural to talk to her. I told her it had only been five days. (I was thinking it was too early to do her temple work.) She said, "I know." I thanked her for her wonderful son, and she looked to the foot of the bed and my eyes followed her. There stood Grandma Coufal, her husband Michael, the two people who had adopted Mother Holmes when she was 9, and two other people. I readily recognized one as her birth mother. For some reason, I knew that the other was Mary, a sister of Mother Holmes who had disappeared when she was 22 years old. They were all deceased. I recognized them as each looked like they did while here on earth.

"What about the promise?" Grandma Coufal said to me in a very stern voice. I knew exactly what she was referring to. When she was in a rest home at the age of ninety-three, we had visited her. Grandma was a good Catholic lady and always attended her church. As she sat in her wheelchair, she looked up at John and said, "I just want to be with Michael." It had been forty-five years since Michael died. John took her hand and told her that he knew what to do to fix it. We would do their temple work after she passed away so they would be together for eternity. She looked up at him with tears in her eyes. She had no idea what he was talking about. He said again, "Grandma, we will fix it, won't we LaVelle?"

I said, "Yes, grandma, we will fix it."

She looked at John, with the faith of a child, and said "Johnnie, if anyone can, you can!"

"We will Grandma, we promise," John said.

Well, the promise had not been kept, as Grandma lived for ten more years. After she died at the age of 103, I always had it in the back of my mind to do her temple work, but I did not get around to it. When we got back home from our visit to the nursing home, John had done Mike's temple work. However, the rest of the promise was not fulfilled. I had not done my part. (A person must be deceased one year before their temple work can be done for them.)

When she asked what about the promise, I said, "Grandma, do you remember when you lived in this house and you had the farm to run?" (Mike had built the home for Clara, and Mom Holmes had bought it after she died)

She said, "Yes, I know that you have been busy."

I was working full time, had several children still home, was teaching gospel doctrine, and helping John with his business. What she said next was, "Now you are moving to Gunnison and you can do our work in the Manti temple. There are many of us waiting." I was stunned that she knew these things.

She told me they were in holding and could not move on. I said, "Clara, I cannot do the work myself." She said we would need to come back to Nebraska for additional information. She gave me further instruction as to what I was to do. By now I was aware of many more people in the room. I could not see them, but I knew that there were many depending on me to prepare their temple work to be done. She told me to "seal Dorothy, John's mother, to her and Mike." I looked over at John's mother's birth mother, and she smiled and then was gone. I asked Clara if there was another child that had been born to John's mother. She told me there was, but not to concern myself with that at this time. I asked her if she would be at the funeral in the morning. I do not know why I asked her that. She smiled and left.

The room became dark again, and I was once again aware of the clicking fan next to my bed. I lay there trying to decide if it were a vision or a dream. Had they really been here with me in that room? Yes, they had! I had never fallen asleep. Why didn't she give me names, dates, or places? I laid there trying to take this all in. Suddenly, the room became very sacred to me.

I called out to Linda in the next room. I felt like I wanted to share my experience with her. She did not answer, and I wondered if they were now with her. I got up and approached her room, and I could hear the soft music she was playing. I woke her and told her we were not the only ones here in the house that night. Others had come, left a message and instructions, and were now gone. We sat there and hugged and cried because such a marvelous thing had occurred. She asked me to stay with her, and it was hard for either of us to sleep. At about 4:30 a.m., she was resting well, so I went back to my room and pondered everything that had happened earlier.

In the morning as we prepared to go to the funeral, I shared my experience with John. Later he expressed some of the emotions he felt as I had shared things with him. He felt surprise, joy, and envy that they had come to me. He was very supportive of the things that needed to be done. I explained to him that I was sure Clara was allowed to come to me because I was the one who had been negligent. He had done what he promised. I wondered what was ahead of me and how I was to get help for all the others who were in the room.

Once we got back to Utah after the funeral, we moved to Gunnison. We had only been there a few weeks, and though I had done nothing to start on any of the work Clara had requested, I felt the spirit of that sacred night with me as I tried to get settled in our new home. I also felt the spirit of the adversary, because I would get depressed and sad about leaving the family and our big home. The new one was so small and needed a lot of work, and I was grateful for the children's efforts to come see us.

It was July 23, and Kim, Kaylene, and Daniel had come to see us. When I went to bed that night, I had a dream of a huge book in front of me. But as hard as I tried, I could not see the names. I woke up and a voice said to me, "There are 62 of us." Completely overwhelmed with the thought of it, I was exhausted and fell back to sleep only to see all these people standing in front of me.

I was so tired and pleaded, "Oh please, leave me alone; I need to sleep." They all put their hands in front of them and turned around. They started to walk away with their heads down, and they looked so sad. I felt so ashamed and said, "Wait, please, please give me some names!" I woke up, and the name 'Sharon' came to my mind. I immediately thought of my sister's daughters Sharon, Debbie, and Ruth. I knew I had the wrong group.

Who was going to help me with this assignment? Here we were in a new little town, and who would believe my experience? I just wouldn't tell anyone, I decided – they would think I was crazy!

The second week we attended church in Gunnison, I saw a little sign on the door that indicated there was a family history room in the church open two nights a week. I decided to go there and get acquainted with the people in charge. I felt my prayers were answered. I met Elle, who became my dear friend. Not only did she believe the spiritual experiences that I had had, she had had many of her own and was so close to those on the other side of the veil. I did tell her my story eventually, and she completely believed me. She helped me get the paper work done for Clara and for her and Mike's sealing. In October, John and I went to the Manti temple to do their work. It was a sweet experience, though I was so weak I could hardly do it. Those who were in the sealing room with us said they felt a very special spirit there.

The reason it had taken so long was because I had been so ill with something that would not go away. It got worse and worse. There were times for a few weeks that I even wondered if I was going to die and spent time in the hospital. Through testing, they found that I had only one functioning kidney and that it had become severely infected. A doctor from Gunnison was the physician who finally found the antibiotic that healed me. Three doctors in Provo could not find the right medicine. I was told through a Priesthood blessing that I would be healed because of my faith. I had spent a week in the hospital.

I was still recovering at Thanksgiving, but I felt prompted that we needed to get back to Nebraska soon. I put both Clara and Mike's names in the Manti temple, knowing that the temple is for both the deceased as well as the living and we needed their help.

We left the Sunday after Thanksgiving and we went by way of Denver. We hit a terrible snowstorm and visibility was almost zero. I told John this was the craziest thing we had ever done. It was the middle of winter, we didn't know where to go when we got there, and we did not know who to talk to. I suggested turning back. He said, "No, we must go on to Nebraska!"

I had gone through notes from Mom, and they made little sense. Oh, how I wished I had listened closer when mother Holmes was trying to tell me who all her relatives were all those years ago. I did find in an old notebook I had with me the name Bob Shonko, and had put a note by it saying, "Mom's half cousin, maybe." When we got settled in a hotel room, (Mom's house had been sold by then), I looked up Bob's phone number, called it, and a very grumpy lady answered. Bob was not home. I told her who we were and that we were trying to make a family tree. I asked if they had any information to help us. She was sure he did not. I asked her if I could call him back when he got home. She said, "He is at the doctors, and I don't know when he will be here."

I thanked her and said, "I will try later." She was not happy about that.

I called back a few hours later. He was totally opposite from her, and invited us right out. We visited for a while, and I asked him if he had information on the family that may be helpful. He said, "I will look." He left the room and was gone ten or fifteen minutes. I was sure he could not find what he was looking for. Finally, he came into the room with a stack of papers a half-inch thick. He said, "This is all I have. You can make copies, but I want these back."

John and I looked at each other. Bob handed them to me, and I felt such joy and gratitude. What I held in my hand was better than finding a gold mine. They gave family information for thirteen families who came from Bohemia and Czechoslovakia in the 1800s. I cannot tell you how blessed we felt to have found this man and the sacred papers he had tucked away, not because he had a purpose for them, but he had felt that he should keep them. Bob had cancer, and his condition soon worsened. He died in 1999.

The very first page provided this information: In approximately 1867, thirteen families came to America from Czechoslovakia. It gave the names of the families. They came by ship and docked in Galveston, Texas. This was right after the African Americans had been given their freedom. The Shanka families were afraid of the black people, so they returned to the old country. Five years later, they returned to America via New York. The other families settled in Spill Ville, Iowa. After ten years, they moved to Abie, Nebraska, by covered wagons.

The information contained names, birth dates, marriages, children, and death dates when possible. The next day we found a copy machine – and that was a task. We drove about 60 miles and finally found a bank that had one. We also visited many local cemeteries. For the next several months, I spent as much time as I could on this project, doing more research and getting the names that I had temple ready, so the family could help me do them.

On Nov. 29, 1998, I entered in my journal that it had been a busy last five days preparing for Thanksgiving for thirty-two people, and that the day had been wonderful. Most of the family were able to stay over to help with temple work on Friday.

John, Eric, Heidi, Emilie, Justin, and I set out for the temple on Friday morning. The grandchildren did the baptisms, and John and I did the initiatory work. When we got home, Cindy, Adam, Linda, and Eric went to the temple to do the endowments for Grandma Holmes and John's great, great grandparents. Work was also done for Emil Dusatko, Clara's brother who I had been so impressed to do work for. I felt very much that he had been called on a mission on the other side and could not fulfil it until his work was done and he had received the priesthood.

My heart had been full as we drove to the temple on that Friday morning. I could hear the voice of Clara saying, "We are in holding, and you can do the work in the Manti Temple." I supposed that by that time, John and Justin were used to all my tears by now. These were happy tears. I was happy that the work had begun, and that the family was willing and worthy to help with this important work. I knew that they would be blessed. Other names were taken home by the children so they could complete the endowments in their assigned temples.

I was grateful for a new program the church had put in place so that this work could move forward in both Canada and the United States. It had only been available to us since August. I shared my holiday experience with my friend Elli. She assured me that there was another family gathering that weekend, and they were rejoicing for what was being done for them. There is still so much to be done. We will get it done!

I called this chapter Second Birth because so many were and are waiting to be baptized so they can progress in the life after this one. We believe that in order for people to progress in the next life they must follow the example of Jesus Christ and be baptized in this life. If they don't have the chance while they are allowed, we believe that people can be baptized for them by proxy in the temple, and then it is up to them in the spirit world to accept the proxy work done for them. This goes for other temple ordinances as well. Baptism was called a second birth by Christ, and it is the gateway to God's highest kingdom.

Else what shall they do which are baptized for the dead, if the dead rise not at all? Why are they then baptized for the dead?

1 Corinthians 15:29
Bible

And now, my dearly beloved brethren and sisters, let me assure you that these are principles in relation to the dead and the living that cannot be lightly passed over, as pertaining to our salvation. For their salvation is necessary and essential to our salvation, as Paul says concerning the fathers – that they without us cannot be made perfect – neither can we without our dead be made perfect.

Doctrine and Covenants 128:15

Chapter 21

Finding What They Did in Gunnison

Even though some said that John had brought me to Central Utah kicking and screaming (not literally), I was beginning to believe there was great purpose for us there. I knew I would not have gotten the work done for Clara and her family if I still lived and worked in Salt Lake, or perhaps the doctors up north would not have found the right antibiotics for my one working kidney. I had learned that I had probably been born with only one, or if there were two, the second was small.

The first Sunday that we attended church I went to Relief Society, and there was a feeling in there I had not experience in the women's meeting before. The women looked so sad, did not do much visiting before the meeting started, and some were crying. I was sure there had been a death in the ward. The first counselor conducted and then turned the time over to the president just before the closing prayer. The president stood up and read a nice quote from the Reader's Digest Magazine, and I thought that was unusual. The sister who offered the prayer was also crying.

I told John that I thought their Relief Society was rather strange, but then this was a small town. He said he felt a different feeling in Priesthood, too. The following Tuesday, the two counselors from Relief Society came to welcome us and tell us they were glad we were there. Just before they left, I thanked them. I said that I was looking forward to getting to know their president more as well. They looked at each other and one said, "Well, Sunday was her last day. We may as well tell you because you will hear it from someone. She and her husband were going into talk to the bishop after the meetings to tell him that they wanted to have their names taken off the records of the church." I told them, "I felt something was amiss on Sunday, I surely did not expect that." These Relief Society sisters loved her, and that is why they were so sad.

On the following Sunday, I was called to be in the new presidency. I had to learn who these people were quite fast. I did so enjoy the women I worked with. They were so genuine, and we taught each other a lot. My question, "What do these women do all day?" was answered. They do everything that we do up in the bigger city, only they could do more because they did not have to travel as far.

I was later called into the Stake Relief Society Presidency. I learned to love these people also. Visiting other wards was enlightening. The stake president asked us to speak in one ward on loving thy neighbor. I thought that sounded easy, and then he told us that there was a second part: "Love thy neighbor, beginning with your spouse." That took on a whole new meaning.

There were presidents that I really admired. When we visited the Axtell Ward, I had not yet met the president. I noticed a sister in a wheelchair in the corner and a couple of women talking to her. I saw a lot of ladies with another sister and assumed she was the president. When it was time for the meeting to start, the sister in the wheelchair took her place in front and was introduced as the president. I later learned she had diabetes, lupus, and severe rheumatism. I so admired her and would draw a lot of strength from her and her example in a few years.

197

Our president wanted the stake to make 220 little T-shirt dresses for the Church Humanitarian Department. We assigned each ward so many dresses according to the size of their ward. We met with our sewing machines at the cultural hall in the stake center to do the project together in one day. It took a lot of organization. Our President had a big "gong" bell, and each time ten dresses were finished she wanted it to gong. After about thirty dresses, we said enough with the gong. We were all getting headaches. We had two goals that day: to make the 220 dresses, and to not blow up the church with all those sewing machines going. One of our high councilmen was an electrician. He checked out the wiring for us and said we were good to go.

We worked on the house a lot. We did more than we intended to in the first place; I really needed another bathroom. The house was small, but it did have one large closet we converted into the second bathroom. The house was over one-hundred years old. The lady who lived there before us used the bathtub to do her laundry. In preparation of starting to remodel, I wanted to remove some old wallpaper from what was going to become the laundry room. I pulled off the first layer of paper and could see our neighbor's house through the siding on our house. We finally got the remodeling done and got to the point of having the ceilings redone. The man was there to give us a bid, and a family of mice ran across the living room floor. I was so embarrassed. I told him that was just the way we entertained our guests.

Had we not bought this house, I may not have met Elle, as it turned out we were neighbors. We would have attended another Church of Jesus Christ of Latter-Day Saint church on the other side of town.

John decided to open a store for the items he was distributing geared to men and their businesses. He had built up quite a few accounts and needed a place and office for him. When we talked about it, I decided I wanted to have a ladies clothing store as well as his inventory for the men. We opened our store in 1999 on Main

Street in Gunnison. I really liked going to buyers-market and enjoyed the customers who came in. It was called Spirit Mountain Apparel.

Justin made the basketball team and been well accepted in school. He had changed some and become very quiet. That was his personality, but after a couple of weeks, I realized he was quieter than usual. I wondered if the move had been hard on him. He said he liked the smaller school and that "basketball was okay, and the guys were great." Something was wrong. He had said some negative things about his coach, but would not elaborate. I was worried about him.

Now, I had raised enough ball players in my household over the years to know that much goes on behind closed doors in a locker room. Some of it needs to, but some coaches take advantage of those closed doors. That was supposed to make them "men." Justin had never complained about a coach before, and he had seen his share for his young age. I knew something needed to be addressed. He promised he would talk to his dad when he got home. He did, and things seem to work out.

Justin's senior year was so different. They had a new coach who was highly respected by the boys, and he trusted that they knew what they were doing. Those games were so exciting. I didn't know if my heart was going to make it. One game, I had to go out during the fourth quarter. Our team was behind. When I came back in, I sat by fans of the opposing team and I heard them say to each other, "We have this game in the bag." I turned to them and said, "No you don't. Our team is known as the comeback kids for a reason; they will come back!" As soon as I said it, I felt a little foolish and pompous, but my team saved me – they did come back and win the game.

Another game, which was with Manti, Gunnison's biggest rival, was close. Emotions were high, and people were making spectacles of themselves. I had not seen anything like it for a long time. I thought about the Stripling Warriors in the Book of Mormon, who were young men asked to defend their people. I wondered whether these players would join forces if necessary, if they were required to fight against evil. I decided they would. I wondered the same about the cheerleaders and decided they would, as well. Then I wondered about the parents, and I couldn't come up with an answer. I did not know, but this rivalry had gone on for years. I told Justin of my analogy the next day. He said he was sure that I was the only one who was thinking of the Book of Mormon during that game. You never know!

They did win the state championship that year. The school had not won the state championship for over 20 years. It was so exciting. Most of our family went to Cedar City to support the team. Justin was on the starting line-up both years, and people said that he had made the difference. He was able to play every position and was good. His parents were so proud.

After the championship game, we all headed back to Gunnison. The team got there at about midnight and Main Street was lined up with townspeople to welcome and cheer them on. The fire trucks were out when the bus stopped. The boys all climbed on them and the sirens and bells were going. The police had plenty of reason to do disturbing-the-peace arrests at midnight, but they were cheering as loud as the rest of us. Yes, moving to Gunnison had been a good experience for Justin.

It was not only in basketball that Justin had a made a difference. A few mothers thanked us for bringing him there. They had been worried about their sons and they thanked Justin for just being himself. I don't know if he knew that he had helped them to find themselves and their testimony of the gospel. They had kind of saved each other.

After graduation, Justin went up to Utah State in Logan, Utah. It was one of the saddest days for me. I knew this day would come, and now here it was. We had children in our home for 40 years, and now we were empty nesters. Some of the kids asked "Mom,

Dad, are you going to make it?" Justin's mission call came toward the end of the year. He was going to Italy!

As for me and wondering what the women do in small towns – well, they do it all. Teach their children in righteousness and help their husbands in businesses or farms. They are educated, talented, and very, very busy. Most love the Lord and serve him to the best of their ability and are humble as they go about their daily tasks. Do they have their challenges? Of course they do. These are the steppingstones, provided for us to grow, become humbler, and find our relationship with our Savior.

My John was inspired to come to Central Utah. The family knew of my negative, resentful, and reluctant reaction to this move. I look back now and know I would not have missed this chapter in my life for anything!

Take my yoke upon you, and learn of me; for I am meek and lowly in heart: and ye shall find rest onto your souls.

Matthew 11:29
Bible

Learn of me, and listen to my words; walk in the meekness of my Spirit, and you shall have peace in me.

Doctrine and Covenants 19:23

Chapter 22

New Decade, New Century, New Life Changes

"Mr. Holmes, you and I have a big problem. Don't you do anything strenuous until I see you on Monday. You are a walking time bomb!" I could hear the doctor talking to John over the phone. "You have a 97 percent clogged artery that needs to be fixed," he told my husband.

John asked, "What do you mean? I thought you fixed everything earlier when you put the 4 stints in last week."

The doctor responded, "Well, we missed one and we need you to come in Monday and get it fixed. Just don't do anything before that!"

John had been mowing the lawn nine days earlier when he came in, wiped his face off, and said, "I am going to the hospital!" Then he went into the bathroom. I was cooking dinner and talking on the phone with a missionary mother whose son had just traveled to Italy with Justin. She was telling me they arrived there and were in good hands with the mission president and their new companions. I was trying to listen to her and John at the same time. He said, "Are you coming with me?" I didn't know what was going on. I thanked the sister and hung up, turned the stove off, and ran out the door after him.

He said, "I'm having a heart attack!" The hospital was three blocks away, and when we got there I ran into the hospital and said, "My husband needs help!" The emergency team was out that door so fast. I was so grateful for them and their fast action. The same doctor who had found the right kidney medicine for me was on duty. He checked John's vitals, then very quickly gave him a shot in the heart. A $5,000 shot, I might add, but it saved his life and stopped the attack. A lot of damage had been done. They got him into the ambulance after he had a priesthood blessing, and it took off for Provo.

I went into action and made arrangements for the store, pets, and some other things. I called David, filled the car with gas, and headed to Provo. Our good friend, Andrew, took the lead, and his wife and I followed him. No one wanted me to travel alone. As we were nearing Nephi, the calmest feeling came over me. I knew he would live and that I would not lose him at this time.

When I arrived at the hospital, most of the kids were there waiting for me. "He keeps asking for you, Mom."

I said, "I got here as fast as I could." John was stable and resting. They had done more tests and planned to take him into surgery the next morning to insert stints. Over half of his heart was dead. The boys insisted on getting me a room nearby, and I left a few hours later. When I got to the room, all I could do was thank Heavenly Father that John had survived this. I was so thankful for the comfort I got from the Holy Ghost, and I wished I could give him a big hug. That thought made me start laughing. You can't hug the Holy Ghost, you silly, I thought to myself. I didn't sleep much as I kept calling the hospital to check on John.

They had told me they would take him about 7:30 a.m. When I got there at 7, he had already gone in for the procedure. We were told afterward that things went well. Four stints had been put in two arteries. We were given some instructions, and they released him the next day.

He didn't get his strength back, nor could he breathe well. He suspected something more was wrong. I tried to get him to walk, per doctor's instructions, but it was too hard for him. It had been a week and he finally agreed to go outside. He walked as far as our neighbors, and I thought he would collapse before he got back home.

That is when he decided to call the cardiologist and tell him what he was experiencing. That's when the phone conversation occurred, with the doctor telling him there was another stint that needed to be put in. "Why didn't you do it when you did the other ones?" John asked the doctor after their conversation. He was told that he was too weak, and that the doctor thought it would be too hard on him. He needed to come in first thing Monday morning and they would take care of it. He was also told to go straight to the local hospital if anything went wrong.

So here we were, a whole nine days later and the weekend to wait this out. The anger he felt alone was enough to cause him stress on his heart. Why didn't the doctor fix it during the original procedure? Was John really too weak? Was the doctor in a hurry because it was a holiday weekend? Or was it just careless work?

We got him back to the hospital, and they put three more stints in him and sent him home the same day. It took a long time for him to get strength back. He was eventually told he needed to get rid of as much stress as he could and should probably give up his business. I asked the cardiologist how bad it was and how much time he thought John had left. He said if things go well, maybe three to six years.

He tried to continue with his business, but it was too hard on him. My little business was okay, and money was tight. We had Justin on the mission, and we were debt-free now except for about $50,000 now in hospital bills. I really wondered what we were going to do. I prayed and fasted about it, but we couldn't figure anything out. Adam and Cindy stepped in for several months and helped with Justin's mission. I knew if we went back up north, the stress of living up there would shorten his life. Jobs that paid anything were just not available here, however.

One day as I was preparing a talk for a stake Relief Society assignment, I was reading in the Doctrine and Covenants in section 112 and my eyes wandered over to section 111. I read:

> *Concern yourselves not about your debts, for I will give you power to pay them. Tarry in this place and regions round about; and the place that is my will that you should tarry, for the main, shall be signalized unto you by the peace and power of my spirit, that shall flow unto you. This place you may obtain by hire. And inquire diligently concerning the more ancient inhabitants of this city; for there are more treasures than one for you in this city. Therefore, be ye as wise as serpents, and yet without sin; and I will order all things for your good as fast as ye are able to receive them. Amen*

(Doctrine and Covenants 111: 5&7-11)

I read this at least three times and then picked up my scriptures and went into where John was sitting and read them to him. He asked me to read them again. Tears were rolling down his cheeks. We didn't know how we were going to it, but we knew what we had to do. We felt very strongly that we should move my business to Richfield, Utah and he would try to find work there.

Eventually, he was feeling strong enough and thought of a plan. He went to see a man in Richfield who had had a similar business to what John had, only he was more into T-shirts and trophies. John asked him, "Have you ever had an outside salesman?" He said, "I've never even thought abought it." John told him he would like to be one, and he would bring his accounts with him. They worked everything out, and John was happy with the outcome. John worked for this company for eight years on a part-time basis, and it worked out well for us.

The kids came down and helped me get the store set up in a building that John had found. It had been a wood shop, so I had to do some work in it to get it looking decent enough to put a ladies clothing store in it. I did much of the work myself.

Justin was doing well on his mission but found people were not to receptive. We had been told it was one of the hardest missions there was. He struggled with the language the first few months. Then, they put him with a companion from Ukraine who did not speak Italian or English, so together they worked it out. He did not write us another word about the language barrier again. It had been a shock to him to have just arrived in Italy to find out that his father had a heart attack a few days after he left.

We decided that we should move to Richfield. I would get so tired at the end of the day that I almost felt like I would fall asleep at the wheel. I just wasn't like I used to be. In 2001, we put our Gunnison house up for sale. I was sure it would take a while because some houses there had been for sale for two years. To our surprise, it sold in about a month. At this time, Alysia and Brad had come to live with us. They now had two young boys, and we all lived in our "great big" 900-square-foot house. Brad worked in Salt Lake during the week. As we were looking for a house to rent in Richfield, we were looking for the six of us. We found a place to rent in Richfield that accommodated the two families well.

In mid-September, John was watching the morning news on TV. He called to Alysia and me to come. It was September 11, 2001, a day that we will never—or should never—forget. Islamic extremists hijacked four airliners and carried out suicide attacks against the United States. After take-off, the terrorists took command of the planes, transforming ordinary commuter jets into guided missiles. Their targets were the twin towers of the World Trade Center in New York City.

Another target was the Pentagon outside Washington, D.C. American Airlines Flight 77 circled around the building before it slammed into the west side of it. A fourth plane crashed into a field in Pennsylvania, and all 45 people on board were killed. Theories were that this plane was headed for the White House or Camp David. Over 3,000 people were killed that day.

The three of us, along with millions of others, watched in disbelief. Had the third world war begun? Most of the nation stopped that day in shock and horror because of what we witnessed on television.

President Bush was shuttled around the country that day because of security reasons. He returned to the Oval Office and addressed the people declaring, "Terrorist attacks can shake the foundation of our biggest buildings, but they cannot shake the foundations of America. These acts shatter steel, but they cannot dent the steel of American resolve." He further said, "We will make no distinction between terrorists who committed these acts and those who harbor them."

I went into the store later that day – not that I had any customers – and I was glad because an elderly woman came in. She lived alone and needed someone to talk to and express her concerns. We sat and talked. At one point, John joined us, and was further comfort to her and myself.

The people of our country turned to God with whatever beliefs they had for about six months. Churches were full across the nation. However, then we saw complacency set in again, and people returned to their normal ways. The attack affected the economy in many ways. Jobs were lost because people were not spending money, and some businesses were forced to close. Many troops were sent to the Middle East, and thousands of lives were lost.

I had been vacillating about closing my store for several months now, but not just because of the economy. I was getting concerned about my own health issues. I chalked it up to getting older, and I knew I was losing strength in my whole body. John supported me and said it was my decision. We had not discussed it for a few weeks. One Sunday while singing in the choir, the thought came: "Close the store!" I returned to my seat to sit by John after the song and told him, "I am closing the store."

Later, when we were in the car driving home, he asked, "How can you be in a choir singing a song one minute, and the next you are sitting by me, telling me you're closing the store?"

I said, "It was that still small voice that overshadowed all the voices around me, including my own, and I knew from where it came."

So, early in 2003, I closed my little store in Richfield. The economy was taking another hit, and more stores were closing. Mine was very slow. A Walmart was being built, and I knew I could not compete with them.

For though we walk in the flesh, we do not war after the flesh.

2 Corinthians 10:3
Bible

Ye hear of wars in far countries, and you say that there will soon be great wars in far countries, but ye know not the hearts of men in your own land.

Doctrine and Covenants 38:29

Chapter 23

John says "Bingo"

"There he is, I see him!" The Salt Lake International Airport was so crowded and colorful, with flags and banners being held by people from nations all over the world. The 2002 World Winter Olympics were being held in Salt Lake City, Utah, and the opening ceremonies were the next day. The athletes and trainers had been here for a few weeks. Now the spectators and families were pouring in.

However, there was only one person I was waiting to see at the airport after two years of his being in Italy. My 6-foot-5 baby boy, Justin, was back on United States soil. We were so happy to see him, and I am sure he was equally happy to be home. With the world in such commotion, I spent a lot of time in prayer in behalf of him and his companions. Many of the family came to greet him and it was a little chaotic, but that was okay. He was home!

He came home to a different house and town. One of his buddies, who had returned from his mission a few months earlier, was waiting for him to get home. He had life planned out for them the next few years. Justin had matured a lot and had his own ideas of how his life was going to go. Playing around with the guys was not his thing. When he heard how much playing some of his friends did on their missions, he was disappointed in them. They say we parents send a boy on a mission, and the Lord sends us home a man. I thanked the Lord this was the case with all four of our sons. There weren't many employment opportunities in Richfield, and he soon went back up to Logan. He found employment and went to college in the fall.

He kept telling me about a girl he wanted to meet named Jessica Lamprecht. He was a little gun shy. Another girl who said that she might wait for him prior to his mission did not even tell him when she got engaged. I had to write the "Dear John" letter. Eventually, he and Jessica started dating, after she sent him a note in class asking what his name was.

They were married in the Salt Lake Temple the following June. We had the reception in Idaho Falls, where she was raised and her parents lived. Their reception was so fun, and everyone danced. I danced with all my sons and sons-in-laws. John danced with all his daughters. We all laughed so hard when Craig cut in when Justin was dancing with his new bride. He started dancing with Justin and then stuck a $20 bill in his pocket.

Justin and Jessica lived in Logan for a few years, and he continued to work for the same company and go to school. Jessica worked for a dentist part time. Then they moved to Idaho Falls and lived with her parents. He graduated from Idaho State University. The company had transferred him to the store in Idaho, and he worked for them until he graduated and found other work. He often said that every time he went to work, it reminded him why he was going to school. They have blessed us with four more beautiful grandchildren.

I had been called to be the Humanitarian leader in the Richfield ward, and we had quite a few activities. The Salt Lake humanitarian department gave us some of the upholstery from an airline that was re-covering their seats in the airplanes. They worked out well for us to make school bags and fill them with supplies. The curtain material was used for hygiene kits.

I was told that books were needed in some countries, especially ones that helped teach children to read. I set a goal for 300. At

1,200, John and I loaded his truck and my car with boxes of books and took them to Salt Lake to the Humanitarian Center. When we retuned early in the evening, there were 31 more boxes of books under the carport. The city library had a book sale, and what they did not sell, they had brought to us. We had to censor all the books before we could send them to Salt Lake. They couldn't take any that were religious, political, or had sexual content in them. This time, I made arrangements with Deseret Industry (a non-profit thrift store provided by the church) to deliver the books to Salt Lake for us. I really enjoyed this calling. I always found great satisfaction in helping others.

The owner of the house we were living in kept giving hints that they wanted to sell. However, we were not interested in buying the home. John was having more trouble with his legs, and it was so hard for him to do stairs. The owners were not too interested in fixing it up either. It needed new linoleum in the kitchen and new carpeting.

We started to look for another place to live and thought we had found the right place, but something was wrong. I got the feeling we were not supposed to move. I was sick, and something was the matter. It was not a physical sickness, and I had not experienced it before. That afternoon, we had told the people that we were going to move into their home. Now I laid in bed and felt sicker than I had in a long time. I thought, "Is it my spirit that is sick? Is it sad?"

I laid there and thought about it and what we were about to do with the move. I began to realize that it *was* my spirit letting me know that moving would be the wrong thing to do. I went to John and told him we can't move. He said, "I know. You are going to be called to be the next Relief Society president in this ward, and it is going to happen soon."

I responded: "No, I've done that, and besides, they would not call a sister who just rents a house and may not be here long." He insisted it was going to happen.

I didn't sleep much that night, and still wasn't happy with the house. Would the Lord call me again to fill that position? I was so much older, I had a hard time with names, and I really didn't know the sisters, especially all the widows. There were two pews of them in church each Sunday, and a whole bunch who couldn't attend because of their health. This much I did know.

The following day, we got a call from the bishop's secretary wanting to set an appointment with John and myself. We went in, and the call was extended to me to be Relief Society president. All John could say was "Bingo," as he smiled at me.

I asked, "Are you sure?"

"I am sure, and so is the Lord," said the bishop. I left with a heavy weight on my shoulders. I was thinking of all those widows. There were fifty-nine of them. Then I said to John, "Well, at least this time, I won't get pregnant." Ironically, our landlady called a few days later and said she had just received a $25,000 credit card, and to go ahead and pick out my carpet and flooring for the whole upstairs. I did.

Picking my counselors was a process. I knew immediately who I wanted as my secretary. I had worked with her in a family history class, and I was impressed with her organization skills and knowledge of the sisters. I prayed about who to have called as my counselors. Finally, I had a name for the first counselor. Nothing felt right for the other position. On Saturday night, I was looking at the ward directory trying to see if I could get some inspiration, I looked at one name and thought, "I don't even know who she is." I continued looking through the directory and went through it several times. Her name, Billy Conder, kept coming back to me.

The next morning, I was in choir practice again, and the thought came to me that the next sister who came through the north door was going to be my counselor. No one came in that door for several minutes. When a sister did, I did not recognize her. When I sat down in the congregation by John, I tapped the sister in front of me on the shoulder and asked who the woman was. She said, "Billy Conder. She works in the primary." My heart started to pound, and I submitted her name immediately. When the call was extended to her, she said she knew it was coming. She knew, she just didn't tell me. The Lord doesn't work that way.

We became fine friends, and I so appreciated her. We had a wonderful, spiritual time in our presidency. One of the first things I told these sisters was the work was serious business and the work of our Savior, but that we shouldn't take ourselves too seriously. We needed to laugh and find joy in our efforts. My first counselor was of a very serious nature, and I am sure she thought I was sacrilegious.

On Sunday, August 31, 2003, we were set apart as the new presidency of the Richfield 4th Ward Relief Society. The most wonderful thing happened to me when I was being set apart, something that I had prayed for since I had joined the church.

I had not thought of my father that day. I had many other things on my mind. The bishop set me apart, and was going to give me a personal blessing. There was a pause, and I was sure he couldn't think of anything to say to me when I heard my father's voice say to me as clear as I ever had, *"Vellie, I am here with the brethren."*

Only my father called me "Vellie." He had been deceased for 18 years. He was there with us. It was overwhelming, and such a spiritual and sacred experience. The tears rolled down my face. I could not tell you one thing that the bishop did say once he commenced with the blessing. All I knew was that my father had accepted the Gospel of Jesus Christ and held the Melchizedek Priesthood. My prayers had been answered.

When I met with the bishop on Tuesday night to go over some business in the ward, I asked him if I could share something before we started. I told him what had transpired on Sunday when he had set me apart. He looked at me with a serious look on his face and said, "That is wonderful," and went on to say, "After I set you apart, the words were all there for me to give you a blessing, but I could not get my mouth to work. Nothing would come out, and I felt stifled. Now I know why. It was to give your father time to intervene and say that *he was there.*"

The first thing I wanted to do as a new presidency was meet all the sisters in their own homes. We started with the 90-year-olds and worked backward. If these sisters died on our shift, I at least wanted to know who they were and something about them. Visiting with these older sisters was one of the choicest experiences I had. They were so full of wisdom and knowledge. The thing they taught me the most was they were just young spirits in older bodies.

We were involved in many funerals. Some were so sweet and you felt the spirit of the comforter there to give the family peace. Others were hard on the family; they seemed to lack the understanding of the gospel and that death is part of the plan of salvation. Each one had circumstances that were so different.

Death can be so sweet at times. Sister Ethelyn was 93 years of age and so frail. She lived with her daughter and her husband, and they took wonderful care of her. We knew she was in her last days, and the last time I visited her, I felt like I was in the presence of an angel. She just glowed as she laid there with her beautiful white hair. She took my hand and thanked me for coming. She then slipped off to sleep. She joined many more angels during the night. It was my privilege to know her.

Another sister did not live in our ward, or even in Richfield. She lived in a neighboring town. A good friend invited her to come to our church with her. She came regularly and fit right in, and it was clear she was trying to learn and understand. She interjected many good thoughts in our lessons. I had the feeling I needed to go see her. When I did go to her home, she told me that she was hoping that I would come. I stayed for two hours and she told me her story.

Her family had been members when she was a child, but then her father moved them to Arizona and joined another religion.

She said even as a little girl she felt close to the Savior and always believed the story of Joseph Smith and the restoration of the gospel. If a family member mentioned anything about the Prophet Joseph, they were punished severely. Usually they were sent to the hot huts and locked up for a few days until they were cleansed and promised never to speak his name again.

When she was old enough to break away, she did so and had nothing to do with her family. She was always afraid if she got back in the church her father would find out, and she did not know what he would do. Finally, after meeting the friend who brought her to our ward, she knew she needed to come back to the church and face what consequences may come. She had studied and had a wonderful testimony. She said even when she was in the hot hut, she felt either the Savior or Joseph was with her. Her husband was not a member of the church, but with much fellowshipping from the elders and others, he joined. It was a wonderful occasion when we went to the temple to see this family sealed for eternity. She did eventually make some contact with her family. Her mother had been heart broken when she left. Her relationship with her father remained estranged.

One day, I was going home after doing some shopping when I got the feeling I needed to visit another sister. I was her visiting teacher and had been there a few days before. I was in a hurry because I needed to get home and get a few things done before I went to work. I had gone to work part time for a decorating company. When the prompting came, I told myself there wasn't time, and I best go on so I would get to work on time. The feeling came again, and still I fought it. When I turned the corner, I found myself in her driveway. I had no clue why I was there.

I knocked on the door, and one of her children answered and was crying. I saw his older sister on the couch, and their cousins were there and were also crying. I asked if their mother was there, and she came from the kitchen. I said, "I am sure I have come at a really bad time." She grabbed my arm and pulled me into the house. She was crying, too. They had just received news that her brother's two-month old baby had died. She told me what she could about the circumstance of his death. It was devastating to them all. I knelt down, extended my arms out, and said to the children that we needed a group hug. They ran into my arms and clung to me as I hugged them. I can't remember what I said, but it brought them out of the shock they were feeling, and it was a little better.

Her father drove up a few minutes later to take them to be with the family. The sister thanked me for coming. She said I made such a difference in a terrible moment. After that, her children called me the praying lady, even though we didn't pray at that moment, we only hugged.

For one of the Relief Society birthday parties, we were going to do an enactment of Third Nephi from the Book of Mormon. I was trying to find a brother who would play the part of the prophet Nephi. All the men who I had in mind who would do justice to the part were not available the night that we were going to do it. One morning at about 4am, I woke up with a brother on my mind. He had only been a member of the church for a few months. I was sure he would not want to do it. I couldn't go back to sleep, however, and kept wondering if he would do it. Had he even read that part of Book of Mormon and how the people on this continent knew when the Savior was born? Did he know the signs that had been prophesied?

In the Book of Mormon, we read that the people on the western continent knew of Jesus Christ's birth because there would be signs given. One of these signs was that there would be a day and a night and a day, with no darkness. There would be no darkness, even though the sun would set.

The Book of Mormon tells us also what took place during those five years between Samuel the Lamanite prophesying of Christ's birth and the fulfillment of that prophecy. The Book of Mormon also tells of Jesus Christ's visit to the western continent after his resurrection and how he left his Nephite disciples after the forty days that he spent with them. He told them there are other sheep he must go to, just as he told his Apostles in Israel. (John 10:16; 3 Nephi 15:17)

At about 10 a.m., I called the brother on the phone and told him why I was calling. He jumped at the opportunity to do it. He had just recently read Third Nephi. He said he loved it, and it was one of his favorite parts of the Book of Mormon. I had found my Nephi! His wife played the part of Nephi's wife, and their children were Nephi's children in the play.

The Relief Society Declaration had been introduced a few years earlier, and we made it one of our study guides for the years I served. I felt a need for more spirituality in our ward. I had wonderful sisters who could carry out the social and homemaking part of the program. They were so talented, and their contribution just added to the spirit we as a presidency were attempting to bring.

As we visited sisters, we realized that even though many said they believed in the Book of Mormon, many had not read it from cover to cover. That was our goal, and we challenged the women in the year of 2005 to read it entirely. Many took our challenge; it did not hurt that our prophet challenged the whole church to do it in General Conference that year. I think the sisters took his challenge more seriously than ours.

Many did complete their reading challenge. One sister who was in labor with her fifth child had about nine pages to go. She took the book with her to the hospital, and either she or her husband completed the book between contractions. She finished her goal. It was late in December, and she knew that with a new baby and the busy Christmas season, if she didn't finish before the baby was born, she wouldn't finish at all.

We submitted the idea that we would like the young women to join us in Relief Society at least once a month to the bishop. We would combine opening exercises and then excuse the Mia Maids and Beehives and ask the Laurels to stay with us for the lesson. The purpose of this was to help the young woman's transition into Relief Society easier when they turned 18. He approved, and the program was very successful in our ward. Other wards who tried it did not see the successes we did. Cindy had shared this idea with me, and it worked very well in their Las Vegas Ward. The general board had requested that we pray about and come up with ideas that would help our young sisters when they graduated from high school. Many were becoming less active because they felt misplaced.

During my time as Relief Society president, I stood among righteous women. I felt much love for them and was very humbled. So many were far more qualified than I was. I knew the things we taught one another were eternal truths and correct principles, and I would defend them with my life because of the righteousness that they are built upon. Even now, my love and understanding of the scriptures continues to grow, and I find great delight in them.

I served in this position until 2006. By then, I was on dialysis and found that I had cancer. My love for the Savior, our Heavenly Father, and the gospel of Jesus Christ would bring me so many blessings during the next seven years.

Who can find a virtuous woman? For her price is far above rubies.

Proverbs 31:10
Bible

And behold, I tell you these things that ye may learn wisdom; that ye may learn that when ye are in the service of your fellow beings ye are only in the service of your God.

Mosiah 2:17
Book of Mormon

Chapter 24

I Will Wait Upon the Lord

In 2004, I was coming up the stairs one morning and I could hardly make it. I had to pull myself up by the railing. I wondered what was going on; I seemed to be growing weaker every day, and just did not feel normal. I finally went to my doctor in Richfield. The test results showed that the functional kidney was in big trouble. He sent me to a nephrologist in Provo. Again, the test proved that the kidney was failing. I was told that I would need to go on dialysis in a few months.

I felt there must be an alternative way to receive help. The next day I called our chiropractor, told him my situation, and asked if he knew anybody who could help with natural medicine. He did. I called the man he suggested, and he said to come up the next day. John was hesitant and did not like the idea. So, this time I told him, "I am going, with or without you!" He went.

The man was a homeopathic doctor, and he was able to help me for a little over a year. My kidney did not improve much, but at least it was stable. The doctors never did find out what was wrong with the kidney. One said I had a virus, another said it was just overworked. I do know I was grateful for the help that I got. The homeopathic doctor's own father had been on dialysis for over four years, and he was really interested in trying to keep others stay off it if possible. It is not the greatest life. Eventually, the homeopathic medicine could no longer help me. I needed to see a nephrologist again.

I made an appointment with the nephrologist in Provo again, but I requested another doctor. I was able to get in the end of January to see him. The first thing he said to me was, "I don't know if I want you for a patient. I do not need you as a patient, and you fired my colleague!" I was quite taken back. John was furious, and if I had not been so sick, I would have walked out. Medicare at that time assigned me to this clinic because it was the closest nephrology clinic to Richfield, and their doctors worked in conjunction with the small dialysis center in Richfield. He sat down and started to review my history and said I needed to go on dialysis immediately.

He then left the room, returned a few minutes later, and said, "I just moved a mountain for you." I asked what he was talking about and he said, "I have made an appointment in forty-five minutes to have the ultrasound and all the tests needed to put in a fistula." The dialysis machine pumps all the blood and cleans it like a kidney does, and the fistula is where they access you and connects to your heart. It would go in my neck temporary. In a few months, it would mature and then I would dialyze through the one they would put in my arm the next day. He again left the room and when he came back in, he said, "I have just moved another mountain." I had never met anyone so arrogant. When this doctor retired, he hugged me and said I was one of his favorite patients. We were both very stubborn.

I had the two surgeries the next day and began to dialyze three times a week for four-hour sessions. It made me sick and weak, and I was already so weak. I continued in my calling in the church and my job. Was it easy? No; I look back now and wonder how I did it. I knew that the Lord was helping me.

We had a family gathering in the spring, and I wanted a priesthood blessing. John asked Justin to give the blessing. He began and then seemed to be struggling with it and he kept pausing. In the blessing, I was told that I would be completely healed, even if it meant I would get another kidney. I was told many other things that gave me comfort and peace, and was assured of the love our Savior had for me. When Justin completed the blessing, he apologized to me and said, "Mom, I am sorry for all the pauses. The words I was to pronounce upon your head only came to me in Italian. I had to pause and translate them into English so that you could understand what I was saying."

The blessing gave me great hope, and I knew I would get well. They put me on the transplant list and said there is usually a two year wait unless I had a donor from the family or a friend. Many of the children did offer to be tested, but I refused to let them do it. I had my own reasons concerning each of those who offered. Mostly, I was concerned that later in their lives they might experience kidney failure, and I did not want them to go through what I was.

I started on dialysis on February 1, 2006. The following April, I rolled over in bed one night and I felt something pull in my breast. There was a definite lump. We needed to go to Logan for a family event that weekend. When we were driving home, I told John what I had found a few days earlier. He was so worried. I went to the doctor a few days later, and he confirmed my suspicion. I was between stage three and four with breast cancer. My left breast needed to be removed.

We got home late in the afternoon after an appointment at the Huntsman Cancer Center. Heidi was instrumental in getting me in so quickly. I told John I was leaving for a while. I wanted to go visit some of our elderly sisters, though not to tell them what was going on with me. Most did not even know I was on dialysis. I tried to keep it very quiet. I knew by visiting them, I would forget my own troubles and possibly help them. They did love the visits, and I enjoyed visiting them. I had learned long before this time in my life that when we are faced with great personal challenges of our own, engaging ourselves and helping others makes our own burdens lighter.

John's health was still deteriorating, which made us a great pair. Mostly it was his legs, and he was having trouble getting up and down our stairs, even to get in the house. I was sitting at work a few days later looking at the classified ads in the newspaper. I was looking at a house for sale in Richfield. It was a one-level, easy-entry manufactured home. I called the realtor, and she told me it had gone under contract that morning. I really didn't think much about it until she called me back a few weeks later and said, "The contract fell through; would you like to look at it?" We went over, and I liked it. John was not impressed.

A few days later, he walked into our house and said, "We are supposed to buy that house." By now I was used to him changing his mind, and it always seemed to work out. He said he was going into his office to call the owner, who he knew personally.

I asked, "Don't you want to go see it again?"

He said "No, we are just supposed to buy it."

I said, "Well, I do," and I called the realtor to make an appointment to see it again.

When John was talking with the owner later in person, the man sat back in his chair and said "John, do you want to hear something really weird? I had a dream two nights ago that you and I were sitting here in my office, and we were talking about you buying my house on Seventh North." The offer was made, and he accepted it. John was in no way trying to cheat the realtor out of her commission by going straight to the owner. However, we had never had a home like this before, and who better to ask about it than the man who had it brought in, set it on the foundation, and looked over all the other particular's John wanted to know about? When John told me about the owner's dream, I had chills just go through me.

We were going to move in after my cancer surgery. John made up his mind that when I came home from Salt Lake, I was coming to my new home. Neither of us were in much condition to pack and move. Our wonderful kids, though they could not all come at once, sacrificed and came to help as they could. The actual day of the move, Linda and her husband Eric came and got us moved. Kim helped get the house in order. Our son Eric was also there, and between all of them, we looked like we had lived there for years by the time I left on May 17 for my surgery. Kim was able to stay in Salt Lake for a few days while I was in the hospital. It was so nice to have her.

Dave and Teresa brought me home. It was nice to come to our new house. I loved it. Teresa helped me with personal things that were required for me after the surgery, and then John had to take over for a while.

My request on the kidney transplant list was canceled. I had to be cancer free for five years before I could even be put back on the list, then wait for two more years for the donation. By then, I would be in my 70s. I hung onto that blessing pronounced by Justin and knew that if I did my part, the Lord would do His. And **I would wait upon the Lord.**

Behold, God is my salvation; I will trust, and not be afraid: for the Lord Jehovah is my strength and my song; he also is become my salvation.

Isaiah 12:2
Bible

And I will also ease the burdens which are put upon your shoulders, that even you cannot feel them upon your backs, even while you are in bondage; and this will I do that ye may stand as a witness for me hereafter that ye may know that I, the Lord God, do visit my people in their afflictions.

Mosiah 24:14
Book of Mormon

Chapter 25

Golden Keys to His Kingdom

I had learned many years earlier that it does not matter what happens to you in this life, but it's what you do about those things that really matters. Sometimes you cannot do much about them, but you can always control your attitude, and that was exactly how I intended to be with this challenge in my life.

A few months after my surgery and being on dialysis, I came across a paper I had written at some point in my life. It served as a reminder of how I had hoped I had responded to different trials I had faced in the past, and I was determined that I would not change my feelings just because a new one was here. It would be my life style for several years. I had written:

> *"Let us thank the Lord when we have trials in our lives, lest we may never know our inner selves. We may not know what inner strength we have, or if we will be able to overcome our own weaknesses. It is through trial and tribulation that we become strong and closer to God.*
>
> *To enter their presence, we must know God, our Father, and his son Jesus Christ. We must*

*know when we have experienced the promptings
of the Holy Ghost and have Him as our constant
companion. It is only through the experience of this
life that we can grow to a state where we will receive
from our Father all that he has to give us. May the
trials and burdens that we carry be the golden keys
to His Kingdom."*

I have learned also that as we reach the unknown and tread on our own uncharted waters, that faith lights the way. If we keep that faith cultivated, we will never walk in darkness. We cannot let a season of doubt, disillusion, and discouragement ever take over.

I had settled into my life of rising at 4:30 a.m. to get to dialysis by 5:15 a.m. so that I could get some rest and get to my job by noon. It was working well for the most part. There were bad days when I just wanted to sleep. I did, however, meet some great people who almost became like family. We spent so much time together sharing a common challenge. We formed the Kidney Lunch Bunch and met on non-dialysis days. We had a lot of fun together. We found that we could tolerate what we were going through if we kept our own and each other's spirits high. We definitely decided dialysis was not for wimps. We wanted to put a sign up saying that, but the head nurse did not think the hospital administrator would like that.

Some of the new friends I made were short-term, as I saw thirteen die on dialysis the first two years that I was there. Their bodies gave up, and some chose to go off the machine. We knew that in a few days or up to a week, we would receive news that they had moved on to a better life.

We cannot take our kidneys for granted. Once the poison they remove from our blood stream has built up to a certain point, it takes our life. The machine doesn't do 100 percent of what the kidneys do, but they do eliminate much of the damage and poisons from our bodies. It was a wonderful blessing to have dialysis available. Forty years earlier, it was available to only the very well-to-do. The machines were quite primitive. I was told that before computers came into our lives, the only way to tell if you had been on the machine long enough was if you passed out from plummeting blood pressure or vomited. That can all be monitored now with computers.

One of my good friends on dialysis was Mike Stratton. I first met him the day that we moved to the manufactured home in Richfield. I was standing by one of the trucks that were being loaded, and he drove up on his motorized wheelchair. He was looking for me. He was new in town, and he said, "I will be at dialysis Monday." He had moved here from Cedar City because he was told that it was easier to get a transplant at this facility. He was on the early morning shift like me. He said he would see me at 5 a.m. Monday and away he went.

He was put on a chair next to me, and we became good friends. Mike was about 50, and one leg had been amputated due to his diabetes. His heart was bad, but he was still optimistic that he could get a transplant, an artificial leg, and then have somewhat of a normal life. His wife and children had abandoned him.

He was a member of The Church of Jesus Christ of Latter-Day Saints and had a wonderful testimony of the gospel. His favorite subject was anything about the church and its principles. Sometimes in the early morning when I saw him going to the center in his motorized chair, we would race. He thought it was so fun when he won.

He had met a divorced woman in the church and fallen in love with her. He wanted to marry her, but had nothing to offer her. One night he got brave enough to go to her house. There was mud in front of the driveway. He got stuck in the mud, and while trying to get himself out of it, his motor scooter tipped over. He said he must have been there for over an hour before someone noticed him and helped him get up. He did not try to see her that night, as he was covered with mud. He gave up after that. He continued to tell me how much he loved her. She had some physical problems of her own, and would have understood his if she only knew how he felt.

Mike went to the hospital in Provo often for the next few years, and it seemed each time he came back, his condition had gotten worse. The last time he came back, he said, "This will be my last time. I have decided to go back to Cedar City to die." There was nothing more that could be done for him. He wanted to share a scripture with me from the Doctrine and Covenants: *"Fear not, let your hearts be comforted; you rejoice evermore, and in everything give thanks…All things wherewith you have been afflicted shall work together for your own good."* D&C 98:1,3.

He did not come when it was time to dialyze again. I was told that he would be taken back to Cedar City that night. I had a very bad day on the machine myself, but felt I needed to tell him good-bye. When he saw me at his apartment door, he hobbled to it and hugged me and said, "I knew you would come; you are my best friend!" We talked a moment, and then those who were transporting him needed to get him in the vehicle and leave.

On Sunday night, I called the rest home where he was staying. He said, "There was something that I wanted to share with you when you came to see me on Friday, only there was not enough time." He told me he had a Priesthood blessing earlier that day, and in the blessing, he was told he was being released from his sick and frail body and was going home to serve the Savior and teach the gospel that he loved so much to those who waited to hear it. When I returned to the center on Monday morning, I was told that he died that night in his sleep.

Everyone loved Cindy, another dialysis patient. She was one of the most delightful, cheerful people I had met. She made everyone feel special, and always had open arms to greet them. Cindy had been on dialysis for nine years, and her body had rejected two transplants. They were trying to prepare her body for another one. The second rejection caused her to gain over 50 pounds. They tried many things to get the kidney going, but it didn't want to adjust to its new home. Finally, the doctors gave up, and she was back to where she started, only with all that extra weight. This did not get her down; she maintained such optimism and reflected that in all she did and in all she spoke. She was an example of what we are taught: that the wise optimist depends on the wonderful and glorious promises the Lord has made to us. She demonstrated great faith. The last time I spoke with her, she was still hopeful of getting a kidney. She had been approved for a third one – something rarely done.

Our friend Amanda was on dialysis, too. She did not speak English, only Spanish. Cindy spoke Spanish, so she was our translator. At one point, Amanda needed a place to stay for a week while an apartment was being prepared for her, and the social worker asked if she could come stay with me. My concern was how we were going to communicate for a week. I told myself that with love you can break down any barriers. I told her to come and stay with me. It was an interesting week, and sometimes we would have to call Cindy on the phone, so she could translate for us. It was really kind of fun. Amanda was of another faith, and she eventually was baptized into our church. I attended the baptism. I did not understand a word but, oh, how I felt the spirit of the occasion.

My dear friend, Leona, joined us at dialysis. Her husband, Tie, would bring her over from Ephraim, and he was so attentive to her needs. They were only married five years when he had a sudden heart attack and was taken from her. That was hard on her as he was the love of her life. She eventually moved over to Richfield, and we became good friends. I knew she was so lonely. She went to Texas for a while with her only son, but that ended in a very unfortunate relationship; they said they never wanted to see each other again. When she returned to Utah, she had to live in Salt Lake for insurance purposes. I still occasionally see her and talk to her on the phone. She is very dear to me.

As for me, I took my share of trips to the hospital in Provo. One night, I woke in the middle of the night and found pus where the tube was entering my artery that led to my heart. It was infected. I woke John, and he got me to the hospital. My doctor was called, and he called my nephrologist to get instructions. They had to act immediately; if it would have hit my heart, it would have killed me. They had the medicine to inject into me to stop the infection, and then I went by ambulance to the Provo hospital. Three doctors said to me after I was better that I should have been a dead woman. It had come very close to my heart.

It was during this stay at the hospital, I had another encounter with the evil one. I was on very heavy drugs and fighting for my life; the doctors told me that in another few hours the infection would have hit my heart. Once it does, there is nothing they could do. The second night I spent in the hospital, I was in a semi-sleep when suddenly, my mind was full of demons.

They were horrible creatures with long arms and legs that looked like snakes. They came at me like a sword, and were hanging from large, ugly chandeliers attached to heavy chains that rattled when they were moved. I was in my hospital bed placed in a huge, ancient, dark room filled with ugly décor. These demons would swing toward me, grabbing out for me and making awful noises. Their heads were shaped like two-headed frogs, hissing and screeching as they swung from the chandeliers and darted out at me. First one would come at me, then two at a time, and then all of them at once. They kept reaching for me, and I could not get away. I was screaming out, but no sound would come from my throat. I do not know how long this went on, I only know I was exhausted and wanted to give up. Physically, I was so weak. I was fighting so hard to keep them away, and my spirit felt like it would succumb to the evil ones. I just didn't care. It was as if all the will to live was drained out of me both physically and spiritually. I felt like I was drowning in evilness. I was pleading for help, and then the next thing I knew, in my mind I started singing the hymn,

"I Need Thee Every Hour." I sang it over and over, and it gave me strength and determination to pull myself out of this dark place. Again, by the power of the Holy Ghost, this evilness would be forced to leave me. I murmured the words, "By the power of the Holy Ghost, leave me!" Slowly, I calmed and lay there in the hospital room repeating the song over and over in my mind. The words; *"I Need Thee, Oh, I Need Thee; Every Hour I Need Thee, Oh, Bless Me Now My Savior; I Come Too Thee!"*

When I told my experience to my sons the next day, I asked them if they thought it was the drugs that caused my mind to be taken over like this, or the increased weakness in my body. Eric said, "Mom, Satan will use any means that are available to get to us. It doesn't matter if it was the drugs or something else. He will use any tool to take our bodies and destroy our spirit."

Another time, I had a stroke while on the dialysis machine. They didn't think anything was wrong because I could not tell them, but the technician could see something was not right. When the head nurse got to me, she told them what was happening. Once again, I was rushed to Provo. I was there a few weeks, had therapy, and felt like I was good as new. I did realize later that I had lost a portion of my memory. They also told me that I had a slight heart attack.

I had quit my job at the decorating company. John seemed to be getting worse, and could not do a lot. In 2008, he lost his job. I had known he was not able to carry his load at work and wondered how long the company could carry him, as his sales were down. He was on a salary plus commission, and the commission checks were getting smaller.

One morning after John had been out of work a few weeks, I had been at the computer a long time. When I came out into the room, I was dressed up. He asked, "What have you been doing, and where are you going?" I told him I had been putting a resume together, and I was going to find a job. He felt terrible and argued with me. I knew he was not able to work, so I felt like I should.

I went to Workforce Services and applied for a few jobs. Later that afternoon, a man called me and told me I was just what they were looking for in the Richfield area. It turned out it was demoing products for a national company. There were also many reports to be done by computer. They needed a lead person, and my starting salary would be $13 an hour. It was only part-time, and it worked with my dialysis hours. I took a state and national test that were required, and I took the job. What a blessing. I had the job for over three years. There were days I would get off dialysis and come home, change, and go straight to work. I knew that I was very blessed and was given extra strength to do this.

The children also were helping us financially, and that, too, was a great blessing I will always be grateful for. I knew it was a hardship for some, and each did what they could.

I continued to stay active in the church and attended my meetings every Sunday. I taught Relief Society six years while on dialysis, remained a visiting teacher, and was called to be over the special music for Sacrament meetings. I knew staying busy and optimistic would help me to get through this. Yes, I was still waiting upon the Lord with love for, and faith in, Him.

And not only so, but we glory in tribulations also; knowing that tribulation worketh patience.

Romans 5:3
Bible

And this because of their exceeding faith, and their patience in their tribulations [no power will operate against them.]

Alma 60:26
Book of Mormon

Chapter 26
I Can See Clearly Now

July 16, 2011

"Today has been the hardest day of my life," I wrote in a notebook. "We have taken John up to Utah Valley Hospital for an angiogram on his heart."

It took only forty-five minutes, and the nurses came to get Alysia, David, Eric and me to meet with the cardiologist.

I knew the news would not be good. I certainly hoped it would be better than what I was about to hear. He told us John needed four to six arteries and one valve replaced leading to his heart, and they would need to take the veins from his legs. His legs were full of fluid and damaged from the fire 30 years earlier. And, of course, his weight was against him, and he was also diabetic. He weighed over 300 pounds. There was only about 50 percent chance he would make it through the surgery. The cardiologist said his lungs were very weak and feared pneumonia would set in. He would not walk quickly, if ever, and a heart patient needs to walk. There were many risk factors due to his legs.

Today was Friday, and the doctor said he would like to do the surgery on Monday. John said he would like the weekend to think about it and put some things together. This was heavy news for all of us, and much was going through all our minds. If it was successful, he could live another few years or more, but the doctor said he had 3-12 months if he continued the way he was.

Eric took John home in his car, and David drove me in ours. Then the two boys drove back to Salt Lake together. John and I sat up and talked late into the night. Peace was with us, there was no fear, sorrow, or regrets; just joy for the plan of salvation and the knowledge that however long he had left, we would be together again. We expressed our gratitude for the life and family we had together and for what was still to come in the eternities.

We kissed good night and I went to my room. The only comfortable position he found was sitting on our couch. I could not stop the flow of tears as I knelt and pleaded with our Heavenly Father to help my husband with the decision that he needed to make in the next few days. If it was time for him to step through the veil, I would not stand in his way.

As I knelt and uttered these things from my heart, the image of me kneeling in a tiny room close to the hospital came to my mind. It was from when he had his first heart attack. I had felt the Holy Ghost with me as if he were putting his arms around me to comfort me whispering, "He will live." It was different this time. The same peace came over me and the sweetness of spirit; however, the thought came to me this time that, "time will be short, at best, with your sweetheart; make it as peaceful and bring as much joy to him as possible, and all will be well." I was pretty sure at that moment, that John would decide not to have the surgery, but knew it was his decision.

Some guilt set in me then. For the last few years, at times I had felt some resentment toward him. Every time I tried to get him to go to the cardiologist, he would not. He said that if he did, he would not come out alive, but in a black bag. As I knelt and prayed that night, this resentment completely left me and did not come back. I had asked the Lord so many times to help me get over this resentment. I did not like feeling this way. It was as if my eyes were opened and I could see clearly now; John had these feelings about it, and I had to respect them. Now I could see clearly what he had been fighting, and there was no doubt in my mind how brave and courageous he had been and was even now.

I got up from my knees and slipped into bed. The tears continued to flow. Sleep would not come, even though I had been up for twenty-three hours. I went in to where he was sitting and I sat next to him on the couch. He took my hand, and finally I slept. We both slept for a short time, and then I decided to put all these thoughts on paper.

I had felt for many years that when he steps through the veil and returns to Heavenly Father that he would be called on a mission, one of many. His Patriarchal Blessing said he would teach the gospel to those who have not yet been permitted to hear it. He would teach it in simplicity in many languages. Oh, how he loved to teach the gospel. Many were waiting to hear his testimony of Jesus Christ and his gospel so that they could move forward.

Those thoughts remained with me through the night. I knew my job was to make him as comfortable and joyful with the remaining time we had, and I was better prepared to hear his decision in the morning.

Looking back on that time six years ago, I now know that when John did decide to break his appointment with the doctor, his thoughts to not have the surgery done were for a purpose. He felt then if he had had it done, he would not live through it. Because of the promptings he had, I had him these additional years to help me through a difficult time in my life with cancer and dialysis.

On Saturday afternoon, he asked me to come sit with him and talk. He had made his decision. He was not going to have the surgery. He expressed many of his thoughts with me and asked how I was doing with it. I asked him if I could read something to him. I got my notebook and read what I had written down the previous night. The tears came, and I could hardly talk, but he needed to know that I understood. We were in complete harmony on the matter. We had both received the same answer to our prayers.

I had overwhelming images going through my head of me trying to take care of him and so many, many other things, such as work and fighting my own physical battles. I would rely on the Lord more than any other time in my life.

I had learned so long ago that when things go wrong, don't ask "Why me?" But to think "this is my assignment, and I will take care of it."

Two scriptures came to my mind as I tried to sort all of this out and see the picture come more clearly to my mind.

The Lord will give strength unto his people; the Lord will bless his people with peace.

Psalm 29:11
Bible

And it came to pass that there came a voice unto them, yea, a pleasant voice, as if it were a whisper, saying; Peace, peace be unto you because of your faith in my Well Beloved, who was from the foundation of the world.

Helaman 5:46-47
Book of Mormon

Chapter 27

His Spirit soared Like a Lion

Our lives changed drastically from that day. It had been twelve years from the time John had his first heart attack, when he was told he would have three to five years. Already, we had been given six years plus. We knew those had been a great blessing. Now, this doctor said he had "maybe a year." Would it be longer if he did not have the surgery?

When John told the doctor, he responded, "If I had to make the choice, that is what I would do, also." He had started to go downhill fast. He was unable to walk more than 10 feet at first, and then it got less and less. His breathing was labored, and when he tried to lay down, he felt like his chest was going to cave in. We tried different positions with the aid of pillows. His feet were swollen and painful. He had constant open sores that drained on his socks and pillows from his feet and legs, and they had to be changed several times a day.

In September, the family held a 73rd birthday party for him in Richfield. I reserved the park, and everyone came except Cindy and her family. They had been there over the Labor Day weekend. We started in the park, and then had to move to the church because of the weather.

John did not attend his own birthday party, though I had a wheel chair for him. The children came over to the house one family at a time to visit with him. When it came time for cake, we called him on the phone and the mighty Holmes chorus sang "Happy Birthday" to him.

I needed to get additional help to take care of him. In October, I called hospice. I could no longer bathe him. Julene, his nurse, had several good suggestions, including ointment for the water blisters on his legs where the grafting was from the fire. His legs leaked water constantly from the blisters. Hospice also sent a chaplain, Charlie Black, and he and John became great friends. Charlie was amazed at John's attitude on death and said that he taught him a lot.

There was one very energetic home care person who came three times a week and was always dancing. One day while she was bathing John, she started dancing and swung her leg above his head. That did it. Here he was, already stripped of his dignity. He didn't know if she targeted his head on purpose, but the whole incident was unnerving to him and he requested a change. The next one we got was referred to as "the sergeant," but her bark was worse than her bite. He told her he loved her before he passed on and made amends with the dancer.

I continued to work as much as possible, but it was getting so hard to leave him. Sometimes he would want someone to sit with him, and sometimes not. We had two volunteers from hospice; one was in her eighties and she would come and bring her knitting. The two of them could talk about anything. He called the other one "the whirl wind." She would run in, say hi, tell us about her family and all her trips, and then she was gone again.

Our old friends Bob and Mary Alice, their daughter Lora Lee, and her husband, John, were so helpful to us. They checked on us every day. Their friendship meant everything to us. Bob would come at about 6:30 a.m. on my dialysis days, and Bob and John would have a McDonald's sandwich breakfast together. Mary Alice would walk our dog, Vincent, and she volunteered to come and take care of John if I got called up for my kidney transplant.

The children were wonderful, each doing what they could from where they lived. David and Teresa were there two times a month helping in many ways. Eric and Heidi came as often as they could, as well as Linda and Eric. Their phone calls meant so much to me as well. Alysia was having her own battle with thyroid cancer and doing chemo and radiation treatment.

John had a desire to give each of the children a father's priesthood blessing. Each made it there one by one, so he could fulfil that desire. I had the privilege of hearing, recording, and putting them on the computer. I also requested one from him, and will treasure mine the rest of my life.

We had many visitors; some would come not knowing what to say to a dying man, while others brought good tidings to us. Whatever the case, John made them feel at ease with his humor and quick wit. They always left feeling uplifted and having received words of wisdom from him. People would say they came to cheer us up, and it would turn out just the opposite. One day when Linda and her family were there, John said he was going to "kick the bucket soon." Three-year-old Olivia said she wanted to "kick the bucket with Grandpa."

One Saturday evening, I was out walking the dog and I passed our bishop's home. He had offered to help with our utilities. Money was getting tight, and there were two large insurance policies on John. Both premiums had increased, totaling over $600 a month. I had done everything I could to pay those premiums. I could not let them lapse. I had cut down on my work, and I was getting exhausted. It took more time and effort to take care of John, and I needed to be with him. I had thought a lot about his offer, and decided I should talk to him again about the matter. I went up to the porch and rang the doorbell. He stepped out on the porch, and we talked about the utilities. He did not give me an answer. He was looking at me as if he were looking right through me, and he finally said, "No, Sister Holmes, I do not want your utilities.

I want your house payment." Tears filled my eyes; I had not seen that coming.

He later told me that the visit we had was a very spiritual experience that he needed. He had been out of town that Saturday morning, and on his way home he received a phone call that his daughter had been in a car accident in Logan. She was not hurt, but her car was totaled. He drove to Logan to help her, then drove back to Richfield to find additional family problems waiting for him. He was not in a good mood when I rang his doorbell. As we talked, he was overcome by the spirit. He, too, did not see it coming, but felt impressed to take the house payment. He thanked me as I was thanking him. He said he had wondered how he was going to put himself in the right frame of mind to hold meetings on Sunday, and how to feel the spirit he needed to conduct himself as a church leader.

John's condition worsened in November. Sometimes, I would just go into my room and cry because there was so little I could do for him. His courage and endurance were amazing. I watched him physically deteriorate. I also saw another change was coming. His spirit soared like a lion. I could see him draw closer and closer to our Heavenly Father. The discussions we had about the gospel were a treasure to me. His knowledge and understanding of the scriptures were a gift to him, and I would miss that so much when he was gone. By the end of November, he was on very heavy morphine for the pain. We knew that each attack he had in his chest may be his last one.

Julene said she was sure he would not be here for Christmas. Christmas came and went, and so did Easter and Mother's Day. He would take a few steps back and then stabilize. Those who visited continued to see the mighty spiritual growth. Nor did his sense of humor taper off. He would make us all laugh, and there was such a good spirit in our home. He was an example of endurance and expressed love to all that came. When I would share something about a family member or friend he would say, "Bless them."

There were times I felt extra help in our home, angels both seen and unseen. One night, we were in his work room. He had gone in to look at some of his pictures and reminisce. I was so tired from dialysis and work. I was trying to help him get up. I did not have the strength I needed, and wondered how I would care for his legs, feet, and other needs. I was sitting there asking myself how I was going to do it. Then I felt we were not alone in the room. In fact, I knew we were not alone; I had help. I got up and with great ease attended to his needs and helped him get settled for the night. I asked him if he felt what I had, and he said, "I saw my worn-out wife begin to move as if she had rested for hours instead of 15 minutes. I saw you with the energy and vitality of a much younger woman, and I wondered where it came from."

I told him, "We received extra help tonight," and I felt this several times during his last months.

He didn't complain much. He did ask a few times, "How long will this go on? What more do I have to do?" My answer was that his work was not finished, and when it was, he would be called home. There were still more lives for him to touch.

He had a blessing in February. In all the blessings he had, he was told he would have courage and strength to go through this. John was one who always said, "Give the blessing time to work." When I asked him in the latter part of April if he wanted another Priesthood blessing, he said, "no." In May, when he learned that David would be here on May 12, he said he wanted David, Bob, and our friend, John, to give him a blessing.

Dave and Teresa came, and again they wondered how he could still be hanging on. David told me after the blessing that in all the blessings he had given, he never felt like he did when he gave this one. He said, "the feeling was electrifying as I placed my hands on Dad's head, pronouncing the words that came to my mind."

In the blessing, John was told the time for him to step through the veil had been sped up. That loved ones were gathering to meet him. Others were being prepared to hear his testimony of Jesus

Christ. Preparations were being made for him, and he was to align himself with the prophets.

We knew time was short, but how short? We did not know. He asked me what I thought aligning himself with the prophets meant – having the knowledge of the prophets? The faith? He seemed puzzled. We discussed it off and on for a few days, and he felt satisfied that it was having the faith of the prophets and the desire to teach of Jesus Christ and our Heavenly Father.

John did ask me at one point, "Would be wrong to ask for a release from this life?"

I told him, "No, as long as it is qualified with, "Thy will be done."

He slept a lot that week and didn't feel like many visitors. He did keep saying, "It will be soon."

I was scheduled to work that Saturday. He thought it would be all right, but I had my reservations. When Saturday came, I got up and got ready for work. When I went to help him, he had already done things for himself. I was surprised. He looked at me and said, "I am going soon." He had said this so many times, but I decided not to go to work. I made arrangements for my work, and we had an enjoyable morning together and he ate a nice breakfast.

He wanted to watch television. I asked if he minded if I went to work for about an hour. We had nine events the next weekend, and I needed to prepare for them. I was scheduled for four of them myself, but I had the feeling I would not actually be there. He said, "Go ahead," and I called Mary Alice to see if she could sit with him and she did.

I left at 1:10 p.m. As I stepped out the door, I stopped, backed back into the room, and said, "I love you." He said, "I love you, too."

At 2:15 p.m., I had my work finished and was at the pharmacy to get some supplies John needed. Every time I went to reach for one, however, the thought came to me, "You won't need this." I did not buy anything for him. On my way home, I called him to tell him I was coming. He said, "Please hurry."

I got home at 2:40 p.m., said goodbye to and thanked Mary Alice, took care of a phone call, and then turned to him and said, "What can I do for you?" He said he needed the chair. By now, he used the portable toilet I stored in his bedroom. I went in to get it. I heard him pull himself up on the walker, heard a big sigh, and then he fell over the walker. He had fallen before, but this time it was different.

I turned and said, "John, are you with me? John, John!" He had me pinned into the bedroom, as he was right in front of the door. I managed to get around him and reached for a pulse. I looked at his face, and his long eyelashes were resting on his cheeks, with his eyes closed and a hint of a smile. It was now 3:04 p.m. on May 19, 2012, and my sweetheart was gone!

I have fought a good fight, I have finished my course, I have kept the faith.

2 Timothy 4:7
Bible

Wherefore, fear not even unto death; for in this world your joy is not full, but in me your joy is full.

Doctrine and Covenants: 101:36

Chapter 28

Love is a Many Splendored Thing

Where was the phone? I had just had it, and I needed to call the hospice nurse. I needed to call David. I needed to cry. I was out of breath, and nothing worked. I just held him, was he really gone? His face was so peaceful. Again, I felt for his pulse, wondering if in my haste I missed it.

I found the phone. The hospice nurse on call sent two policemen to lift him from the walker, and they were there in an instant. Yes, he was gone. David formed a network to notify the family. Friends came, and our new bishop of one week and his wife came. They were so much comfort to me. The bishop had visited John earlier that day. His body was on the floor, and I sat next to him, stroking his hand and arm and watching the change in his mortal body, and seeing the last sign of any life drain from his face.

They came from the mortuary to take him. They all stepped into the other room and said I could take as much time as I needed with him. Only then did the tears come. Eventually I let them take him, and inside my mind I was screaming, "Take me with you, take me with you!" I knew it was not my time, and I hoped he knew how much I loved him.

I knew he had stepped through the veil and was on the other side. I felt so many emotions, and especially joy for him. He could now go on those missions that he was promised he would. He could teach the gospel, one of his greatest loves. Had he aligned himself with the prophets? I did not know, but he had great faith and wisdom.

Alysia was the first to arrive, followed by Dave and Teresa. They were so much comfort to me. Craig and his wife Cindee came later. The rest were making arrangements to get there.

John had written an outline for his funeral, including those who would give prayers and talks. He wanted our daughters to sing the song "The Olive Tree." He loved the words in that song, and to hear his daughters sing. He had asked them years earlier to sing it when the time came. He also asked for the inscription on our headstone above our names to say, "Love is a Many Splendored Thing."

John's viewing was Wednesday night. When we got home, Kim decided she wanted to put his petrified frogs in the casket with him. He had two; he brought the bigger one home years earlier and insisted on keeping it. He loved showing his petrified frog. We found a baby one later and kept it, too. Kim was on a quest to find them, and she did. She put the box of frogs in the casket the next day, and all the children put some small item in that was a momentum of his. I put a letter I had written in his hand before we closed the casket. Justin said the family prayer, and then the grandchildren were all asked to come up and push the casket from the Relief Society room to the chapel. Justin and Jessica's little girl, Brylee, broke away from her parents and ran up to the casket crying out, "My papa, my papa!" She stole the show.

I could not have asked for a better tribute to him than was given at his funeral. Eric gave a talk on the plan of salvation, and the girls' song was beautiful, though they were having a hard time.

John's testimony, which he had written, was read. David told the story about the time there was a pile of wood at one of our homes and the wood had nails in it. Dave had stepped on one of the nails. His dad later asked him to go out and pull all the nails out of the wood and put them in a jar. Some of those nails were bent and rusty. In one of our moves after that, Dave had found that old jar of nails. His father had kept them for many years. Before John's death, Dave was out cleaning our shed again, but he did not find the old jar of nails. Instead he found some shiny new nails in their place. That is how he described his dad in the last part of his life. His spiritual growth had soared like that of a lion finding its own power. John had drawn on his own spiritual stamina and growth.

After the luncheon provided by the sisters of our ward, everyone headed for Logan, where he was going to be buried the next day. I came back to the house with Melissa and Jason, but I was quite disoriented. I could not find my money, or remember what I was going to take even though I had made a list. I was sure glad to have Jason, Melissa, and Madi with me.

While we were driving north, I could tell Jason had been touched by things said at the funeral, and he had many questions about the church. We talked all the way to Alysia's, about a two-hour drive. He had more questions after we got there. Justin was at the house, and he joined in the conversation to help explain things.

The cemetery was beautiful. It was the Friday before Memorial Day, and it was a lovely spring day. The Color Guard was there representing all our armed services, the gun salute was given, and I was presented the flag that covered his casket. Alysia read a poem she wrote, and David dedicated the grave. Linda's friends gave us another luncheon, and Kim's husband, Mark, gave the blessing on the food. Then the family had to leave for their homes.

I stayed at Linda's until Tuesday, so I could dialyze Saturday and Monday. I missed John so much, and I could feel his presence everywhere. Still, I could feel nothing but joy for him.

It was hard to get into any kind of a routine once I got home. Eating was a joke. I would get hungry, but didn't feel like cooking. I ate out a lot, and that got old fast. In June, I received the insurance money. I tried to be conservative with it. I paid off some bills, and bought a 2007 Buick Lucerne. I test drove several makes but kept going back to the Buick. The last time, I was test driving on the freeway. I felt like John was sitting there next to me saying, "You know you want it, go buy it." I did! It has been a great car for me.

To those who may be readers or listeners of this, I do have a few words to say about marriage. I certainly am not an expert, but draw from fifty-five years of being married to one person. It was a marriage I had set my goal to have long before I met my John. I knew I wanted an eternal marriage, to be married in the House of the Lord, his Holy Temple, for all time and into the eternities.

You must face challenges with faith, knowing that neither of you are perfect beings. You must work together to strengthen the bonds between you, striving to be one in heart. This does not happen overnight. It can take decades. Don't give up on each other. Learn to know their most intimate feelings. Work through any bad times together. There was a time when John's own mother said to me, "Why don't you divorce him?" I was shocked, and felt sad that she did not know her own son well enough to see the divine potential in him. He was a valiant spirit and a son of God, who loved Him.

Be faithful to your covenants – in thought, word, and specifically action. Learn to communicate, even if it begins with shouting; calm yourself, bridal your tongue! Pray, and make it a priority. Pray together and make it meaningful. Don't let your pride rule your life. We all have it. Sometimes we need to pray when it is the last thing we feel like doing.

Life is so busy nowadays. We are being pulled in so many directions, and Satan is having a hay day with that. We get so busy with life. Slow down, allow the spirit to come into your thoughts and guide, direct, and teach you. In our busy days, we forget to live a life that will help us return to Heavenly Father. Let that be your goal; the blessings are there for you and will not be withheld.

Sometimes we must put away the things of the world. Yes, I know that there are many, many good things out there. Try to make the decision between good, better, and best for the whole family – especially your spouse, who needs to be the most important person to you. Live so that their hurt is your hurt, and their concerns are your concerns. We live in a world where the question in any partnership (including marriage) is unfortunately: "What is in this for me?"

Your marriage is two people that are ever changing. None of us are completely the same as we were five or ten years ago. Hopefully, we are better than we were in the past, and are worthier to obtain exaltation in the celestial kingdom. Each man and each woman must be individually worthy of that blessing. Always, and I mean always, include the third partner in your marriage, and that is our Heavenly Father.

I do believe love is what you have been through together, and there is so much more to love than making love. It is when your two spirits unite, and you feel excitement because of your thoughts and goals, and you know it will be wonderful to be together forever. Does this just happen? Good grief. No! You must make it happen, and each must figure out his or her way! Do not give up on each other. I leave this thought with you also: Husbands, tell your wife you love her, even when her actions do not merit it; wives, tell him you love him when his actions do not merit it. Find something positive about each other. It will take you a long way.

It was a few months before I got back up to Logan to see the headstone. It was wonderful to see our names, an image of the temple where we were bound together for eternity, and the inscription that John had requested: "LOVE IS A MANY SPLENDORED THING!"

⌒𝓂⌒

Let the husband render unto the wife due benevolence: and likewise, also the wife unto the husband.

1 Corinthians 7:3
Bible

Thou shalt love thy wife with all thy heart, and shalt cleave unto her and none else.

Doctrine and Covenants: 42:22

Chapter 29

Receiving My Gift of Charity and Love

The kidney transplant was getting close – or so they kept telling me. I was at the top of the list. It had been seven years now. Being on dialysis was taking its toll on me. Some of the kids had said they did not know who was going to go first, dad or mom.

My only concern now was, "Am I getting too old?" Then one of my doctors told me she had attended a conference in Denver, where she had learned of an 81-year-old man receiving a kidney. That was good news to me. I never gave up on the blessing that Justin had given me seven years ago that I would be healed, even if I was to get a new kidney. I knew then I would wait upon the Lord, and I would continue to do so now.

I wanted to stay close to home in case the call came. I would only have a few hour's window to get things organized here and get to the transplant center in Murray, Utah. The first call came the end of September. I went up, all prepared and ready, but then the nurse told me that it was not the match they thought it was. I should go home and wait for another call. Some thought I should be angry about the situation, but I was not. I knew if it were not a complete match, it would only cause more problems. I stayed calm and waited. The second call came while I was having dinner with a friend. She got so excited that I needed to calm her down. She was driving me to Scipio, Utah to meet Eric, who would take me the rest of the way. We got about twenty-five miles out of town, and I got a call to turn back. This one was not going to work either.

On Oct. 21, 2012, a third call came in the afternoon telling me to be prepared to come in about six to eight hours, but not to leave until they called me. Finally, the call came, and the nurse said, "*Come.*" The doctor had left on a plane for Arizona to take the kidney out of the patient who was the donor. She would hand carry it to the plane, fly to the transplant center, and put it in me. Once again, I got there, and this time and it was a perfect match. The transplant team told me it took off the moment it was hooked up.

I remember thinking, "I just want John," as I came out of surgery. The nurses told the family I had been saying it for a while as I came out of the anesthetic. I said it again when they took me into my room. So many of the family were there, and they had kept those who weren't there as informed as they could. Dave stepped up to my bedside and told me it was him and that dad could not be there. It took me a minute to realize why! Alysia stayed with me for the night, and she was so helpful. The nurses were already overworked.

I went to Eric and Heidi's home in Bountiful to recuperate. They only kept me in the hospital for four days. Over the next two weeks, Eric and Craig took turns getting me to the hospital early in the morning to get blood draws. The kidney was working wonderfully and showed no signs of rejection. I had heard so many stories about having to stay in the hospital at least a month, or having to get new carpet and furniture in my home, or get rid of my pets in order to protect my weakened immune system. None of that was true. I did try to give my cat away twice, but both times he found his way back home.

I later found out the donor was a 35-year-old woman. I wrote a thank you/condolence letter to the family, but I never heard back from them. I wanted them to know that their loved one gave me the gift of life. The information was all kept very private, and I respected that. I felt I had received one of the greatest gifts— of charity and love—whether it was the donor's decision or her families.

In November, Ruth came to my home in Richfield. She was so much help to me, especially when I could not figure out how to empty the vent in my dryer and I thought someone had switched clothes dryers on me. I was on some strong pain pills for a while. She also got me hooked on the television series *Downton Abby*.

One of the things they had prepared me for was the fact that I needed to stay away from people and stay isolated for at least two months. I couldn't be in crowds or attend church, and I needed to wear a mask when people came. Cindy and her family came for Thanksgiving that year, and she prepared the food.

At the end of December, I was not feeling well. Every day, I thought, "tomorrow I will be better," but every day I was worse. Mary Alice kept telling me I seemed weaker and did not look well. A couple of days into January, I could hardly move. I called my doctor, who told me to get to Provo right away. Eric came again and got me there as quick as possible.

After much testing, they found I had a virus that about 40 percent of transplant patients get. It was very contagious, and I was put in isolation for about 12 days. I guess I was sicker than I thought. Eventually, I gained my strength back. Mary Alice went to get my medicine when I got home, she came back empty handed because my co-pay was $1,000 for a 10-day supply. I was not prepared for that. I had sent her with $40. I got that worked out, and there was a program to help me. I had to take the medicine for two months.

I relied so much on blessings of the priesthood during these years. They gave me so much comfort and strength. Usually these blessings were given by John when he was still alive, or one of our sons. At one of these, Craig was giving it and said that I had been a beacon to many people in my lifetime. Afterward, I asked him if I had ever been a beacon to him. He said very tenderly that I would never know how many times.

Melissa's son little Max was born in April of the following year. I so wanted to see him, Melissa, Madi, and Jason. She called and said their daughter, Madi, was going to be baptized in the early fall and they would have Max blessed then too. They were now living in South Carolina. I asked if she could wait until November around Thanksgiving and I would fly out and spend time with them and be there for both the baptism and blessing. Madi readily agreed to wait.

I had a wonderful time there. They treated me like a queen, showing me all the sights and telling me about the history. The plantation they lived on had so much history itself. The tour of the mansion alone was worth the trip. I saw tributaries, something I had never seen before – and those trees, they were something to see.

Little Max was adorable, and Madi was such a cute little second mother and quite a young lady. I was amazed at all the things she could do. She made bullets with her father, who had taught her a lot about guns. The plantation was a private hunting place for the owner, his associates, and their families. The owner employed Jason as a grounds man. Madi loved the horses, had ducks, sang, was a great swimmer, was in plays, and just an all-around girl. Melissa had provided her with many opportunities, places to go to, and things to learn.

I knew that it was time to get involved with John's genealogy from Finland. I also needed to continue work on Clara's line from Bohemia. It was something I had really procrastinated doing. I had no excuse now. I needed to do something with all the papers that had been saved in that old dilapidated box that was saved from the fire thirty-three years ago. Wow! Had it really been that long? Truly there is a time for all seasons, and it was my season to get going on this! The box contained what little information we had that our home teacher in Sandy had found at the genealogy library in Salt Lake back in 1977.

Some work had been done, but we hit a lot of walls. Mary Alice, an expert genealogist, did a lot of research and found some more information for us. Now there was a new computer program out called "New Family Search." What a wonderful tool it has become for the church and for all who wish to search out their ancestry. The church combined forces with an online family research called Ancestry.com.

I didn't know if I could learn all this at the age of 72 because I could not retain things like I used to. I was called to be a Genealogy Consultant by our bishop, and now I had to learn. I was happy that many I worked with over at the center were my age or older. We all felt our inadequacies, but we also knew that with the Lord's help, we could accomplish what we had to do and still learn new things.

No, there were no excuses. I had been blessed with a new fantastically functioning kidney, and my health was probably as good as it was going to get. The two things I had problems with were with my legs and back. Being on dialysis depletes your body of the good thing as well as the bad. My bones were weak, and I had osteoporosis. Yet, I had been given so many blessings. Now it was time that I started giving back gain.

I felt I had been preserved to do this work. Did I know if I could find many of those who were waiting to get out of spirit prison so that they could progress? These would be unfamiliar waters for me in many ways. These people were from Finland. John used to say, "Honey, will we ever find them?" I would reply that, "They may be lost to us, but they are not lost to the Lord."

I asked myself, "Is John finding them on the other side? Is he teaching them the gospel?" I knew what the New Year would bring – a lot of time at the Richfield Family History Center.

I will send you Elijah the prophet before the coming great of the great and dreadful day of the Lord: And he shall turn the hearts of the fathers to the children, and the hearts of the children to the fathers, lest I come and smite the earth with a curse.

Malachi 4:5-6
Bible

After this vision had closed, another great and glorious vision burst upon us; for Elijah the prophet, who was taken to heaven without tasting death, stood before us, and said: Behold the time has fully come, which was spoken by the mouth of Malachi – testifying that he [Elijah] should be sent, before the great and dreadful day of the Lord come—To turn the hearts of the fathers to the children, and the children to the fathers, lest the whole world be smitten with a curse—Therefore, the keys of this dispensation are committed into your hands, and by this ye may know that the great and dreadful day of the Lord is near, even at the doors.

Doctrine and Covenants 110: 13-16

Chapter 30

The Lord's Work Hastens; Miracles Still Happen

We have all heard someone say, "The day of miracles is over," or ask, "Why doesn't the Lord let miracles happen, like in the good old days?" When I have heard these things, I have felt sad for the individual who said it. If we open our eyes, we will see miracles all around us. I don't just mean when the white bud on a peach tree turns into a tasty pink and orange fruit, or the caterpillar turns into a beautiful butterfly, or when we hear the cry when a new baby is born, or how we depend on the sun to rise each morning and set in the evening. These are miracles that were organized to happen when the earth was created.

Even more than these natural miracles, we have miracles happen each day in our individual lives. Some do not recognize them to be what they are. People usually give credit to another person, or take credit themselves. They do not realize that all knowledge flows from heaven, from an Eternal Father, and His Son, Jesus Christ.

The internet was one of those miracles. Yes, as with all good things we know there is great opposition, and we know we must be careful and even prayerful that we do not get caught up in some of the bad things it offers. The Lord knew that the time would come that He would need to be hastening his work in order for the gospel to be proclaimed to all nations. That's why the internet and other technology were provided. The Lord gave the gifts needed to the individuals who brought this technology forth. Surely, these are all modern-day miracles.

I found much joy is in the family history center as I resumed the work for John's family, and a few of my own ancestors whose work had not been done. The new Family Search website is one of those miracles the Lord made happen, so we could find our families and connect generations.

I had the opportunity to work with brother Paul and his wife Martha. They were the directors of the Family History Center in Richfield. Paul inspired us. He was not only knowledgeable, he was very funny and patient with all of us, and he lived so close to the spirit. He had his own health battles with benign tremors and always used a wheelchair or walker. He did not feel well, but when he entered the history center, his mind was always quickened. He was amazing as he taught, helped, and assisted us in our work. Martha was his constant companion and knew the new Family Search program better than the rest of us, including Paul. She would get us out a predicament when we found ourselves in one, especially in the Finnish records. She would fix our problem and just say, "Oh, you kids!"

Here I was, learning this new program and researching the records of Finland. I was trying to learn their culture, how they named their children using the father's given name as their last name, and I was very confused. I saw my own miracle come as this knowledge unfolded. With the help of Paul, I was able to find many of John's family. It was amazing, and I felt the spirit of Elijah so strong. People would come into the center and wonder what was so special about this building. What they were feeling was the spirit of Elijah, and with that spirit came a very sacred feeling;

we saw many quiet miracles occur as people found their deceased ancestors and did their temple work.

Paul and I had been looking for John's father's grandfather for about three months. We had his grandmother and where her baby had been born. She had named her baby boy after her father. There was no marriage record to be found, and finally we decided the child had to been born out of wedlock. After spending so much time trying to figure out who he was, I said I wanted to go to another line and work on it. He agreed, and for about two months that is what I did. I found several families during those months.

I walked into the center one day and Brother Paul said, "Sister Holmes let's go find that grandpa!"

I said, "You mean the one we spent weeks looking for?" He nodded, and we went to the computers. For almost three hours we sat there looking. I was following his direction and interjecting some of my own thoughts as to how we could find him.

We finally had it narrowed down to two men. He said, "One of these is your grandpa." By that time, it was time to leave our shift, and we said we would continue next week.

For two nights I could not sleep. I tried to figure out the formula he used to find these two men. Paul seemed to know every way there was to trick the computer, and it almost always worked. I was stifled. On the third day, I was driving by the center and saw his car. I went in and asked for about two minutes of his time. I asked him how he had concluded that "grandpa" had to be one of these two men. He looked at me, looked into my eyes, and said, "LaVelle, sheer inspiration." I knew he was telling the truth, and that was the only conclusion I had come up with as well. I left and could hardly wait until we met again.

When it was my assigned day I went to the center. Paul was waiting for me. We sat in a corner of the room because I had so many papers to spread out. We went to the place on the computer that we had previously been and brought the names and information up on these two men. We quickly ruled one out, since nothing seem to fit as we looked at it again. When we went to the second name, we found not only him, but also his parents, a brother ten years older than him, and his sister. We studied it a moment and then he pointed to the younger brother's name. He was the same age as the mother of the child. Paul said, "There's your grandpa!" A feeling started to come over me that something was wrong. I knew that the younger brother was not our grandpa – it was the older brother. Then I had one of my own miracles. It was not just Paul and me in that corner. We were surrounded by so many of the family members. We both felt them and knew they were there with us. I could feel their joy. They had been waiting for us to find them, and I am sure helped in every way they could.

I was glad I was sitting by the corner because I was so overtaken by the spirit and emotion that I turned my head to the wall and fought back the tears. Paul was having a hard time controlling his emotions as well.

Now, the papers that were preserved from the fire held even a greater meaning to me. I felt even a greater connection to those whose information was found because of the few names and clues in that old dilapidated box, and for the prompting I received the day I put it under the bed. It is hard to describe my feelings. I know that some were allowed to help me, and they gave me guidance as I searched for the additional names, dates, and places in the computer.

There are other wide-spread miracles I have witnessed in my life. Lowering the missionary age to the age of eighteen for the elders and nineteen for the sisters brought untold miracles as missionaries surged in number. They could now reach out earlier to those who had been prepared to hear their testimonies all over the world. I was able to be a small part of that in Richfield as I accompanied many sets of young missionary sisters when they were teaching men who were ready to receive the gospel. For legal and safety reasons, they had to have a third sister with them if they entered a home where no other women were present. So, I saw a glimpse of this marvelous work.

One of the men I went to see with the young sisters was named Royal. Royal had quite a life and was a good man. He had lost his wife, and his family lived in other states. He did not see them often. He had bone cancer and was in a bad way. He studied the Book of Mormon with us and became quite a scholar of it. On January 30, 2015, he was baptized. When we were visiting him several weeks later, he was somewhat depressed. He told us that now he had found the true gospel, and by that time he had received the priesthood, but because of his health he was not able to serve the Lord. That made him sad.

We talked to him about temple work and asked if he had any idea if any of his deceased family had been members of the church. He did not think so. We asked him to gather names and dates and places or whatever he had or could remember by our next visit. He had a few names and places, and he met us at the Family History Center. In less than two weeks, we had found nineteen of his deceased family members who had not had their temple work done. He was overjoyed and knew his prayers were answered. He was able to go to the temple and witness the youth doing the baptisms and confirmations for them. We are still working on him getting to the temple to receive his own endowment.

It was in November of 2014 that I once again rolled over in my bed and felt something. Was the lump I felt in my right breast what I thought it was? One more time, the doctor confirmed my suspicion, and now my right breast needed to be removed. As I talked to the Lord about this surgery, I felt it would just be one more hurdle to get over and then I could and would get back to my work.

On Dec. 1, 2014, Craig took me to the University Hospital for the surgery. Again, my prayers were answered. I only needed one pain pill after the surgery and did not require radiation or chemotherapy. I would only need to be on cancer pills for the rest of my life.

I went to Linda and Eric's home in Logan to convalesce from this surgery. Linda and her children Olivia and William were my nurses. I was able to attend some of the grandchildren and great-grandchildren's holiday programs while I was there. I did resume my work at the family history center right after the turn of the year.

Verily, verily, I say unto you, the hour is coming and now is, when the dead shall hear the voice of the Son of God: and they that hear shall live.

John 5:25
Bible

I beheld that the faithful elders of this dispensation, when they departed from mortal life, continue their labors in the preaching of the gospel of repentance and redemption, through the sacrifice of the Only Begotten Son among those who are in darkness and under the bondage of sin in the great world of the spirit of the dead. The dead who repent beyond the veil will be redeemed, through obedience to the ordinances of the house of the God.

Doctrine and Covenants 138: 57-58

Chapter 31

No Bologna in Heaven

I cherish the dreams I have had with John in them since his passing. When I wake, I feel so close to him. Most have seemed so real they have awakened me, and I feel inclined to write them down. It helps to reflect on them when I especially feel lonesome.

In one, I had gone to church on a Sunday morning. I had some papers in my hand and took them down near the front of the chapel to give them to a sister. When I turned around, I saw John standing at the back of the chapel. I was so happy to see him and that he was there with me. We smiled at one another as I walked up to him. He took my hand and led me over to the left side of the chapel, third row, where we had usually sat before he died. We sat there and continued to hold hands all throughout Sacrament meeting. When the assigned sister gave the prayer and said amen, he then rose and turned to me and said, "I need to go now." I smiled and said, "I know," and he was gone. When I awoke from my dream, I had the sweetest and most beautiful feeling.

In another dream, we were both in a very large building similar to a high school for about 3,000 students. John was in the front of a classroom facing a lot of people sitting and waiting to hear him speak. I was talking to him and asking if he could come with me when he was done. He did not answer. Finally, I stepped out of the room and stood at the door and listened. The things that he was telling them were so wonderful, I could tell why they were so anxious to hear him. I left and was going to all parts of the building doing different things, talking to a lot of people, helping in any way that I could. It seemed much later, and I became anxious to get back to him and afraid he would be gone. He was still in the room, but this time he was alone. I was glad because now maybe he could come with me and see what I had been doing. When I asked him, he declined and said he could not come. That made me sad, but once again I understood. He told me the time would come when we could do things together again.

When I woke from the dream, it was so understandable. We were in two different spheres, both doing what we needed to do – him teaching, and me, I'm not sure. Whatever I do, hopefully I am doing some good because he certainly was. I was fascinated that it seemed like we were in a school. He was teaching the gospel, and I was trying to keep things running as smooth as I could.

Another dream concerned his father. I had passed through the veil and was standing by John. We were surrounded by people, some I recognized and others I did not. I felt a special connection to all of them. It was a joyful time, and they were thanking me for what had been done for them. I felt much love and gratitude for them for giving me the privilege and for doing their part as each generation had been allowed to come to earth.

In a distance I could see John's father standing with his arms folded. He did not approach me, and I did not move toward him. I kept visiting with those around me. It was a wonderful time, but I felt like I needed to be with Father Holmes.

He had little use for me when he was alive except that John and I had given him nine wonderful grandchildren. One reason for his attitude toward me was that he did not think I would be faithful to John. The other reason was that I had taken his boy, and John had joined the Church of Jesus Crist of Latter-Day Saints. Father Holmes did not think we were Christians. I looked at him again, and there was a softening that came over him. He stretched out his arms and he moved toward me. I moved toward him and we embraced. I knew he had accepted the gospel and that he was grateful for the work that had been done for him and his people, those who I now call my people as well.

Probably the funniest dream I had was when I was dreaming that I was asleep in my bed. I woke up because I heard someone moving things in my refrigerator. I got up, slipped into my robe, and walked in the living room to peek around the corner and see who was there. It was John, and he was frantically pushing things around in the refrigerator. He looked up and saw me and asked, "Where is the bologna?" I said, "I don't buy it anymore because you are not here to eat it." He was very disappointed and said, "I thought for sure you would have bologna, because there is no bologna in heaven! There are a lot of other good things, but I still like my bologna!" When I woke from this dream, I was a little bewildered and found it to quite amusing. I sure do hope there is watermelon in heaven!

Another dream was strange and woke me right up on the night of March 10, 2015. I was dreaming that I was sitting on a bench in the middle of a field. On my right side were many large and sometimes wild animals. They were all used to me and were grazing and enjoying the warmth of the sun. At my left were many small animals: chickens, ducks, rabbits, squirrels. I saw in the distance a man walking toward me in a grey suit. He was walking in the middle of the gentle animals. As he got closer, I realized it was John. He said he came to talk to me and had to make some important decisions. He asked me if I still loved him. I was surprised at the question. He said he did not think I did. At first, I assured him that I did, but the more he said to me, the more defensive I became. Why would he question my love? Finally, he said, "Well, I have my answer." He picked up a suitcase, which he did not have as he approached me, and started to walk away. He continued to walk from me through the small animals and he did not look back. I sat there bewildered and in despair.

I got up and started walking toward the large animals; suddenly, they went wild. I called for John and in an instant, he was there with me. He calmed the animals, and they went back to their grazing. He started to leave, and I whirled around and caught his arm. Only then did I notice how soft and smooth the fabric of his suit was. He turned toward me, and our eyes met. No words were spoken as we looked into each other's eyes. It seemed like the fifty-five years we had spent together on this earth passed between us, and I felt a lifetime of emotions in only a few seconds.

I felt hurt and wanting to hurt, anger and joy, love for him and not loving him, always needing him, calmness, and yet turmoil. Each of our children's birth flashed before me. I saw times when we made decisions together and other times when we did not. I saw times I felt begrudging about this and I did not want to forgive, yet wanting to be forgiven. Should I let this drive us apart? No, too many good things had come from our marriage. I saw in his eyes rejection, yet I saw wanting and being wanted. I felt ever changing, yet constant feelings of love and learning from each other.

The scenes of the last months that we spend together rolled through my mind and I felt something that even then, I did not feel. Suddenly, I felt a spiritual connection between us that was so powerful that I began to tremble. I became so weak I was sure I would collapse. Then he took me in his arms and strength entered my body again. I was surer than ever that our two spirits were connecting with love more than they ever had before we came to this world and while we were together during this mortal probation. He told me he would always be there for me.

Then I woke up wondering what all this meant. It was maybe just a dream, yet I couldn't think there was no meaning behind it. What do we know about dreams? Much has been written, so many opinions given by the experts that study the human mind. I decided there must be a lesson for me in this dream. I do know, too, that the Lord has used dreams to teach, guide, and direct his people sense the beginning of time.

First, I never should take our love for granted. Second, we had something so special, something some never find. It was confirmed to me, again, how life is so precious both here and in the spirit world. There is much to do here, and there will always will be a lot to do there; we can experience the joys our Heavenly Father wants us to, and we change and grow with these experiences. The covenants we make in the Holy House of the Lord are binding no matter where in the universe we are. Also, I came to realize that the emotions we feel can be bridled if we apply the everlasting principles into what we are feeling and take control of our whole self. Perhaps this dream meant nothing, but I know that I feel I will never take whatever is good for granted again.

It took some time to figure out what this dream may have meant. John was in heaven, where it is peaceful (small gentle animals). I was still in the world where there is much commotion going on around us including wars and rumors of wars (large animals). John, as my eternal companion, would be there for me because of the love we had for one another and all that we had gone through together when he was here with me.

As for his leaving with the suitcase and saying he had some decisions to make, I felt he would be continuing to teach the gospel to others who had not had the opportunity of knowing about it while they were here on earth. Others, who it would take all his commitment and dedication to our Savior to teach. He needed to know I was still in complete harmony with him and had my love to sustain him. The love that he will always have.

I felt again, as I did when he had to make the decision concerning heart surgery in 2011, that I would not stand in his way.

I have recalled a dream he shared with me before he died. He had dreamed he was teaching ancient Chinese people and how much he had learned to love them. I had asked him, "Was I with you?" He said, "No, you couldn't come with me yet, but you will be!"

If we live in the spirit, let us also walk in the spirit. Let us not be desirous of vain glory, provoking one another, envying one another.

Galatians 5:25-26
Bible

Wherefore, lift up thy heart and rejoice, and cleave unto the covenants which thou hast made.

Doctrine and Covenants 25:13

Chapter 32

Oh Our Fair Ones

In 2016, I celebrated my 75th birthday. The family put on a fantastic celebration for me with so many surprises. I will reflect on that day for the rest of my life. Those who were in attendance were "Our Fair Ones." There were a few who could not come because of distance and time of year, a new baby who didn't come, a grandson on a mission, and one that could not get off work. The party was fun, with tributes, stories, games, talents, music, and, as always, good food. I also learned that on my birthday in 1649, England's King Charles I, was beheaded. Also, the Lone Ranger, a favorite radio show, was heard for the first time in 1933.

The grandchildren sang one of my favorite songs, "We'll Bring the World His Truth." I taught this song when it was first introduced to the primary. I was the primary chorister in the Bountiful Ward. I cannot explain the powerful affect it has on me since I first heard it.

What a beautiful family. There are over 80 of us now, counting in-laws, grandchildren, and great-grandchildren. Over the next few decades it will continue to increase. In a few generations there will be hundreds. They are beautiful in spirit and body. I have felt impressed for several years that I should write my story and share it with my posterity and others. The things I want to share the most are my testimony of the gospel of Jesus Christ and my love for my Heavenly Father and His son Jesus Christ. Everyone has a story, and each is unique; this has been mine. Just the story of a simple woman who loves her family, friends, and life, who gives thanks to Him from whom all blessings flow—starting with life itself. I put my God and His son before anybody, for I know that when I do that, all other things will come together.

Last August, while shopping in the produce department, I was reaching for a bag of green grapes when the thought came in my head, "LaVelle, you need to go on a mission." It startled me; it was a quiet yet very clear voice that I heard, and it came completely as a surprise. I finished my shopping, but could not get the thought out of my head. For the next few months, I told myself every reason that I should not go on a mission. My health was a concern, and my dog. I was already thinking of selling my home and moving to Logan where John was buried so I could be closer to family. The excuses were all there, yet the thought was still there also. The song "We'll Bring the World His Truth" was forever going on in my head.

We had a family gathering in Logan at the end of August. Dave, Eric, Justin, and son-in-law Eric Jensen were there, and I took the opportunity to talk to them and get their input on the fact that I was thinking of selling my home. I said nothing of going on a mission. In October, my house was listed by my son-in-law Eric, as he was a very successful realtor. An offer came in January, which I accepted. As it turned out, it did not go through. About a week later, a second offer came, and it was far better than the first. They offered my full asking price in cash.

I had gone in and talked to the bishop just to see if I was too old to go on a mission. I asked him the question, and he never did answer me. (What a wise man!) Before I left his office, I had been entered in the online missionary system, had my picture taken, and was given a missionary book. I walked out of the church wondering what just happened. I felt it was all good; I had peace about selling my home and starting a new chapter of my life.

Tonight, March 16, 2016, is the night before I close on the sale of my home here in Richfield Utah. I sit here to finish this chapter of my book, which I felt so impressed to share with you. It is by no means the last chapter of my life, and there are some thoughts I want to share now.

My patriarchal blessing tells me that my mission in life is to publish glad tidings to all that I associate with. The glad tidings spoke of includes the good news of the Gospel of Jesus Christ. I'm meant to share my testimony and love of the Savior and of our Father, and to tell you each how much you are loved by them. Please always know that our Father loves each of us. He wants you to succeed in every way that is good in this life. He wants you to return to him, and many blessings await each of us if we will learn all we can of him, trust him, and trust that by obeying the commandments, we will receive untold blessing throughout eternity for us and our love ones.

I know He does hear and answer our prayers. Some are answered quite quickly, some we must wait upon him to answer, and sometimes he even says, "No!" I have learned that when that happens, it is because there is something much better in store for us. We must be humble, submissive, and repentant. It is also so important to be forgiving of others, lest we cannot progress, and our hearts wax cold.

I pray that you listen to the Holy Ghost when it comes to you, heed it, and act accordingly. Sometimes it is not a warning, but a direction that God wants you to go in that will benefit you. Sometimes, bad things come in a disguise. They look so attractive that we can find no reason not to pursue them, but if the warning comes to avoid it, **run, run, and then run faster** in the other direction. The cunning one wants you, and he wants you in the worst way. You have something that he will never have; your wonderful body.

You are choice spirits of our Heavenly Father, preserved to come in this dispensation of time. You were valiant in the pre-existence, and you are now. You can determine if you are going to return to Heavenly Father with honor or not. Each of us has been born of royal blood. We must try our hardest to learn the commandments, to know why they have been set in place as they have, and to believe the promises that will come to us by keeping those commandments. In this manner, we will have everlasting joy, not just momentary pleasure. If you can't see why a commandment should apply to you, don't try to reason it out. We should not pick and choose. Let us learn to put our trust in the Lord and lean not unto our own understanding. I have used that formula, and believe me, it works! Don't ask me how. It just does!

We were chosen to come now. We may have to stretch ourselves to do that which is required of us, and we may have questions which put us in a spiritual wrestle to find the answers we seek. That is okay; having questions is a good thing, because that is how we learn more about our Savior's gospel. I know I have learned the most when I have had my own spiritual battles. It makes me stronger, so I can testify of Him more.

We live in troubled times. Well, guess what? There have always been troubled times. The world is ever changing, and there is much corruption and will continue to be. It is lurking around many corners; the evil one is trying to keep us from the glory of God. But by following the prophet, staying close to our Savior in every way, and doing the simple things—like saying our daily and family prayers, as well as reading and pondering the scriptures— we will have peace in our souls and strength to go on, no matter what is going on in the rest of the world.

Our Savior will return. How will He find us? Will we be living the commandments and enjoying the blessings by doing so, or will we find ourselves choosing the ways of the world? Remember, God is the same yesterday, today, and tomorrow. Let us be the sons and daughters that honor Him, and He will honor us as the final curtains are drawn on the earth's mortality of mankind. Learn who you are and continue to fill your full potential.

Please, I urge you to have family home evenings. I wish our family had held more of them. Teach your children about God. If you do not, the world will teach them about things that may give them worldly pleasure, but it won't teach them how to obtain eternal blessings. Acquaint them with the "Proclamation to the World." It was written for the world.

If the time ever comes where you find you or your family in a situation where it feels like the world is completely against you because of your belief in the Savior's true and complete gospel, do not despair. Stand by the prophet and his apostles; they will not deceive you. You may feel alone, but you will not be. God our Father, the Savior, and the Holy Ghost will be with you, as well as a host of angels. Do not deny them! In time, the blessings that await you will be beyond your wildest dreams and to your utmost satisfaction.

I want to tell you of my love of the scriptures. I am so grateful to those in ancient days who, in many cases, gave their lives to preserve the Bible so it could be passed down through generations of time. We can in no way appreciate what they sacrificed to do this for us and mankind. I know the Book of Mormon is true, and that it is a second witness to the Bible and of Jesus Christ. It was preserved to come forth in these latter days; the Lord had designed for it to come now for our benefit, as well as for all his children. We must share it with everyone to whom we are given the opportunity. Each time I finish reading it, I feel like I am saying goodbye to some old friends. I pray I may be worthy to someday be in the presence of those I read about in the Book of Mormon, or at least be worthy to get a glimpse of them.

I visualize the great prophet, Mormon, hundreds of years ago, looking out at his people and how they had come to the state they were in. He cried out, "O, ye fair ones." (*Mormon 6:17, Book of Mormon.*) He was in despair; tens of thousands of his people had turned away from God and all He taught, even after so many blessings had been provided. We are in a battle today, the greatest of all battles, and we must put on the armor of God and do all we can to help win this battle. Those who accept, love, and follow Jesus Christ are His "fair ones."

Mormon asked, "How could ye have rejected that Jesus, who stood with open arms to receive you?...But behold, ye are fallen, and I mourn your loss...Behold, ye are gone, and my sorrows cannot bring your return.

"...The Eternal Father of heaven knoweth your state; and he doeth with you according to his justice and mercy." (*Mormon 6:17-22, Book of Mormon*)

Fair ones, may we heed the warning that is given here, and change this remorseful scene to a joyful one when it is our time to return to our Heavenly Father. May we always give glory to Him and His Son, Jesus Christ, when our probation and journey in this mortal life ends. Let us serve Him, love him, and love each other. May we keep the commandments and cherish the covenants that we have made so that *He* will stand with arms stretched wide open and say, '*My fair one, come, come unto me.*'

I think back to that paper I wrote in a small United States History class so many decades ago, where I testified of the Prophet Joseph Smith. I knew then as I testify to you now that he was and is a prophet of God, preserved to come forth in our dispensation and be instrumental in the restoration of the fullness of the gospel of Jesus Christ. It was restored so we can enjoy all the blessings of this life and throughout eternity if we choose to follow our Savior. He was pre-ordained for his mission as were all the previous prophets in ancient times, each working under the direction of Jesus Christ. These are the glad tidings I am to share, and I do share them with you, my fair ones; my family, my posterity, my friends. We are all the children of God. Remember always that you are loved and are of infinite worth.

So, what about that mission? Well, tomorrow I close on my house and in a few weeks, I go to Richland, Washington, to live with my sister Ruth while I serve a mission in the Family History

Center there. I am returning to my roots. Washington is where I first heard of the gospel of Jesus Christ and where my testimony began and flourished. Perhaps I can return and help someone waiting there gain their testimony of the wonderful Plan of Salvation and of the love and blessings that our Father in Heaven has waiting for them. Another great adventure awaits me.

So, to all my wonderful family and my dear, dear friends......

I love all Our Fair Ones!!

The Lord is my shepherd; I shall not want. He maketh me to lie down in green pastures: He leadeth me beside still waters. He restoreth my soul: he leadeth me in the path of righteousness for his name's sake. Yea, though I walk through the valley of the shadow of death, I will fear no evil; for thou art with me; thy rod and thy staff, they comfort me. Thou prepareth a table before me in the presence of mine enemies; thou anointest my head with oil; my cup runneth over. Surely goodness and mercy shall follow me all the days of my life; and I will dwell in the house of the Lord forever.

Psalms 23:1-6
Bible

Epilogue

Reflection on the Mission, May 20, 2017

My son Eric drove with me to Richland. It was so good to see Ruth and her family.

The director of the Richland Family History Center met with me a few days later. He showed me what I needed to do, and I got acquainted with their routine and some of the consultants. I was familiar with the things they had, and was impressed with the books and materials available. We went downstairs and met the assistant director, and he asked if I had been shown the storage room.

It was full of boxes, old computers, etc. At the far end were some large binders, each three or four inches thick. There were over three dozen of them. I was drawn to them, and inquired about them. They contained family histories. Some were brought in by families who did not want them, but had felt they should not throw them away. Many belonged to a brother whose mother had done years of research. Before she could finish her work, she passed away from cancer. There had not been enough consultants to continue the work needed to complete her work.

I stood there and I was completely drawn to these binders. I felt the Spirit of Elijah stronger than I had ever before, and I felt there were many in this small storage room saying, "At last we will be found." I asked if I could work on the binders in my spare time.

I finished up with the director and walked out of the family history center. I got in the car and drove off, only to pull off to the side of the road because I was overcome with emotion. I was afraid I may cause an accident if I kept going. I totally was not prepared to have the experience I had just had. The spirit I felt became stronger, and the tears flowed. At last, I knew why I was here; there was a special assignment for me. I asked for Heavenly Father's help as I undertook this work.

So, my project began. I spent my spare time extracting names and matching them up with what was already in the computer. I did a lot of research to connect these families together. Some days it was routine, but when I made a major breakthrough, it was so rewarding.

I did most of my work in the 1700 and 1800s. I would find missing parents, spouses, children, and sometimes whole families because of one name.

I had found a family written in the first census in 1790. The parents and six children were listed with their names, birthplaces, birthdates, and their deaths. When I compared it to the work in the computer, everything was a match. I thought to myself, "this is an easy one," but for some reason, I could not turn the page. It was like it was stuck. I compared everything again and knew something was wrong. After some time, I finally decided to continue although the feeling stayed with me that something was not right. The next day, I again worked on this family to no avail.

That night I had a dream where a small boy was standing, looking at me with a pleading look on his face. I woke up and knew this little boy belonged to this family but had no way to prove it. Who was going to take my word? My dream didn't have a paper trail. I contacted my director, who said to continue and maybe something would give us a clue. He was right.

Several days later, I found a letter written in 1830 from an aunt to a niece concerning this family. In the letter, she listed the father, mother, and all six children, as well as their dates and places of birth. In her last sentence before she closed, she wrote that there was another little boy who died at the age of 3 or 4. He had been born between census and did not show on any other family record.

I knew this was the boy in my dream. He did not need to have any of his ordinance work done because he did not live to the age of accountability, but he needed to be sealed to his family for time and eternity. I felt elated to find this letter. I again called my director, and he had me call the Salt Lake Family History Center. When they heard the story, they gave permission to get this small boy sealed to his family immediately. I cannot imagine the joy that was felt by these parents when he was sealed to them for time and eternity. I felt great happiness for them!

I had found two families that lived in the same town. The fathers were born the same year and had the same name. Their wives had the same name, also, and there were 23 children. Some shared the same name and same year of birth. They lived in the early 1800s. My question was whether there were really two men, or whether one had married two women with the same name. I knew I had to straighten this family (or families) out if I could. After prayer and research, I inquired with other workers if they had ever done any research on this family name. No one could recall doing so, but one sister told me there were seven books downstairs that had that name combined with other families.

When I looked at these books, they were each two-three inches thick. I stood there and thought to myself, "Oh help! This will be like looking for a needle in a haystack!" I pulled a book out that could be a possibility if they were in alphabetical order. I laid it on the table and walked over to get a chair. When I returned, the book was open. When I looked down, I saw the name of the man or men I was looking for. I could not believe my eyes. There **were two** of them; they were cousins, and both had been named after their grandfather. Both were born the same year and married women with the same name. One had eleven children and the other twelve. With this information, I could make sure the information in the computer was correct. It took time and research, and it was worth every moment of it.

While shopping one day, pushing an empty cart, I lost all strength in my left leg and was in great pain. I had cracked a bone behind my knee. I thought, "I really don't need this!" I had only been there for six weeks, and I was determined to not let this stop me from my work. So, with help from Ruth, a cane, a walker, and the young elders to get me into the history center, I was able to carry on.

I found sisters who were alone in the ward I attended. I asked them if they had a family home evening group. They did not, so we formed one. I grew to love these women. We had a lot of fun, as well as some inspiring spiritual discussions. I also became friends with the people who worked other shifts at the history center.

I was also invited to meet monthly in another family home evening group. It was hosted by the stake Patriarch and his wife. They had such a lovely, sweet feeling in their home. On Monday mornings, we attended an institute class where we studied the powerful book of Revelations.

I was also called to teach gospel doctrine, teaching the last few classes of the Book of Mormon, and then the Doctrine and Covenants until May of the year 2017. Teaching is one of my passions.

I had always wanted to go to the Columbia River Temple, and now I took the opportunity whenever I could. I experienced many sweet things there. I learned the story of how that temple came to be. Now it stood in the place that we had hunted rabbits so many years ago.

I so enjoyed the privilege of living with my sister, Ruth, and getting to know her again. Knowing her better is loving her more. We shared so many of the same values, including our belief in Jesus Christ. We sometimes laughed and talked as only sisters can do. I got to know her family better as well, and I shared in their successes and trials. I love them more now.

On May 19, 2017, David flew to Pasco to drive me to Logan, Utah, where I was to live. I knew that at some time after the passing of John, I would move there. What I did not know was that I would take a detour to Richland, Washington, to have an unforgettable year in my life.

My daughter Linda and her good husband, Eric, had bought a home with me in mind to live in. They had it ready for me to move in upon my arrival. With the help of her sisters, who lived far away, and other family members, the home was furnished with all that I needed.

As I have worked for the dead as well as served with the living there is a prayer in my heart that I hope each of us can come to understand. It is said so well in both the Bible and the Book of Mormon:

> *And the King shall answer and say unto them, Verily I say unto you, Inasmuch as ye have done it unto one of the least of these my brethren, ye have done it unto me.*

Matthew 25:40
Bible

> *And behold, I tell you of these things that ye may learn wisdom; that when ye are in the service of your fellow beings ye are only in the service of your God.*

Mosiah 2:17
Book of Mormon

Glossary

Brief descriptions of terminology used by the
Church of Jesus Christ of Latter-Day Saints

Note: These explanations and definitions are meant to clarify the unique terms used by the Church of Jesus Christ of Latter-Day Saints mentioned by LaVelle throughout her memoir. More information about any of these topics can be found online at www.churchofjesuschrist.org

Age of accountability: The age in which children are believed to understand enough to be accountable for their actions on a spiritual level. It is scripturally stated to be at eight years of age, and at this point children can choose to be baptized. Before this point, they are believed to be free of sin due to the Atonement of Jesus Christ and do not need baptism because they are not accountable.

Angels: Scripturally, angels are messengers from God. There are accounts of angels in both the Holy Bible and the Book of Mormon. Members of The Church of Jesus Christ of Latter-Day Saints believe in the ministering of angels in the present time as well as the accounts given scripturally.

Apostles: In the New Testament, Jesus Christ called twelve men to be His apostles. They led the church at the time and shared the truths Christ had taught them. Members of the Church of Jesus Christ of Latter-Day Saints believe that Christ has once again appointed twelve apostles through his modern-day prophet. They, with the prophet, lead the church through revelation from Jesus Christ.

Armor of God: Based on the scriptures Ephesians 6:11-17 in the Bible, it is a metaphor for righteousness. Putting on the Armor of God symbolizes protecting oneself through virtues such as faith, hope, charity, courage, obedience to commandments, etc.

Baptism: In the New Testament, Jesus Christ was baptized by being completely immersed in the River Jordan. Members of The Church of Jesus Christ of Latter-Day Saints believe that in order to follow the path that Christ modeled for all people, baptism by immersion is a necessary and sacred action. Baptism is considered the first step in a commitment to follow Christ. A person may be baptized after turning 8 years old (see *Age of Accountability*). Members believe that they covenant (or promise) God that they will always remember Christ, take His name upon them, and keep His commandments. In return, they are blessed with the Gift of the Holy Ghost given through confirmation. (see *Confirmation*).

Beehive: A class in the Church's Young Women's program for girls aged 12-13. In 2019, changes were made to the Young Women's program and the former class names of Beehive, Mia Maid, and Laurel are no longer used.

Bible: Also known as the Holy Bible, this is a scriptural account traditionally made up of both the Old and New Testaments. It contains records and prophecies of the ancient Israelites, as well as the life, miracles, and teachings of Jesus Christ. Members of The

Church of Jesus Christ of Latter-Day Saints use the King James Version of The Holy Bible for their studies.

Bishop: The person who presides over a local congregation (see *Ward*). Like all callings in the Church, the role of bishop is unpaid. The Stake Presidency over an area extends the call to be a bishop (see *Stake*). A bishop traditionally serves for approximately five years before a new one is called, though there are instances where the call may be longer or shorter depending on his circumstances. His responsibilities include leading the ward (particularly the youth), caring for the poor and needy, overseeing missionary work, managing ward finances, and many other obligations. He is assisted by two counselors, an executive secretary, clerks, and the leaders of the other ward organizations (such as the Relief Society president).

Bishopric: Comprised of the bishop and two counselors, a bishopric presides over a ward (local congregation) in The Church of Jesus Christ of Latter-Day Saints.

Book of Mormon: The Book of Mormon is another testament of Jesus Christ to be studied along with The Holy Bible. It contains the writings of ancient prophets on the American continent who taught and followed the prophecies and teachings of Jesus Christ. It tells of a group of people who left Israel around the time of the biblical prophet, Jeremiah, and were led by God across the ocean. The culminating part of the Book of Mormon is the account of Jesus Christ's visit to these people in the Americas, fulfilling the prophecy he gave to his apostles in Israel that "other sheep I have, which are not of this fold." (John 10:16)

Branch: Similar to a ward, a branch is a local congregation of The Church of Jesus Christ of Latter-Day Saints. The main difference between a branch and ward is size; a ward is typically a large congregation of several hundred, whereas a branch is much smaller. A branch is led by a branch president and his two counselors.

Branch President: The leader of a branch, which is a smaller church congregation. Their role is similar to a bishop's (see *Bishop*).

Church service; Calling: Members of the Church may be given a variety of jobs to help run the organizations in the ward. These jobs are called "callings" because each member who receives a job is "called" to do it. For instance, a bishop may extend a calling to a member to be a teacher in one of the organizations of the church. Even roles such as bishop and stake president are callings, and all callings are unpaid. Members fulfill their callings to the best of their abilities as an act of service. Throughout LaVelle's life, she served in various callings such as visiting teacher, Relief Society president, Primary president, etc.

The Church of Jesus Christ of Latter-Day Saints: Established in 1830 as a restoration of the same church organized by Jesus Christ in the New Testament (see *Restoration*). The Church was restored by a man named Joseph Smith Jr., who became its first prophet. Since that time, the church has spread to many countries across the world. It continues to be led by a prophet, twelve apostles, and many other local leaders. For more on the history of The Church of Jesus Christ of Latter-Day Saints, visit churchofjesuschrist.org.

Confirmation: Confirmation is an ordinance, or sacred, formal act performed after baptism (see *Ordinance*). Men holding the priesthood, or power of God (see *Priesthood)* confirm members into The Church of Jesus Christ of Latter-Day Saints by placing their hands on the head of the person being confirmed, with one priesthood holder offering the confirmation prayer. While the baptism that occurs before the confirmation shows the member's willingness to keep the commandments, remember Christ, and take His name upon them, the confirmation is where God keeps his promise and blesses the new member with the Gift of the Holy Ghost (see *Holy Ghost, gift of*).

Covenant: A two-way promise made between God and his children.

Dedicating a grave: A prayer offered by someone holding the priesthood (see *Priesthood, Melchizedek*). In the prayer, the grave is dedicated and blessed to be protected until the Resurrection (see *Second Coming of Christ*).

Dispensation: An era of time throughout history in which God's people have been led by a prophet. The times of Abraham, Noah, Moses, and Christ himself are examples of some of the dispensations throughout time. Members of The Church of Jesus Christ of Latter-Day Saints believe that Jesus Christ restored his church in the 1800's through the prophet Joseph Smith, thus starting what is believed to be the last dispensation before the Second Coming (see *Second Coming of Christ.*)

Divine nature: Members of The Church of Jesus Christ of Latter-Day Saints believe that the spirits of all men and women on earth are actual children of a Heavenly Father (God) and that His son Jesus Christ is our brother. Due to this belief, members believe that all humanity has divine nature because we are the offspring of God, and that earth life is our chance to learn more about Him and become like Him.

Doctrine and Covenants: A book of scripture used in The Church of Jesus Christ of Latter-Day Saints. It contains modern day writings and revelations from the Prophet Joseph Smith and other modern-day prophets as they were directed by God in how to restore his church to the earth.

Eternal marriage: Members believe that marriage on earth is only valid until death unless the couple is sealed for both time and eternity in one of the Lord's holy temples (see *Temple Work; Sealing*). If the couple is sealed and keeps the promises and commandments that they made in the temple, their marriage will continue in the afterlife (see *Plan of Salvation* and *Exaltation; Celestial Kingdom*).

Exaltation; Celestial Kingdom: Members believe in life after death where they are judged and assigned to live in one of three kingdoms. Placement in a kingdom is determined by the intentions and actions of the person in question while living on earth. Those who made and kept promises to follow God and all his commandments are worthy of the highest kingdom, called the Celestial Kingdom. In this kingdom, they will live with their families, Heavenly Father, and Jesus Christ.

Family Home Evening: Traditionally held on Monday evenings, Family Home Evening is a chance for a family to come together and strengthen both spiritual knowledge as well as family bonds. Groups of college students or widows who may not have close family may also gather together to form Family Home Evening groups.

First Vision: A miraculous vision that Joseph Smith, Jr. had in the spring of 1820. Young Joseph went into the woods near his home to pray about which of the many churches was correct, and he saw Heavenly Father and Jesus Christ in a vision. They told him that none of the churches on earth at that time was Christ's true church. Years later, Joseph would be instructed to restore Christ's original church (see *Restoration*).

Food order: Those in need of food or other necessities can speak with their bishop about their welfare needs. The bishop may instruct the Relief Society president to fill out a food order allowing the family to get the things they need from a church storehouse.

Genealogy: Also referred to as family history, genealogy consists of researching ancestral lines—both personal and public. Genealogy is especially important to members of The Church of Jesus Christ of Latter-Day Saints who perform ordinances such as baptism and temple work by proxy for their ancestors who never had the chance to learn about and accept the gospel of Jesus Christ on earth (see *Temple Work*).

General Conference: A world-wide meeting of The Church of Jesus Christ of Latter-Day Saints held the first weekend of April and October each year. During these meetings, the prophet, apostles, and other church leaders address the members of the Church. It is held in Salt Lake City in the Conference Center, but it is broadcast world-wide.

Gospel of Jesus Christ: The teachings of Jesus Christ including principles such as faith, repentance, baptism, confirmation, and enduring to the end.

Gospel Doctrine: An hour-long adult Sunday School class held as part of Sunday worship. In this class, members study from one of four standard books of scripture—The Bible, The Book of Mormon, The Doctrine and Covenants, and The Pearl of Great Price.

Heavenly Father: Another name for God or God the Father. He is the head of the Godhead. Some religions believe that God the Father, Jesus Christ, and the Holy Ghost are the same being. Members of The Church of Jesus Christ of Latter-Day Saints believe them to be three separate beings. Heavenly Father is the supreme creator and the spiritual father of humanity. Members believe he sent all people to earth to fulfil his holy plan (see *Plan of Salvation*).

High Priest: An office in the Melchizedek priesthood. Worthy priesthood holders who are called to certain callings, such as bishop or those at the stake level, are ordained as a high priest. The other office in the Melchizedek priesthood is called Elder. Elders and high priests meet together as a quorum on Sundays to study the gospel and their priesthood responsibilities.

Holy Ghost/Spirit: The third member of the Godhead, along with Heavenly Father and Jesus Christ. Members of The Church of Jesus Christ of Latter-Day Saints believe each member of the Godhead to be a separate person. The Holy Ghost, unlike Heavenly Father and Jesus Christ, does not have a body of flesh and bone. As a spirit, he is able to touch the hearts of people during their lives. The Holy Ghost has many roles, the most important of which is to testify of God and His Son, Jesus Christ. Other roles include providing comfort, warnings, inspiration, etc. Those who are confirmed a member of The Church of Jesus Christ of Latter-Day Saints are given the Gift of the Holy Ghost.

> **Holy Ghost, Gift of:** The Gift of the Holy Ghost is promised to members who make and keep their baptismal promises. It is the privilege to receive continuous guidance and inspiration from the Holy Ghost throughout their mortal journey.

Home teaching/ Home teacher: Home teaching was a way for members of the Church to reach out and serve, strengthen, and teach their fellow members. Home teachers were generally a pair of men, or a man and a youth, who were assigned to visit a few families in their ward or branch. During their visits, they taught spiritual truths, checked in on the family, provided service, and assisted them in priesthood ordinances when requested. Currently, the Church no longer uses the term home teaching, but has replaced it with a new program called Ministering.

Institute class: Scriptural classes held on the collegiate level but welcome to all members 18 years and older.

Jesus Christ: The second member of the Godhead. Members of The Church of Jesus Christ of Latter-Day Saints believes each member of the Godhead to be a separate person. Jesus Christ is the only begotten child of Heavenly Father, meaning that God the Father is both his spiritual father and earthly father. Given his divine parentage, Jesus Christ was able to perform an Atonement for the sins of the world. He lived a perfect life free of sin, which made Him the only person who was able to make such a sacrifice. Members believe that Christ suffered for the sins of mankind in Gethsemane, died on the cross at Calvary, and was resurrected from the dead three days later. Members believe that eternal happiness is achieved through faith on His name and by following the example He set in life.

Joseph Smith: The first prophet of the restored church, often called the prophet of the restoration. Throughout time, there have been many prophets called of God, such as Moses and Abraham. Joseph Smith was the first prophet called in modern day. Joseph received a miraculous vision of God the Father, and His Son, Jesus Christ in 1820, and in 1830, he restored Christ's church under Their direction. Joseph Smith and his brother Hyrum were later martyred in 1844 and the church members were driven west to settle in what later became the state of Utah.

Latter-days: This is a term to describe the present era in which we live.

Laurel: A class in the Church's Young Women's program for girls aged 16-18. In 2019, changes were made to the Young Women's program and the former class names of Beehive, Mia Maid, and Laurel are no longer used.

Mia Maid: A class in the Church's Young Women's program for girls aged 14-15. In 2019, changes were made to the Young Women's program and the former class names of Beehive, Mia Maid, and Laurel are no longer used.

Mission: Missions come in many forms. The most familiar is that of nineteen-year old women and eighteen-year-old men, who leave their families for eighteen months to two years to share the gospel (proselyte) in an assigned area. They teach others about Jesus Christ, serve, and strengthen the wards and branches in that area. Missions can also be based solely on service rather than proselyting (called service missions). Senior couples may also choose to go on missions (called senior missions), where they serve together in a specified area for a few months or years—whatever they are able to do. LaVelle served a senior mission alone when she moved to Washington to serve as a genealogy missionary. Her sons served proselyting missions when they were nineteen.

Mission call: In order to serve a mission for The Church of Jesus Christ of Latter-Day Saints, the person who wishes to serve must fill out mission papers and submit them to the church. At church headquarters in Salt Lake City, missionaries are assigned to the areas where they will serve, which could be almost anywhere in the world. A letter is sent to the missionary relating where they will serve, the language they will be speaking there, and the length of time they will be gone. Receiving a mission call is an exciting event, as LaVelle describes in her experience with her sons. These calls are now sent digitally, rather than by mail.

Missionaries: Pairs of unpaid volunteers for the church who have chosen to serve a full-time mission (see *Mission*) for eighteen months to two years. Female missionaries are referred to as "Sisters" and male missionaries are referred to as "Elders." When LaVelle speaks of "young elders," she is talking about pairs of male missionaries assigned to her ward or branch.

Mormon (ancient prophet): Mormon is an ancient prophet in the Book of Mormon, and it is after him that the Book of Mormon is named. The book contains writings from many different prophets over several centuries, but Mormon was the prophet who compiled all their histories into the complete record that is the Book of Mormon.

Mormon (nickname): Mormon is often used as a nickname for the members of The Church of Jesus Christ of Latter-Day Saints from their belief in the Book of Mormon. Although Church leaders have recently asked members to call themselves by the full name of the Church, members used to commonly refer to themselves as Mormon or Mormons, as LaVelle does often in her book.

Moroni: The son of Mormon. Moroni is the last prophet to contribute to the Book of Mormon. He promises that any who read the book and pray to know if it is true will receive an answer from God through the Holy Ghost, testifying of its truthfulness.

Ordinances/Ordinance work: An ordinance is a sacred, formal act performed by someone holding the priesthood (see *Priesthood*). Members believe that certain ordinances are necessary for exaltation (see *Celestial Kingdom/Exaltation*). These ordinances include baptism, confirmation, temple endowment, and temple sealing (see *Temple ordinances*).

Patriarchal blessing: A patriarchal blessing is a special priesthood blessing given to members of The Church of Jesus Christ of Latter-Day Saints by the patriarch in their congregation. In this special prayer, the patriarch informs the member of their lineage in the house of Israel, as it is believed that all humanity is either directly descended or adopted into one of the twelve tribes of Israel. The patriarch will also provide personal blessings, warnings, and admonitions that will help guide and inspire the receiver in their life.

Plan of Salvation: This is also sometimes called the Plan of Happiness. Members of The Church of Jesus Christ of Latter-Day Saints believe that Heavenly Father created this plan as a way for his spirit children—all of humanity—to become like Him. His spirit children would leave the pre-mortal life where everyone lived with God to come to earth and receive a body, just as Heavenly Father has a body. While on earth, people would be tested for obedience as well as form familial bonds. Because all mankind would make mistakes, Jesus Christ chose to be their advocate with the Father and suffer for the sins of the world so all people would have the opportunity to repent of mistakes and return to live with God again after this life. After death, people enter the spirit world. Not much is known about the spirit world, other than it is a place of waiting and learning (see *Spirit world*). With the Second Coming of the Savior, all people will be resurrected and receive a physical body again as Jesus Christ did, and then the final judgement will occur. After judgement, all people will be assigned to live in one of three "kingdoms." Only in the highest, the Celestial Kingdom, is it believed that people can live with Heavenly Father and Jesus Christ and their families for eternity.

Pre-existence: Members believe that before people were born on this earth, all humanity existed as spirit sons and daughters of Heavenly Father in what is called the "pre-existence." Here, God told his children of His plan, and Jesus Christ accepted His role as the advocate for humanity and agreed to suffer for the sins of the world. Because Lucifer (also known as Satan) wanted that role for his own glory, he led one-third of the spirit children against Christ and the other two-thirds in what is called the war in heaven. In the end, Satan and his followers were cast out, never to receive a physical body.

Pre-ordination: It is believed that certain people on earth were chosen in the pre-existence for the roles they led on earth, provided they were worthy of them in life. Examples are the prophets found in every dispensation, including Adam, Moses, Abraham, and Joseph Smith.

Priesthood: The priesthood is the power of God on earth. While all members of the church benefit from having the priesthood restored, worthy male members 12 and up are granted the authority to use it for the benefit of their families and others. All ordinances, such as baptism, the sacrament, confirmation, and temple ordinances, are done through the power of the priesthood,

> **Priesthood; Aaronic:** Sometimes referred to as the lesser priesthood, those who hold the Aaronic priesthood are generally young men aged twelve to eighteen, though adult males who join the Church may also hold it for a time. A young man must hold the Aaronic priesthood before they can receive the Melchizedek priesthood. Their responsibilities are different than those of the Melchizedek priesthood holders.

> **Priesthood; Melchizedek:** The same power of God that Christ used to create the world. This priesthood is conferred upon worthy men aged eighteen and older. Baptisms, confirmations, blessings of healing, and temple

ordinances are a few of the ordinances that require the Melchizedek priesthood to perform.

Priesthood blessing: Receiving a priesthood blessing is one way members can benefit from the priesthood in their life. Those who hold the priesthood and are worthy to use it can give blessings of healing and comfort by the laying on of hands. LaVelle mentions she and many of her family members were given priesthood blessings when the need arose for healing and comfort. While great miracles can occur through the giving and receiving of priesthood blessings, members believe that it is ultimately the will of God that dictates whether someone will be healed.

Primary: This organization in a ward or branch is made up of all children aged three to eleven. Generally, classes in primary are divided up based upon age. Ward members are recommended by the Primary president and called by the bishopric to teach the children about gospel truths. The Primary meets together on Sunday, both in a large group, where primary songs are taught and practiced, and in smaller classes based on age where lessons are taught.

Proclamation to the World: A proclamation given in 1995 by the Prophet of the Church and his apostles at the time. This is a prophetic declaration of the importance of the family unit in God's plan and the roles of husbands, wives, mothers and fathers are outlined for the greatest chance of happiness in this life.

Prophet: A man called by God to lead His church. A prophet holds the authority over all areas of the church. Examples of prophets include Adam, Moses, and Abraham. When Jesus Christ ascended up to heaven, he called Peter to be the prophet to lead His church. When he and all the apostles were martyred, members of the

Church believe there was no prophet on the earth until God called Joseph Smith to be the first prophet of the restored church in the latter days.

Regional games: Organized sports and activities for members from different congregations to play and compete together.

Relief Society: The largest women's organization in the world. All women of The Church of Jesus Christ of Latter-Day Saints aged 18 and older are members of the Relief Society. The ward Relief Society meets together in a class on Sundays to learn from each other as they study the scriptures and the words from the prophets. Relief Society members also participate in service projects, activities, etc. to benefit their wards and community. The Relief Society in each ward or branch is led by a Relief Society president and two counselors. They are responsible for overseeing the welfare of the women in their congregation.

Restoration: Refers to the organization of The Church of Jesus Christ of Latter-Day Saints in 1830. Members believe that Joseph Smith, Jr. was a prophet called by God to restore Christ's church back to the earth. Rather than being reformed, Christ's church was restored back to the earth exactly as it was organized by Jesus Christ in the New Testament.

Repentance: Members believe that when people sin, they draw further away from God. Repentance is the process by which people who have sinned can align themselves with God once again. It includes understanding what you did wrong, feeling remorse, making amends, and promising to do better, while utilizing the Atonement of Jesus Christ.

Resurrection: When a physical body and a spirit are reunited after death, never to be separated again. Christ was resurrected three days after his death, and members of the Church believe they will all be resurrected after Christ's Second Coming (see *Second Coming*). It is a promise given to all people born on earth.

Road show: Short skits or plays put on for entertainment, usually performed by different wards within a stake.

Sacrament: A religious ceremony performed by the priesthood during sacrament meeting on Sundays (see *Sacrament meeting*). Priesthood holders bless the bread (symbolic of Christ's body) and water (symbolic of Christ's blood) and distribute it to the congregation. Taking the sacrament is a renewal of the promises members made at baptism.

Sacrament meeting: The focus of Sunday worship. Members meet for an hour to listen to talks given by other members, sing together, and most importantly, partake of the sacrament (see *Sacrament*). It is followed by either Sunday school classes, Relief Society/Priesthood classes, Young Men and Young Women classes, or Primary classes, also held for an hour.

Satan/cunning one/evil one: Members believe that Satan was a spirit brother who fell from God's grace when he warred against Christ and God's faithful spirit children in the pre-mortal life (see *Pre-existence*). Because he was not granted a body, his desire is to tempt and lead away those who are on earth to get them as far away from God as possible. While most people never encounter him or his followers in a physical way, there are times when members will say they have felt his presence or sensed his followers nearby, as LaVelle wrote in her experience. Satan and his followers can be combated and overcome by the power of Jesus Christ and the Holy Ghost.

Second Coming of the Savior: Members of The Church of Jesus Christ of Latter-Day Saints believe that Christ will come again to the earth. This second coming is described symbolically in the book of Revelation in the Bible. After Christ returns, the resurrection will occur (see *Resurrection*) and everyone will be judged by Heavenly Father and Jesus Christ and assigned to live in one of three kingdoms of glory—Celestial, Terrestrial, or Telestial.

Spirit of Elijah: Biblically, the spirit of Elijah was foretold to turn the hearts of children to their fathers and fathers to their children. Members believe this is referring to genealogy work, where families research their ancestors and teach their posterity. Many people who feel strengthened in their genealogy work say that they can feel the spirit of Elijah helping them.

Spirit world: A place where spirits go after a person dies. It is described as a waiting place. At death, bodies go to the grave and spirits go to the spirit world to wait for the Second Coming of Christ, the resurrection, and judgement. Not a lot of details are known about the spirit world.

Spirit prison: A state of those in the spirit world who did not ever learn about/accept the gospel of Jesus Christ on earth. In the spirit world, they have the opportunity to learn and accept what they were not able to in life. However, because all saving ordinances must occur on earth, spirits in this state must wait until those still living do their ordinance work by proxy in a temple. Once the proxy work is done, the spirits can decide whether or not to accept the work. It is believed those who accept are no longer in the state of "spiritual prison" and can join the ranks of those in the spirit world who teach the gospel to others who have never heard it.

Stake: A stake is a group of congregations in the Church, generally comprised of five to twelve wards and/or branches. The stake is led by a stake president, two counselors, a secretary, and clerks. There are also stake leaders for all the various organizations of the church, such as Relief Society, Sunday School, Primary, Young Men, and Young Women.

Stake Conference: Twice a year, a stake (see *Stake*) will meet for stake conference instead of their normal church meetings. During this conference, leaders of the Church and other stake members are asked speak to the members of the stake.

Temple ordinances: Ordinances are sacred, formal acts, and some of these sacred acts can only be done in the temple. All ordinances that occur in the temple are called saving ordinances and are necessary for exaltation. Because they are necessary, members who are living do them for themselves and also by proxy for ancestors who have passed away without having done them while on earth. It is then up to the ancestor to accept the proxy ordinance (see *Spirit prison*).

> **Temple Sealing:** Also known as marriage for time and eternity. Members believe that in order for couples and their families to be able to remain a family unit after death, they must be sealed together in the Holy Temple. Temple sealings are recognized as a legal marriage, but in some cases, couples choose to be married civilly first and then go to the temple to be sealed in a separate ceremony.

> **Temple endowment:** This is an ordinance in which members learn more about the plan of salvation and make further covenants (promises) that build on those already made at baptism.

Baptism for the dead: Because baptism is a saving ordinance, baptisms are one of the ordinances that can be completed for those who have passed on in the hopes that they will accept the proxy ordinance in the spirit world. Normal baptisms are conducted in church buildings rather than the temple, but all work for departed people, such as baptisms for the dead, must be done in the temple.

Temple Square: The area surrounding the Salt Lake Temple in Salt Lake City, Utah. Many Church buildings are located on Temple Square and General Conference is held in the Conference Center at Temple Square.

Tithing: Mirroring the law of tithing that existed in Christ's original church, members who obey this commandment pay one-tenth of their annual income to the church. This money is used to support the church in things such as building and maintaining church buildings and temples.

Veil: Members of the Church believe that when spirits come from the pre-existence to earth, they pass through a veil, which is the reason they do not remember living with God. In death, people pass through this veil once again. When members say things like "the veil is very thin," they generally are talking about how they feel close to those who have passed on and still feel them with them.

Visiting teaching/ Visiting teacher: Visiting teaching was a way for members of the Church to reach out and serve, strengthen, and teach their fellow members. Visiting teachers were generally a pair of women, or a woman and a youth, who were assigned to visit a few families in their ward or branch. During their visits, they taught spiritual truths, checked in on the family, provided service, and assisted them whenever needed. Currently, the Church no longer uses the term visiting teaching, but has replaced it with a new program called Ministering.

Ward: A ward is a localized congregation in the Church. Generally, a ward will have several hundred members. Wards are led by a bishopric and contain various organizations such as Relief Society, Sunday School, Primary, Young Men, and Young Women. Each of these organizations also has a presidency, made up of a president, two counselors, and a secretary. Together, the ward leadership counsel together to help the ward grow spiritually and run smoothly.

Ward council: A council that meets together to discuss how to best help and lead the ward. It consists of the bishop and his counselors, and presidents from the ward organizations, such as the Relief Society, the Elders Quorum, the Sunday School, the Primary, etc. They generally meet together once a month to plan and discuss how to help individual members.

Welfare Square: A complex in downtown Salt Lake City, UT where food and supplies are prepared and provided to bishop storehouses around the world. The food and supplies are distributed to those in need.

Westward Mormon migration: After the death of Joseph Smith, Jr, the early members of The Church of Jesus Christ of Latter-Day Saints were driven out of their homes and communities in Illinois. Using handcarts and covered wagons, they traveled across present-day America until they settled in what is now the state of Utah.

Willie and Martin Handcart Companies: Two specific groups of saints who traveled west to Utah pulling handcarts. The companies left late and were caught by an early, vicious winter, and many of the saints who were part of these companies died or suffered terrible loss. Some of the most heartbreaking and faith-building stories from the early pioneers come from the experiences of those who journeyed with these companies across the plains.

Word of Wisdom: A commandment followed by members of The Church of Jesus Christ of Latter-Day Saints that outlines a code of health. Vegetables, fruits, grains, and sparingly used meats are encouraged for good health, while tea, coffee, alcohol, addictive drugs, and tobacco are prohibited.

Young Men: The Young Men's program is for all males in a ward or branch aged 12 to 18. It is separated into three quorums: Deacons, aged 12-13, Teachers, aged 14-15, and Priests, aged 16-18. Each of these quorums has specific priesthood responsibilities in the church (see *Priesthood*). In this program, young men are taught gospel truths, participate in various activities, and serve in their ward and community.

Young Women: The Young Women's program is for all females in a ward or branch aged 12 to 18. It used to be separated into three age groups: Beehives, aged 12-13, Mia Maids, aged 14-15, and Laurels, aged 16-18. However, in 2019 the Church changed this so that wards and branches have the freedom to divide young women into age groups that best fit the situation of the individual ward or branch. In this program, young women are taught gospel truths, participate in various activities, and serve in their ward and community.

CPSIA information can be obtained
at www.ICGtesting.com
Printed in the USA
BVHW031157160720
583884BV00007B/146